D1566865

FINDING ROSA

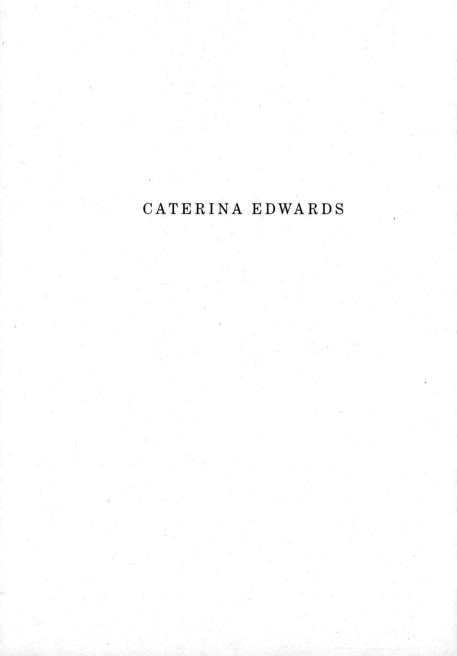

CATERINA EDWARDS

finding rosa

A Mother with Alzheimer's,

a Daughter in Search

of the Past

GREYSTONE BOOKS

Douglas & McIntyre Publishing Group

Vancouver / Toronto / Berkeley

Greystone Books
A division of Douglas & McIntyre Ltd.
2323 Quebec Street, Suite 201
Vancouver, British Columbia V5T 4S7
www.greystonebooks.com

Library and Archives Canada Cataloguing in Publication
Edwards, Caterina, 1948–
Finding Rosa : a mother with Alzheimer's,
a daughter in search of the past / Caterina Edwards.

ISBN 978-1-55365-389-9

1. Edwards, Caterina, 1948– —Family. 2. Alzheimer's disease—
Patients—Biography. 3. Alzheimer's disease—Patients—Family relationships.
4. Authors, Canadian (English)—20th century—Family relationships.
5. Mothers and daughters. I. Title.
PS8559.D83Z465 2008   C818'.5409   C2008-904108-9

Editing by Nancy Flight
Jacket and text design by Jessica Sullivan
Jacket photograph courtesy of Caterina Edwards
Printed and bound in Canada by Friesens
Printed on acid-free paper that is forest friendly
(100% post-consumer recycled paper) and has been processed chlorine free.
Distributed in the U.S. by Publishers Group West

The quotes from "Wanda" and "The Fall" from *New and Collected Poems:
1931–2001* by Czeslaw Milosz, copyright © 1988, 1991, 1995, 2001 by Czeslaw
Milosz Royalties, Inc., are reprinted by permission of HarperCollins Publishers.

We gratefully acknowledge the financial support of the Canada Council for the
Arts, the British Columbia Arts Council, the Province of British Columbia through
the Book Publishing Tax Credit, and the Government of Canada through the Book
Publishing Industry Development Program (BPIDP) for our publishing activities.

Viola: What country, friends, is this?
Captain: This is Illyria, lady.
Viola: And what should I do in Illyria?

Shakespeare, TWELFTH NIGHT

FOR TATIANA, ANTONIA, AND CORINNA

contents

Prologue 1

FINDING ROSA

Environs of Istria
(pre-1945 place names shown in brackets)

SLOVENIA
CROATIA
BOSNIA-
HERZEGOVINA
ITALY
Adriatic Sea
Tyrrhenian Sea
0   100   200
kilometers

0   50   100
kilometers

AUSTRIA

SLOVENIA

•Ljubljana

ITALY

Gorizia•

•Trieste

•Koper (Capodistria)

Piran
(Portorose)

Padua•   •Venice

•Chioggia

Istria

Rijeka (Fiume)•

CROATIA

Rovinj
(Rovigno)•

Cres (Cherso)•

Pula
(Pola)•

Losinj
(Lussino)•

Adriatic Sea

Zadar
(Zara)•

N

•Ancona

Canto di tempo passato
E il tuo sibilare
Giocondo sopra il mio capo
Sei venuta da tanto lontano,
Come me, o Bora,
Per più non tornare alla culla

I sing of time past
And your joyful whistling over my head,
Wind that came from afar, as I did
Never able to return to my cradle

Gian Mauro Siercovich, BORA

prologue

FOR YEARS, I was afraid that I would turn into my mother.

As soon as I could, I left home: struck out in the opposite direction, traveled on. By design and nature, I became my own woman—nothing like her. Still, I remained vigilant, examining my responses to my daughters, monitoring my tone when I spoke to my husband. I feared that if I were not rational and collected, if I did not squelch my anger and emotions, I would become her.

It's an old story. What turned me around, drew me back, was incipient loss. As I observed my mother's mind, then her body, fail, I began to want to know her, Rosa Pia Pagan Edwards—to know the woman she used to be.

At her funeral, in 2001, the presiding priest confused my name with hers. "In Baptism, *Caterina* received the sign of the cross . . ."

It wasn't the usual case of the celebrant's not knowing the deceased. Our family had been among the original parishioners of this church, almost forty years ago.

"Let us pray for our sister, *Caterina* . . ."

In the last few years, I had brought my mother to mass when I was able. And afterward Father John would usually stop at her wheelchair and greet her. "The terrible Rosina," he would smile, then make the sign of the cross on her forehead or pat her cheek. So why was he confused now? I looked at my sister, Corinna, who was standing on my right. She was suppressing a giggle.

I considered signaling Father John, but how? He never looked at me but focused on the coffin or the mid-distance. He continued to make the mistake. Over and over. "Your servant, Caterina . . . The soul of Caterina . . ."

I glanced over my shoulder. Deaths, relocations, and my mother's dementia had thinned out the ranks of her friends. Besides the immediate family, nearly all the mourners (and there were precious few of them) were there to support me, my husband, or our girls. I suspected that between Father John's heavy Italian accent and the foreignness of the service, most of them weren't following what he was saying. Still, two of my friends rolled their eyes and smiled at me.

I was starting to giggle, too. Was the priest losing his memory, as my mother had lost hers? The blind blessing the blind, so to speak. Or—and I felt uneasy at the thought—did the use of the wrong name mean that the blessing and the laying to rest would be misdirected and not take?

Corinna took my hand and squeezed it. My husband whispered, "Doesn't matter." But I suddenly felt more anxious. What if it were a sign? A warning that I was next? The last four years with my mother had been so taxing that I had often wondered who was going to bury whom. And now I felt as if death were being called down upon me.

"O God, to whom mercy and forgiveness belong... command that Caterina be carried safely home to heaven..."

Not me—not yet. I was still searching for the truth of my mother's life. By this time I was beginning to find my way through the lies and the legends. And reconstructing lost memory had brought me to lost history. I was arriving at the forgotten, suppressed, denied history of her homeland and her people.

Not me, please—not yet.

We care because we remember.
We remember because we care.

Avishai Margalit, THE ETHICS OF MEMORY

hurricane rosa

I FOUND MUM in my closet. She was holding up a black, backless sundress and shaking her head.

"What are you doing?" I said.

Mum shot me one of her looks. "You may as well go naked." She extended her arm and dropped the dress onto a pile of clothes between her and the bed. My clothes—which had been hanging neatly when I left that morning for work.

I was twenty-three years old, and Marco and I were newly married. I'd thought that my new circumstance would make a difference, that Mum would stop treating me like a little kid.

"Stop it," I said.

"Save your breath," Marco said to me. "I've been telling her to stop for the last twenty minutes."

Mum pulled a couple of pairs of jeans off their hangers. "Disgusting." She tossed a white filmy blouse over her shoulder. "Wasting your money."

"Mum, you must be tired after such a long trip. How about a cup of coffee? Dad's having some tea and a biscuit." I'd seen and greeted my father on my way through the living room. Marco, who was home studying for his PhD comprehensives, had called to warn me they'd arrived three hours early, and I'd rushed home.

Mum held up a high-necked yellow dress she'd made for me. "Do you wear this? It looks so nice on you."

If I'd been forty-three instead of twenty-three, maybe. Still, I lied. "Of course I do."

She hung it back up in the now almost-empty closet. The top drawer of my dresser was pulled out, but she hadn't upended it yet. "This is my house," I said. I suppressed the urge to stamp my foot.

"As my mother used to say, your nightie still has shit on it," Mum said. "Come on. Help me clear up this mess. Pants on the left, dresses right."

I could feel myself flush. "You made the bloody mess. It was fine, fine, as it was." My voice came out loud and squeaky. "You have to stop." Marco put a hand on my arm.

"Rosina, please." Dad was standing in the doorway. "Didn't I say?"

"Poor me," she said. "Poor, poor me."

The next time they drove up from Calgary for a visit, it was summer, so I was home, ready and waiting. I'd cleaned our tiny apartment, I thought, top to bottom. I was determined: Mum couldn't continue to act as if my place were hers. And, except for a comment on the placement of the hand-me-down sofa, she behaved. While we ate lunch. As soon as I started the dishes, she was up checking out the counter. She pulled out the toaster and found a few crumbs. "Poor me," she said. "*Povera me.*" Fifteen minutes later, dishes, foodstuffs, and pots were out of the cupboards and on the counter. Mum was scrubbing the shelves. "*Quando diventeri donna?*" she repeated between enumer-ations of my inadequacies, not expecting me to answer. "When will you become a woman?" By the time Marco arrived, Mum had scrubbed the oven and was attacking the fridge.

It was the same each time Mum and Dad came to visit in those first years of our marriage. I was young and inse-cure: nothing I said or did stopped or even tempered my mother. She was in her sixties then—a short, round plug of energy, heavy but not soft or fleshy, with strong arms, well-defined calves, and a head of springy black curls. A force of nature, Hurricane Rosa would blow into town three or four times a year and devastate me and Marco and our apartment.

LOOKING BACK, I see that she thought she was doing her duty, protecting us from disorder and decay. She hid mothballs in desk drawers, under blankets, between our sweaters. Once Marco found one in a shoe. Through over-exposure, we became almost oblivious to the sharp stink of naphthalene. By most standards, our home was clean and tidy. But Mum saw impending ruin. *A remengo.* We were going to hell.

In the fourth year of our marriage, we moved from the latest walk-up apartment (mustard-colored linoleum and an avocado-green stove) to a charming old house. The owners, our friends Brian and Nancy, had the main floor; we took the upstairs. More than thirty years later, Nancy remembered Hurricane Rosa and her storm surges. "You had to see her in action to believe her," Nancy said. "And the criticism! I didn't understand a lot of what your mother said, but I'd get the gist: she was tearing you down."

"Endlessly," I said.

"Once you and Marco were away," Nancy said. "And you'd both insisted we weren't to let your parents in. You suspected they might try and replace your bed, even though you'd said no. Well, of course, they turned up, then a delivery truck was out front, and Brian and I tried to stop them. But what could we do or say? Lay ourselves across the stairs? I remember your father bringing up the rear, smiling apologetically. That was what he did, wasn't it? And your mother rewarding the delivery men, who had to carry the new bed up those narrow stairs and the old bed down, tipping them with bottles of whisky. They gave us a bottle, too."

Neither Marco nor I can recall why we'd refused a new bed. We were standing our ground, I suppose. The one time Marco acted uncharacteristically, he got through to Mum. Several years and a house of our own later, Marco came home to the usual scene of Mum ranting and me crying. Perhaps because I was eight months pregnant, Marco screamed (even louder than Mum): "You will not do this." When he threw his keys down for emphasis, they left a dent in the hardwood floor.

Marco's gesture made an impression on more than the floor; Mum changed course. She toned down her criticisms and stopped reorganizing our things. (Still, for years afterwards, she alluded to Marco's "terrible temper," which was particularly unjust, since he is mild mannered and patient.) I suspect the arrival of her granddaughters, first Tatiana and, four years later, Antonia, sapped her fury. At least for a while.

When my father retired from his job at the Southern Alberta Institute of Technology, he and Mum left Calgary and its harsh winters for Nanaimo, British Columbia, and a milder climate. Now they were a thousand rather than three hundred kilometers away from my home, which suited me fine. I was teaching at a local college and then at a university, looking after my little girls, and finding a spare hour here and there for my husband and my writing. In the spring of 1984, I faced a further complication: I fell ill with a systemic arthritic disease. The pain slowed me, aged me. To my surprise, Mum took no notice of my illness. When she saw me walk with a cane, she told me not to exaggerate. And later she denied ever knowing that I had been ill.

The distance, the sea channel, and two major mountain ranges did not protect me. My parents were isolated in their new town, and since Dad was no longer working, they had the impetus and the time to take the two-day trip by boat and car. They may have visited less often, but it was still too often for me. I preferred going to their house and keeping them away from mine. The respite that had come with Tatiana's and Antonia's early years was over. Mum had delighted in everything about her granddaughters until they grew more individual and less malleable.

Hurricane Rosa surged again. But by this time she was more category one than five. Even so, as my parents' Dodge swung into our driveway, my shoulders would slump. Mum would haul herself out of the car and up our front steps, leaving Dad to unload. Before she got through the door, she would start complaining about her knees, her back, Dad's driving, and the car. We would exchange pecks on both cheeks. Mum was on to the landscape— mountain and prairie—*endless,* the heat or the cold, and the condition of our front yard. Dad and I would wave at each other; most expressions of emotion embarrassed his British soul. Mum was already on a circuit of the main floor, checking. "But why do you insist on living in such a godforsaken place anyway? Too far; too, too far."

Dad always took several trips to the car to unload. Besides suitcases, my parents brought a cooler and a box filled with Mum's cooking: bread, egg noodles, *biscotti,* lasagna, apple pies, glass jars of peach preserves and tomato sauce. For their granddaughters—endless socks, underwear, nightgowns, now and then a frilly dress (which the girls usually refused to wear), and, doled out over the year, souvenirs from their annual trip to Hawaii—paper leis, puka shell necklaces, and chocolate-covered macadamia nuts. For Marco and me—sofa cushions, towels, coffee mugs, Wicked Wahine body cream, and an inordinate number of flower-patterned sheets, none of which were to our taste.

No matter how carefully I'd cleaned, Mum still found a corner or a kitchen appliance not up to her sparkling standards. But she was in her mid-seventies by now, and her age was starting to show. She'd let her hair go gray; she suffered from osteoporosis and sciatica and could not stand for long. Since she found the steep stairs to the second floor a strain, my closet remained unmolested.

On their visits, Mum and Dad took over Tatiana's large basement bedroom, so Mum had free rein to root through her granddaughter's drawers and desk. She did so without the high-velocity anger she used to aim at me. Mostly she snooped, lingering (for example) over the tiny school photos of Tatiana's friends. Tatiana would try to stop her—fat chance—then she'd run up the stairs to me. "Mommy, Mommy, Mommy, Nonna's touching all my things, and she won't listen."

"She may not have heard you," I'd say. "You know she's getting deafer by the day," thinking, she won't listen to me either.

PERHAPS BECAUSE I wasn't paying attention, Mum's decline seemed sudden and precipitous. During our weekly phone calls, she sounded like her usual self. She blamed her health problems on Nanaimo, the gray skies and rain, and the vulgar people: *villani*. But when I saw her, she was no longer a force of nature. She was spent, almost immobile. About two years later, Dad announced they were moving again, this time to Edmonton. They had reached that time in their lives, he made clear, when they needed family, needed help.

I was apprehensive when they settled in a condo about six blocks from our house. I was prepared to help. If I didn't, who would? But Mum and Dad could expect only so much from me. Tatiana, who by this time was in high school, took on the cleaning of the condo for a small allowance. I dropped by or phoned every day, ran a few of the necessary errands, and had them over for dinner on Sundays.

But Mum was my father's responsibility, not mine. After all he, Frank Edwards, had married her; he had sworn to be true to her in sickness and in health. I had never had a choice. And for a man in his seventies, he seemed, though somewhat slower and creakier, as able, as competent as ever. He still served on committees for the Association of Science and Engineeering Technology Professionals. He read *Scientific American* and solved math and logic puzzles for entertainment. He managed his wife. He managed his diabetes, weight, and angina pectoris.

Only his eyesight, never good, was getting worse: he had glaucoma and macular degeneration. He probably should not have been driving, though miraculously he never had an accident in those last years. Tatiana, who is a worrier, would tell me once a month that I should do something; I should take away the keys to the Dodge. "He doesn't go far," I'd reply.

"That's not an answer," Tatiana would say, shaking her head at the irresponsibility of middle age.

"I don't have time to drive them to their appointments and to Safeway every five minutes. I'm a working woman. And I know I'd be forced into it. I know it."

"Mommy, really—"

"I'd like to see how often you'd end up chauffeuring them around town. Didn't you promise to go over yesterday and vacuum?"

I had no doubt that my father would outlive my mother: after all, she was older. I even wondered if he would remarry and if I would like my stepmother. He was so gregarious; he would find someone. None of us had any idea of how hard caring for my mother had become for him. He didn't complain much; it wasn't his way to make a fuss. He was from a village in the Midlands of England; he had escaped through his intelligence: scholarships (which must have been rare in the thirties) and the Royal Engineers in the army. But if his situation had changed, his manner—modest, cheerful, and down-to-earth—did not. He'd been raised to grin and bear it, and he did; he joked, he smiled, and he bore it and bore it.

I saw some signs of Mum's mental as well as physical decline. Although once she had been almost as sociable as my father, now she never wanted to go out except to church or to our house for dinner. And even then, they would arrive late because she balked or delayed. I practically had to beg her, my father would say. *Please, Rosina.* And if he did manage to get her out to visit an old friend, she'd ask Dad to take her home soon after they arrived. Or would sit and fall asleep. I accepted her excuses: the pain from the collapsed vertebrae in her back and the ever-present fatigue, but Tatiana suggested that her grandmother was depressed.

Mum would ask the same question over and over again. But she'd done that for a long, long time, Dad said. Whenever she saw Tatiana and her limp hair, she asked her if she conditioned her hair. And Antonia's bountiful curls triggered the question: "Did she have a perm?"

2

We rely on memories of
the past to help us imagine
and make sense of the present.

David Pillemer, MOMENTOUS EVENTS, VIVID MEMORIES

wave me goodbye

MUM STARED and stared at Tatiana and Antonia. Not the way she usually looked at them—with a fond eye—but suspiciously. "Whose daughters are these?"

"Mine. Mine and Marco's."

"Impossible." She shook her head.

It was our first day in Honolulu. Dad had flown us there to celebrate his and Mum's fiftieth wedding anniversary. Before we left, Mum had seemed pleased that we were going with them. "You'll see how beautiful it is," she said. But as soon as we got on the plane, she didn't seem to know where she was or who we were. Between flights at the Vancouver airport, she twice told me that I could go now; she and Frank could manage fine. She sounded as if she were dismissing an employee.

Dad and I agreed that this confusion must be due to exhaustion. She hadn't slept much the night before the

13

trip. And her question about Tatiana and Antonia? Jet lag. But then she asked the same question several times every day we were in Hawaii.

"They are my and Marco's daughters," I would answer.

"Impossible," she'd say. And on the third day, she added, "Maybe with one of your other men."

"What other men? What on earth are you talking about?" I knew I was being silly, but I was offended by this obsession of hers. It dovetailed too neatly with all the times in my youth when she'd called me a slut. "That is what she really thinks of me," I told Marco.

My parents had been going to Honolulu for at least fifteen years. And partly because of Dad's habit of chatting with anyone and everyone, they had made friends with a Korean acupuncturist, a Chinese minister, a Hawaiian gift shop owner, and the property manager of the condominium complex where they stayed. Dad wanted to show off the girls and me to each of them, but—just as in Edmonton—every time an appointment was set up, Mum claimed that she felt too ill or exhausted to go out.

We did go to dinner at the property manager's luxurious penthouse in Nauru Towers, overlooking the Ala Moana marina and park. A widow in her early sixties, Ann Wong was the type of woman I could see my father being married to—the type I would have expected him to want. They were both working-class English (Ann was from Liverpool) but polished by education and their years abroad. Ann's apartment was both sophisticated and kitschy—glass walls, serious Chinese antiques covered by dozens and dozens of Royal Doulton toby jugs. "I'm a serious collector," she said.

Dad had brought her a couple of books from Helen Forrester's autobiographical series set in prewar Liverpool, and Ann, in turn, had passed along a collection of stories by one of his favorites, H.E. Bates. He chatted away to her in a way he couldn't to Mum, or even the rest of us—from a shared cultural context. "Do you remember *Passport to Pimlico? The Lavender Hill Mob?*"

"I have a record at home—" (Victor Silvester)

"Oooh, I used to laugh—" (Gracie Fields)

"Now, she's before my time."

"Not her singing."

Dad sat down at the piano and began to play "The Biggest Aspidistra in the World." Ann sang along enthusiastically. They harmonized on "Wish Me Luck As You Wave Me Goodbye." And, to my daughter's disgust, I joined in on a song from my childhood: "Have Some Madeira, M'dear."

My mother didn't speak to Ann at all, even when she asked her a question. Mum did ask, loudly and in English, who the parents of these pretty girls were. She pointed at Ann: "Was this blonde the mother?" Tatiana and Antonia giggled. Dad kept his eyes on his plate laden with chicken and potato salad. But a few minutes later, he took Ann aside and told her in his best everything-is-all-right voice that Rosa had an overactive parathyroid that kept the level of calcium in her blood high. "And now and then she is a little confused," he said.

I was embarrassed both by my mother's confusion and by my father's need to explain and justify it. Mum had been diagnosed with an overactive parathyroid in Nanaimo, but her behavior betrayed more than a little confusion. She was, as Antonia said, totally out of it. Still,

Dad covered and minimized. And I did not call him on it, make him admit the truth.

What both of us had repressed was a more serious diagnosis, which had predicted dementia. In Nanaimo, when she first began having trouble with balance and walking, Mum had had a CAT scan. The neurologist had told Dad that she had normal-pressure hydrocephalus, or water on the brain. He passed on to me the effects of the condition: a shuffling walk, incontinence, and again, confusion. I am sure that he did not use the word "dementia." Certainly Mum's gait was affected. She did not so much walk as shuffle, hunched over, head thrust forward, taking tiny, slow steps. But she was not incontinent—not then.

Normal-pressure hydrocephalus is the only type of dementia that is treatable. In theory, a shunt can be inserted, the fluid drained. In theory. But the diagnosis is often incorrect. Neil Roberts, a neurologist and friend, had warned me when I'd turned to him for an explanation of normal-pressure hydrocephalus that the CAT scan can show signs of brain atrophy, and the radiologist deduces water on the brain. Even if the fluid were there, he said, the outcome of an operation to insert a shunt can be poor: in most cases, the result is a stroke or major infection. Neil has a laserlike intelligence and a solid reputation as a diagnostician, so I accepted his view rather than that of the (to me) unknown doctor in Nanaimo. Whatever was wrong with Mum was not treatable. And I put the diagnosis and the possibility of dementia out of my mind. Conveniently, I forgot. And Dad never mentioned it again.

He would never admit that anything was seriously wrong with Mum, not even in his last year, not even after the trip to Hawaii. He told me about a TV program on Alzheimer's that he and Mum had watched. Wasn't it a horrible illness? And Rosa had been particularly upset to hear that Ronald Reagan suffered from it—such a pity, and nothing could be done.

So only when Dad was in the hospital and I began looking after Mum did I realize how much he had protected and covered for her. And only then did I realize how taxing physically and mentally looking after Mum must have been.

I suspect that caring for her hastened his death. He came to visit me two days before his heart attack. He was pale and looked tired. "She won't eat," he said. "She complains about my cooking. Well, I don't know how. I never cooked. She complains. And she does nothing. Nothing. I don't know—"

I made some useless suggestions about getting takeout food and having a talk with her. I was distracted and afraid of being manipulated into taking over another duty on their behalf.

"I've been having the most awful dreams," he said. "And my blood sugar—I can't get it down." He looked at me. I didn't respond. He took off his glasses and rubbed his baggy eyes. "I don't know."

But I should have responded. I should have given him a word of support, a pat on the hand, or even a hug. A small gesture. I should have and I didn't.

My father collapsed in the lobby of the condominium building on November 2, 1997. One of the other residents had seen Dad leave for a walk about ten minutes earlier. He'd looked his usual self, she said, though she saw him from above, her condo being on the third floor. I suspect that the sweating, dizziness, and crushing pain—the "coronary event"—began while he was still outside on the sidewalk and that he had to struggle to get back. When he was found, he was sprawled on the floor. An ambulance was called, and (I've been told) it arrived "quickly, in a few minutes." During those minutes, Dad's heart stopped beating, but the paramedics managed to resuscitate him.

Dad was loaded into the ambulance and taken off to the emergency room of the nearest hospital. Only then did Doris, a neighbor from across the hall, knock on my parents' door to tell my mother what had happened. I'm not sure how much Mum understood—perhaps the words "Frank" and "hospital."

Between November 2 and January 11, the day my father died, Mum visited him six times. She obviously found seeing him too distressing, especially during the first seven weeks, when he was in intensive care and attached to a phalanx of noisy, flashing machines. She used every excuse not to go. She was too tired, her back hurt, her head ached. I sympathized; seeing him so helpless and so ill was hard. And it must have been that much harder for Mum to see the man who had been her protection and her security in such a state. Besides, getting her dressed in her winter coat, hat, and boots and maneuvering her into the car and then into a wheelchair and into the hospital was not easy. In the intensive care unit, between the instrument panels, the wires and the tubes, the nurses, and the other gravely ill patients—the elderly lady who had had a heart attack and her rotating parade of many sons and daughters, and the young man with the gunshot wound in his abdomen and his wives, ex and present, brother, and sisters—there was hardly any room for Mum's wheelchair.

Dad was moved from unit to unit, wherever they could find a bed, to less-intensive intensive care, to the burn ward, where at least there were only two beds in each room, and in and out and in and out of the relatively plush cardiology unit. Each time he was moved, I followed with Tatiana's boom box. If I didn't find a free plug behind the snake's nest of wires, I would rely on the batteries for power. His favorites: swing dance music, Italian arias, and Hawaiian songs. Weepy steel guitars muffling the clicks and beeps of the medical equipment.

When I did take Mum to the hospital for a visit, she seemed distracted by everything but my father. She never wanted to be left alone with him. If I was about to leave to use the bathroom or get some coffee, she grabbed my hand. "Don't go," she'd say. Or "Be quick."

"Talk to him," I'd say. "Tell him that you're well. That we're looking after you." For when he could speak (once the respirator was removed), he asked for her. About her. "Mum?" he would croak out, his eyes anguished. "Mum."

But she would not reassure him. "Franco," she would say, then hesitate. "What have they done to you? I should have never let you come to the hospital."

So I told him not to worry; every day I told him I was taking care of Mum. Although panicked and confused about what to do with her, I pretended that I was certain and in control, pretended that I'd assumed my role as caregiver to my mother.

THE FIRST FEW weeks Dad was in the hospital, Mum slept at our house. She was disoriented and difficult out of her normal habitat. The guest room was on the second floor, and the staircase was steep. Getting her up the stairs each evening was an ordeal. Together, Marco and I coaxed, lifted, pushed, and pulled. She would beg us to let her either sleep on the sofa in the living room or go home to her own bed. At night, she never wanted to go to bed, and in the morning, she didn't want to get up, to be dressed and shuttled back to the condo, while I went to the hospital or, more rarely, work.

So we began bringing her to our house for the weekend. During the week, we ate with her at the condo, and Tatiana and I took turns sleeping there. Finding some daytime help was relatively easy. At least it seemed so in the beginning. I hired Mila, a Filipina who had been a nanny to the daughters of some close friends. She agreed to stay with Rosa on the two days that she was available.

One afternoon, a hospital social worker appeared at Dad's bedside. She had heard from the head nurse that I had an ailing mother and that I needed help. (Had I been complaining? When the nurses came in to turn him from one side to the other to prevent bedsores? Or when one of them was changing the bag on the end of the intravenous? Had I? You bet. I talked to whomever would listen.)

My mother was eligible for at least temporary home care. I filled out a flurry of forms, and Mum was assigned to a private agency. The parade of women, home help, and supervisors began. Mum was allotted an hour (more like forty-five minutes), three mornings a week. I let the helper in, then went to the hospital to face the latest diagnosis, the latest complication: fever, pneumonia, brain damage, intensive care, psychosis. The home help woke my mother up, helped her get washed and dressed, and fixed breakfast. She left and I rushed back. At least the condo was only a few blocks from the hospital.

I had to make decisions about my father's treatment alone, with no guidance but my intuition. I asked the doctors to take Dad off the respirator. And I decided to sign a "Do not resuscitate" form. The head of intensive care, a long-faced man, balked. "Do you understand the implications?" he said. "Are you sure this is what he would want?" Dad had no living will; we had never discussed such a situation. So I wasn't sure, but I guessed that over the long term, he would not want a machine forcing the air in and out of his lungs. The tubes came out, and (to everyone's surprise) Dad started to breathe on his own.

For a few days, before Dad developed pneumonia, the nurses talked about his being transferred to a rehabilitative hospital. I started to entertain images of Mum and Dad together in a bright, cheerful nursing home. I would visit, I told myself, every day if I could. No one could expect me to look after both of them, not for the long term. As it was, I didn't know how long I could continue spending long hours with my mother, longer hours at my father's bedside.

I did all the usual, useless things: wetting and cleaning Dad's mouth with a pink swab, massaging his legs with cream, talking to him in my calmest voice, reassuring him. Praying that he would get better. Dad had only isolated moments of consciousness. Suddenly, in a croaking, unfamiliar voice, he would say, "Mum." Or "Where am I?" Or

"Take dictation." In his longest burst of words: "In regards to the problem as stated in the last memo . . . a meeting shall be convened to determine how it can be done." And a few minutes later: "In regards to the management of the problem, contact Corinna; assemble the group."

Despite his delirium, the problem he wanted to solve (I sensed) was that of his care: who was to look after him. How was he to live? And he didn't expect or trust that I could do it alone, or why would he mention my adopted sister, Corinna, who lived thousands of miles away in Puerto Rico? Corinna had always been the competent one, the efficient one.

Soon enough, the question of improvement or convalescence faded. Dad spiked a high fever. His lungs, I was told, were damaged and filling up with fluid.

"Did he ever smoke?"

"No," I said. "No, no, no."

Now the long-faced doctor advised that the intravenous hydrating solution be shut off, and I had to argue that it be continued. To me, the medical position appeared arbitrary and inconsistent: arguing for extraordinary measures one day and starvation the next.

I could see that Dad was dying, slowly, so slowly, and I stopped praying that he would get better and started praying that he would die. For there was no slipping away. He was struggling. *Come on then.* His voice was a howl. Ripping out tubes, flailing at the orderlies. *Why so long? Let me out.* Straining and fighting for release. *Let's go. Let's go. Let's go.* Until the last week, when he fell into a coma. And though my body was fired with the need to get away, I barely left the hospital, spending each night in his room reading or dozing on a foldout chair. I was afraid; I could not watch, and I made myself watch. Until the end, past the end, I stood watch.

Farewell, Captain; may your voyage be a safe one, they used to say in Lussino when a funeral procession passed. He was gone, and he had left my mother behind, left her to me.

CORINNA HAD booked the long, complicated, and tiring trip from San Juan to Edmonton as soon as it had become clear that Dad was not going to leave the hospital. "He's dying," I'd told her. "But it's taking forever."

She arrived January 12, the day after his death. It was minus twenty-six degrees Celsius, with a stiff wind, and although I'd brought a down-filled parka to the airport for her, when she stepped outside, she felt as if she were under attack, her skin pierced by hundreds of sharp knives. Corinna had not visited Alberta in the winter for twenty-eight years; her blood was acclimatized to the tropics. "I can't believe this," she said.

For the next ten days, together we made decisions about the funeral, the priest, the church, the prayers, the flowers, the eulogy, the obituary, the casket, and the mausoleum. We decided who should be phoned in Italy and Canada and what food to serve at the reception. We chose Dad's custom-made, pin-striped suit and a white dress shirt for his burial, but when Mum saw it, she began to scream. "That's Frank's good suit," she said.

"Exactly. . ." And I had thought she'd taken the news of his passing well.

"No, no, no. Not his good suit."

Corinna and I each tried to convince her that this suit was the most appropriate, the most serious one. Mum's voice grew louder and louder, a screech. "What are we saving the suit for?" I said.

"He was her husband," said Corinna, the peacemaker. We led Mum to his closet and pulled out each of his suits. I expected a tear, an exclamation of sorrow at the sight of those familiar jackets and pants. Instead, she inspected each one dispassionately. She pointed to a white mark on a brown wool sleeve. "This one needs cleaning. Frank was never careful." She tugged at a gray-and-blue checked suit with wide lapels and flared legs. "This one."

"That old thing?"

Corinna gave me a "that's enough" look. "Let me iron it at least," she said. And later, when Mum was napping, she said to me, "It's closed casket. So who cares if he looks like he's about to go out to a disco?"

Corinna came for as long as she could; her life, after all, was thousands of miles away. Still, unfairly—because my daughters and husband also supported me—inaccurately, I felt as if I weathered those months alone.

As I write, I can will myself to remember Corinna undressing Mum for bed, gently dropping the white nightgown over her head, guiding her hands through the sleeves. Or Tatiana bent over, sliding slippers on her grandmother's feet. But the images that rise unbidden are of my caring for my mother, just the two of us, cut off, isolated from the rest of the world.

3

Di sicuro e di vero,
non ci sono che le stagoni
The only thing that is sure
and true is the change of seasons
Lussingnan proverb

documents

WHEN I EXAMINED my mother's passport, I felt as if I were spying on her. I knew if she caught me, she would scream, accuse me of violating her privacy, or worse, doubting her word. At least, that is what she would have done a few years ago, when she was still her old self. Now, if she saw me with her passport in hand, she would flail at me, her fist punching my arm uselessly, her voice a screech. "That's mine." If I questioned her, she would not be able to explain why she was angry, why I should not look at her passport. If she opened it, she would recognize the old picture of herself, with dark, not white, hair, with a plump, not a skeletal, face. She would be able to recognize some of the words: Canada, Italy, sex, height, hair, eyes, but she would not understand others: identification, immigration. And most important, she would not be able to read the passport, to read its purpose.

I found the passport in the wooden chest at the foot of the parental bed. I had suspected that they might keep their most precious things there when I couldn't find them in Dad's home office. I looked through the desk drawers and filing cabinet. I was already uncomfortable, flipping through envelopes of bank statements and utility bills, all labeled and in order. But I made myself glance at each bundle so that I wouldn't end up tossing out something I would later need. I was the one in charge now, I reminded myself. I absently noted that they had smaller electricity bills and larger long distance bills than ours, including a surprising number—for my thrifty parents—of phone calls to Italy.

There were five large manila envelopes filled with letters from Italy, England, and Yugoslavia, each marked with the dates received and answered. I saved a few of the more recent letters, written by people whose names I recognized, as a reminder to send them the announcement of Dad's death. I tossed the rest.

Then contracts, forms; credit and membership cards; papers for car, health, and social insurance; records of investments, citizenship papers (including mine and Corinna's); income tax and travel itineraries. A photocopy of a medical report of the operation Mum had to remove a bowel-blocking tumor on a holiday in Arizona. The deed for each house they had owned. Corinna's adoption papers. A signed agreement to guarantee a line of credit for someone I didn't know. The awards for long and faithful service from the Southern Alberta Institute of Technology. A letter from the bank stating that their account of thirty thousand dollars was forfeited because of their "friend's" nonrepayment of the loan. A paper trail through my parents' forty-five years in Western Canada.

I told myself I wasn't snooping. As executor of my dad's estate, as Mum's caretaker, I had to know these facts. A letter to Mum from the Social Insurance office: before she could receive a survivor benefit, in addition to the Canada Pension she was already receiving, Rosa Pia Edwards must appear at the office with proof of her age. She must present her birth certificate and her passport. The pension office noted that the date registered as her birth date with her social insurance number (August 30, 1920) was different from the one my father had listed on his pension forms (August 30, 1917). And I knew that the date on her medicare card (August 30, 1915) was different yet again.

A week after searching my father's desk and files, I finally found an hour when Mum was asleep and I had no pressing chores. The wooden chest was locked. I had found a clutter of keys in the top drawer of the desk, but none were big enough for the large lock. I turned to the bedroom bureaus. Dad's drawers were ordered: one glance at the tidy piles of underwear and socks, the folded sweaters and staircased polo shirts, and I knew the key wouldn't be there.

A place for everything and everything in its place; that had been Mum's motto ever since I could remember. She tried to drill it into me when I was growing up. I was never allowed to leave any clothes on my chair or books and pens on my desk. She inspected my bureau drawers once a week, and if everything was not folded and divided according to her rules, she upended all of them onto the floor. (After I was married, her frustration that her lessons had not taken and that she couldn't enforce her standards in my home fueled the rampages.)

A month or so before he fell ill, Dad had complained that Mum had become messy, disorganized. If confronted, she'd be horrified. "Who did this? Behind my back? Someone. Someone." But he'd be the one who had to straighten up. "She pulls things out but doesn't put them back," he said.

Still, I was shocked at the state of her bureau drawers: scarves, nighties, pictures, perfume, wallets, purses, slips, panties, letters, bandages, belts, magazines, face cream, knitting wool, and fabric, all tossed together. I pushed the drawers shut. A month passed before I was able to face that *casino,* as Mum would have called it—an indiscriminate confusion, a brothel—for I felt no payback, no joy, only guilt and the sense that I had trespassed when I upended her drawers and reorganized them. I found a fifty-thousand-lire note between the pages of her mass missal, a bottle of White Shoulders under a knot of nylons, one hundred American dollars in an eyeglass holder, a china statue swathed in a silk scarf, a photograph of her mother in the zippered pocket of a beach bag inside a larger plastic bag. She must have been trying to hide these things. But from whom? Family or strangers?

That day, since my task was to open the chest, I was happy to move on. A few minutes later, I found the necessary key, long and ornate, in a black velvet pouch in the larger of her jewelry boxes. The passport was in a leather briefcase under a crocheted blanket, a package of sheets, and two embroidered tablecloths at the bottom of the chest. I pulled it out, started to flip it open, and, sabotaged by a wave of unease, laid it down.

I was an adult before I realized that my mother lied about her age. As a child, I did not particularly care. I knew she was OLD. My father was OLD, my aunts and uncles, all their friends, were OLD, relics of other times and other places. And those old times might as well have been a century or a millennium ago; they were so far in the past, so disconnected from my modern, new, soon-to-be-groovy life.

And the places they had come from? My father's country was mine, since I was born in England and left when I was almost eight years old. Most of the books I read as a young girl in Canada were British, so although I did not go to boarding or ballet school, although I did not ramble over the moors or go boating on the Thames or walk in deep woods (I couldn't even find deep woods in Calgary), although I did not have tea or elevenses or a headmistress, I felt as if I did.

And around 1963, when the Beatles became pop idols and Mary Quant a fashion queen, being English, having visited England, brought an unexpected status. It meant you were cool, you were happening, you were now.

But if England was the present, Istria, my mother's birthplace, was the past—hazy and distant and irrelevant.

It wasn't a country; it did not appear on any modern map or in any book that I had read. Throughout my youth, Istria was a fantasy, a mental construct, a sequence of images incubated by my dreams. It existed in my mother's mind, in the reminiscences she exchanged with friends, as the beloved, lost homeland, the wellspring of nostalgia.

I thought of it as another element in those never-ending conversations that adults had—the ones I ignored or half-listened to. *In my day,* they said, *in my time.*

I did not pay attention to Mum's past or her age. I never came out and asked her how old she was. I knew she had been older when I was born—but older than whom? I also knew that she was older than my father, but she never admitted by how much. "A couple of years," she would say if pushed by a friend. This coyness seemed silly to me. But her actual age never mattered until I went away to university and became left-wing and later feminist. Then I viewed her evasiveness as typical of the hypocrisy of the older generation and proof that women collaborated in their own oppression. Saying that a lady should never tell her age proved that her value sprang, at least partly, from her youthfulness; the more inexperienced and the more untouched she was, the better.

Throughout the extensive trip Mum and I took the summer after my BA—England, Italy, and a month in Losinj—I was pumped up with the tenets of feminism. Self-righteous, cocky, I finally confronted her about her age. And she lied.

We were staying for a few days with my mother's nephew Lino and his wife, Gina, in their apartment in Venice. My zia Giaconda, Mum's younger, unmarried sister, lived for forty years with Lino and Gina, but at that time, she was with them only on weekends and holidays; she was working as a paid companion in Padua. She came to Venice to visit us, and just a few minutes after she arrived and hugged us and exclaimed her joy, she began to lament the difficulties in her life. We were in the kitchen, having an espresso.

"I am forced to work *day and night* just to *put bread in my mouth*," she said in her whiniest of whiny voices. "Here I am nearly sixty, and I have no peace, I tell you. I'm working for a pittance. I have trouble paying even my hairdresser." Hot and sleepy, I was only half-listening. I had spent the morning at Ca' Rezzonico, Venice's museum of the eighteenth century, and was wondering whether I was up to shopping that afternoon. Still, the *nearly sixty* penetrated my daze. I thought Mum, the older sister, was in her fifties. I lifted my head and caught the angry look my mother shot her sister.

"Nearly sixty?" Mum's laugh was a short bark. "She always has to exaggerate. Always has to make herself much older than she is."

Zia Giaconda's eyes narrowed. She opened her mouth to say something and then closed it in a tight grimace.

About half an hour later, I overheard Zia Giaconda and Gina discussing Mum. I could hear Zia Giaconda's voice clearly. "She is a selfish woman, that's what she is . . . But to try and keep it a secret from her daughter." They were still in the kitchen, and perhaps because they couldn't see me out on the tiny terrace, they thought I couldn't hear them. But the window was wide open.

"Well, I was left speechless," Zia said. "You saw. No one is to know. It's forbidden."

"But we all know."

"Listen to this. I told her that she should apply for her Italian pension. She has to top up her contributions, but she did work here in Italy for years and years. She is entitled. No, she wouldn't even consider it. She couldn't bring herself to admit she was eligible. I don't need it, she said.

Don't think of yourself, I said. If you don't need your pension, give it to me. I need it. But—there was no way. That's how much love she has for her sister."

I don't remember whether I deliberately searched out her passport or simply came across it. Sometime on that trip, I found and read it.

Rosa Pia Edwards née Pagan, born August 30, 1910 in Lussingrande, Italy.

I held the navy blue book by a thumb and forefinger, as if it were a dirty Kleenex. "You always said . . . well, you said different things, but never 1910." Mum pulled it from my extended fingers and began to turn away, to put it back in her handbag. I wasn't done. "I don't get it. Why lie? Who cares how old you are?"

She gave me her poor-child-will-you-ever-grow-up look. "You don't know how people gossip. I'm a little older than your father, and there are some who will pounce on any little detail and use it against you."

"OK to others. But why to me? And to subtract ten years. That's not a little fudging. It's major. "

She didn't blink. "I was born in 1915. I don't shout it from the rooftops. But it is 1915. That's the truth."

"But it says—"

"It's wrong. The passport is wrong."

Was my embarrassment for her or myself? My mother would lie rather than admit she was a decade older than my father. "How can it be wrong? It is one of the things you can count on."

"Two world wars. You don't know, growing up in Canada, what happens in war. Documents were destroyed." Her tone was calm, matter-of-fact.

"By whom? Are you saying deliberately?"

"Who knows? Tito wanted to obliterate the presence of Italians. Pretend they were never there. Archives were burned."

I was insulted that she thought I would fall for this explanation. "Facts are facts, Mum. Records don't lie."

"That's how much you know," she said.

I never brought up her age again. I thought if it meant that much to her, let her cling to her illusions and think she was fooling me. Besides, I sensed she would stick to her story.

A little more than a year later, I was married and living in another city. I forgot the confrontation over the passport, tucked it away in a fold of my mind. If anyone asked me how old my mother was, I would say that I did not know. And mean it.

Sometime in the mid-1990s—I can't pinpoint the specific time or news story—a report from the war in Bosnia resuscitated the question of the reliability of documents. A mob of Serb soldiers, having shot, captured, or generally driven out the Muslim and Croat inhabitants of a small town and trashed and burned their houses, invaded the town hall and destroyed all signs that those inhabitants had ever lived in the town. They burned birth, marriage, and death records.

I heard my mother's voice, superimposed over the bland tones of the radio announcer. *You don't know.* And queasily I knew she was right. I was learning that the records of a life—a generation of lives and deaths—could be erased, obliterated, a people "cleansed" away by a perverse will.

Not long afterward, I read in a novel, Carlo Sgorlon's *La Foiba Grande*, about a village where the registers were destroyed at the end of a great war. The officials of the new regime pretended that the records had been burned in an unfortunate and accidental fire. But they had been burned to cause statistical chaos, to make a fair plebiscite on the fate of Istria difficult, if not impossible. In the cemetery, all the gravestones bearing Italian names were smashed to pieces. Not just a generation, but hundreds of years erased. But I could not presume that these events were historical; the book was fiction, set in an imaginary village and recounted as a fable. Long ago and far away, a people vanished.

Over a year after finding my mother's passport, I interviewed a witness who saw the remains of the giant bonfire where the registers of her city had been burned. But on the day I found the passport, I didn't know that documents could be destroyed, records falsified. Even so, when I opened my mother's passport, I was not quite as sure and as righteous as I had been that first time. The passport was as I remembered it. *Rosa Pia Edwards née Pagan, born August 30, 1910 in Lussingrande, Italy.* Again, what was hard and certain turned liquid and slippery, sliding through my fingers. *Lussingrande, Italy:* I hadn't noticed that last time. My mother was not born in Italy. In 1910, the island of Lussino was in Küstenland, a province of Austria. It wasn't ruled by Italy until after the Treaty of Rappallo in 1920. So was it a typo? Had she actually been born in 1920 as she sometimes claimed? Impossible. Nor was Lussino in Italy when the passport was granted in 1989.

The accompanying birth and baptism certificate laid out the same facts. It was not the usual government document but a photocopy of a church one, issued in 1947 by the Archdiocese of Zara. It made no mention of any country—only the province of Istria. Had Yugoslavia been left off deliberately to grant Mum some flexibility when claiming country of origin? Or had the signers, Canon D'Antoni and Monsignore Haracich, been uncertain as to which country would finally rule Lussino?

If Mum's year of birth was supported only by this faded form, an error could have been made. The calligraphy is uneven: the word in the space for the year is almost illegible. It doesn't say *dieci* (ten). There is a splotch, then what looks like *ieii,* followed one line down with 1910. The entire certificate feels makeshift.

Each stage of my father's public life was recorded: there are grammar school reports, apprenticeship papers, records of his enlistment in the Royal Engineers and promotions to the rank of captain, war medals, immigration papers, postsecondary school transcripts, and so on. I knew where his parents and their respective parents were buried. I had seen the graves in Earls Barton, a Midlands village, and could take my daughters to see them. (The only relative missing was the uncle Dad was named after, the Frank Edwards who was killed at seventeen years of age in the Battle of the Somme and whose body was never found.)

There were various pictures of my dad as a baby and as a boy and various ones of his father, Fred Edwards, and mother, Ada Tippler Edwards, including a few of her acting in repertory plays. I had inherited her crystal dresser set, a Wedgwood teapot, some Royal Doulton china, the few pieces left of her silver set, and a black apron with bright embroidery that may have been part of a theatrical costume. I had pages and pages of a family tree that traced the Edwardses and the Tipplers back for 150 years. There were no celebrities, no historical figures. My father's family, on both sides, was modest, even humble. Yet its members had left their traces, signs—however slight—that they had once existed.

In contrast, almost nothing in my mother's life was documented. The papers that did exist were suspect. And her family, her parents, for example? I had nothing concrete, no documents, no heirlooms. Not even a gravesite.

As I put the passport back in the briefcase, I heard a familiar screech from the living room. Mum was awake. "Where are you?" she asked when I perched on the sofa arm beside her easy chair.

"Right here, Mum. Should I get you your coffee?"

Her voice was agitated, almost panicked. "Where's Giaconda?"

"In Italy, of course."

"She was with me."

"You must have had a dream."

"I was thinking. I don't understand. We were a happy family."

"What don't you understand?"

"Where did it go, my family? My sisters and brothers around the table. Mamma. I miss them."

"You never told me much about when you were young," I said. "In Lussino."

Mum shook her head. "We laughed a lot."

Mum's words sparked an image in my mind. *My sisters and brothers around the table.* I could see them and little Rosa. The scene together with the perusal of her birth certificate sparked a new longing. I wanted to find my mother out. But also to know the child, the girl, and the woman she had been. That was how my search into the history and the culture that shaped her began.

4

*I do not feel that I am one of those
who remained. I am an aboriginal.*

Ondina Lusa, citizen of Koper

the shell game

THREE YEARS LATER, in May 2001, I made
a return visit to the island where my mother was born.
And her mother was born and her mother's mother, back
and back, hundreds of years. The island of Lussino, now
called Losinj, lies parallel to the Croatian coast in the
Adriatic Sea. At the time, getting there was still awkward,
and Marco didn't want to make the effort. "So you think
this is necessary?" he would say. "We have to interrupt our
vacation in Venice?"

"Necessary for me," I'd answer.

"You have to go to the actual place?" he said, when I
told him that I had booked the hotel, "Haven't you read all
the books?"

"What books? There are hardly any. I've told you that."

"What about all the interviews you've done? What do
you expect to find there?"

My mother's people and her culture. Maybe. Looking at my husband's skeptical face, I said, "How can I know until I find it?"

"It's not as if you haven't been there before."

"I didn't know beans then." My mother's family had been forced to leave temporarily during World War I and then permanently after World War II. When I went to Losinj between the 1950s and 1970s, I knew those facts, but not the context, the history, the meaning. And I had been too young to see, or to want to see, my mother in the place.

The journey was a personal one. Losinj meant nothing to Marco; he would probably be bored. But there were no plane, train, or hydrofoil connections there (the last would start in July), and buses took two days. A car was the only alternative. And since I was easily panicked on Canadian roads, there was no way I could drive on European ones: Marco had to accompany me.

We rented an Opel 235 at Piazzale Roma, the garage at the land entrance to Venice, and took the eight-lane toll highway through the flat delta land, between factories and fields, warehouses and farmhouses. We skirted Trieste and crossed the Slovenian border, where the road abruptly narrowed to one lane each way and the countryside grew greener and wilder. Half an hour and we were in Croatia, the road narrower and narrower, the asphalt pitted, bumps and potholes shaking the Opel.

Then a lineup, a long wait, and a ferry to the northern tip of the archipelago. My cousin Lino had warned us that driving down first the island of Cres and then Losinj to our destination was not for North Americans, not for "you guys used to big cars and big highways." Still, we expected more than a pitted track barely wide enough for two cars.

Marco didn't hesitate. We sped along, around ninety-degree curves, up through an oak forest, then over barren, rock-strewn fields, along the edge of cliffs, the sea a vertiginous drop below. We saw no houses, no huts, only emptiness, silence. I spotted two enormous birds in the sun-bleached sky. The island is a sanctuary for white vultures, home to eagles, falcons, snakes, and lizards.

Once, the archipelago was completely covered with trees.

Once, Robert Graves claims, Lussino was the island of Circe, lush and seductive.

If the lushness and most of the trees were gone, the seductiveness remained. And as we drove along under the cerulean sky and looked out at the wine dark Adriatic, this island seemed a plausible candidate for the island of the goddess Circe, daughter of the sun and granddaughter of the sea.

The first signs of human presence were the *masiere,* the stone walls running in no discernible pattern, marking no boundaries, kilometer after kilometer of gray rocks piled one on top of the other, handpicked to clear the pastures and stop further erosion.

Despite its claim to be Circe's island, I saw no pigs— only the odd goat. When I rolled down the window, I could smell the bushes of rosemary and sage and see the yellow flowers of moly. This was the herb that Ulysses wore to protect himself from Circe's magic and prevent his being turned into a pig, as his men had been, though in the epic its flowers are described as milky white rather than yellow.

Now the road was growing smoother and marginally wider. There were traffic signs, turnoffs, the odd church spire, and a clutch of houses in the distance.

Once, twice, there were soldiers at the door, in the house.

Once, twice, the people were forced to leave their home and their island behind.

On my last visit, I had believed, as so many of us did, that Tito was the good side of Communism. That certainly he took from the rich but that he was reasonable about the taking.

"Now I know better," I had told Marco one of the times he was complaining about the trip. "He was like the other dictators. Now I will see the place differently."

Marco was silent, tense. We drove over the bridge of Osoro and onto the island of Losinj. The bridge also marks a startling climatic change. In the winter, the northern island of Cres (once Cherso) knows snow and the *bora,* a cold alpine wind. Losinj is subtropical, with a multitude of plant species and patches of reforestation. Oncoming cars and buses were more frequent now; suddenly one would be facing us head-on. Marco would swear; I'd shriek. The vehicle would dart back into its lane at the last moment. "It doesn't help," he said, "you yelling." My anxiety was swelling, rising in my throat.

Once, for nearly a thousand years, the coastal cities of Istria and the islands of the Quarnero were part of the Venetian Empire. Until 1945 Istra and Istja were Istria, the

Kvarner was the Quarnero, Koper was Capodistria, Pula was Pola, and Rijeka was Fiume.

Once, for four hundred years, central and northeastern Istria was part of the Austro-Hungarian Empire. Through that period, the majority of Istrians who declared themselves Italian lived in the coastal cities and on the islands, and the majority of Istrians who declared themselves Croatian and Slovenian lived in the interior of the mainland. (And then there were the Austrians, the Romanians, the Hungarians, and the Albanians.)

In the Austrian census of 1910, 43 percent of the population of Lussingrande declared themselves Italian. In 1921, 92 percent of Lussinpiccolo registered as Italian. By 1991, less than 1 percent of the inhabitants of both towns did. I had come to seek out that small percentage, those Italian-Istrians who had not gone into exile during the great exodus after World War II. They were and are called *I Rimasti,* which means those who remained. Both the exiles and the ethnic Croatians have long mistrusted the *Rimasti.* And at times, both groups have denied that the *Rimasti* exist. The more militant of the exile groups have stated that all the Italians left, that none remained. Likewise, the Croatian newspaper *Glas Istre* has declared that Istria always was and always will be Croatian.

Other spokespersons for the exiles, particularly those who settled in Trieste, have acknowledged that some of the Italian ethnics did remain but claim that they were all collaborators and Communists, willing to be assimilated into a Balkan society.

Some of *I Rimasti* did believe in the Communist myth; many Italians fled Yugoslavia in the late 1940s, but some crossed the other way to be part of the revolution and build the new order. A year later, however, many of these idealists, as well as those Italian ethnics who had fought as partisans during the war, were trying to escape Yugoslavia, disillusioned by the ferociousness of the government's anti-Italian campaign: the economic penalties, the executions, the specter of Goli Otok, the Yugoslav gulag.

In the mid-1990s, when Istria alone of all the regions of Croatia rejected Croatian nationalism, the government rediscovered the Italian minority. As no census has been conducted since the departure of so many of Croatia's Serbian citizens during the Balkan wars of the early 1990s, the exact number of Italian ethnics in the country is unknown. The Croatian Ministry of Foreign Affairs declares there are only several thousand. In their newspaper *La Voce del Popolo di Rijeka,* the Italian community claims at least twenty thousand members. When he was still president, Franco Tudjman labeled these remaining few a "fifth column" that weakened the nation. The HDZ (the ruling party) declared that Istria must be "Croatized."

I was on a search for the suppressed, the denied, and the forgotten. The *Rimasti* were here, somewhere. But how was I to recognize them? To survive (I suspected), they had transformed themselves so that they were indistinguishable from the others who lived here: the Croatians and Serbs, who came decades ago, after the exiles left, and the Bosnians and Kosovites, who arrived a few years ago, having been displaced by the recent war.

Once, the cities and the towns of white stone were empty, abandoned. Once? Twice? Three times? Ten times?

THE HOTEL IN Veli Losinj (Big Losinj) was at the head of a promontory, and from our balcony we could look out over the turquoise sea to the mainland mountains. But La Punta was not the luxury hotel promised on the Internet site. It was a sprawling cement bunker built during Tito's rule, with hundreds of rooms, long, dimly lit corridors, and an enormous, marble lobby, empty of furniture and people. And the promised exercise room had no equipment but a padded mat; the disco was closed, the mini-golf course overrun with weeds. "So this is the best in town," Marco said, grimacing at the thin mattress, the skimpy towels. "Spartan."

"Communist style," I said. "I used to think that only the rich and privileged stayed here. I thought if I ever could, it would mean I'd made it."

"Goes to show how wrong we can be." Marco stretched out on one of the narrow single beds. "I'm dizzy." He was pale.

"Let's go down for dinner. Low blood sugar; food always helps."

He moved his head on the pillow. "I didn't like the smell coming in." Abruptly, he sat up. "I can't believe we were so dumb."

The incident he was referring to had happened while we were waiting in line for the ferry from the coast of Istria to the archipelago. The spot is called Brestova, but despite the name, there is no village, not even a house there, only two small booths—one for tickets, the other for drinks and packages of chips. Beside the first booth, a swarthy man had made a loud sound, a call, and dropped into a crouch. He lined up a flat board in front of him, then whipped out three small wooden boxes. His nimble hands shuffled the boxes. A few men from the cars began to gather around him as he started his spiel. The words sounded harsh and strange, but I could guess what he was saying. Try your luck. See the ball, follow the ball, here, there, here.

Bored and hot in the May sun, sipping from a newly purchased bottle of mineral water, I watched the man draw a teenage boy into the game. The boy was wagering his money too quickly, throwing the bills down without observing carefully.

Where? Your eye, my hand. What'll you bet? Come on, here, there, where.

Marco ambled up beside me. I passed him the bottle of water. I could see the mistakes the boy was making, where the man was making the switch, where the ball was ending up. The boy groaned as he made another wrong guess, turning his head and throwing me a rueful glance. He threw down another bill. "There—it's over on the right," Marco said in Italian. The boy showed no sign that he understood; he pointed to the middle box. Then, as my hand was reaching into my pocket, Marco was laying a 100,000-lire note, about $80 Canadian, on the pavement. Here? There? Nowhere, nowhere.

I felt a flash of shame, remembering.

"Four hundred thousand lire. I can't believe it," Marco said. He prided himself on being alert and shrewd.

I shook my head. "We were both taken in." Neither of us ever gambled, not even on lottery tickets. "And I have no excuse. I recently read about these shell games. It's all a trick, an illusion. The ball isn't under any of the boxes."

"The three guys must have been in it together. And we were the mark."

Once, instead of the hotel, a grand villa stood on the promontory. My great-aunt attended her first ball at the Villa Punta. She danced with an Austrian count and ate little creamy cakes. During World War II, the Germans occupied the villa. Then, the British blew it up.

Once, instead of concrete, the builders used the luminous white stone of Istria.

5

I xe resta perche I ga sbaia

They stayed because they were wrong

From a poem by an exile about I Rimasti

wolves in the hills

THE NEXT MORNING, Marco and I walked down the curving road from the hotel to the piazza. A large framed picture of the harbor taken from this road hung over the doorway to my parents' kitchen. And now we were walking into a technicolor projection of the picture. For me, this view was as iconic and as familiar as a postcard of the Eiffel Tower or the Doge's Palace. And every year, an aunt, an uncle, or a cousin would send us a card featuring the view to mark his or her visit. Nothing essential had visibly changed since my mother was a child. The cafés, the houses, the Venetian tower up the hill on the right, even the paving stones were the same. Of course, motorboats were tied up at the dock instead of sailboats. The painted sails with their arcane symbols— sun, moon, or stars—were gone. And when a man on the deck of one boat called out to another man walking ahead of us, they spoke in words that sounded slippery and impenetrable.

Nothing and everything had changed. The familiar scene felt disconnected, foreign to me. I knew the Lussino of dreams and memories, the backdrop to and focus of stories, the home that had been lost, stolen. I knew the Lussino built of the white gleaming stones of nostalgia.

After the piazza, we took the promenade the Austrians had built so that the ladies and gentlemen could stroll in comfort. We tried to visit the cathedral and its Tintoretto, but it was locked. After we passed its yard of nettles and chickweed, we reached a cliff jutting out into the sea and stopped on the observation deck, which had a roof and curved arches to frame the view.

Before World War I, many of the visitors came to Lussino seeking a cure for their ailments. The Medical Faculty of the University of Vienna had certified the climate of Lussino as particularly healthful. And doctors prescribed the warm winters, dry climate, long hours of sunshine, and sea air of Lussino for those suffering from problems of the lungs and throat. Years before the certification, Archduke Karl Stefan, the admiral of the Austrian navy, had chosen Veli Losinj (then Lussingrande) for the site of his winter home.

"Did I ever tell you that Archduke Karl Stefan was made an honorary citizen of Lussingrande?" I said to Marco as we passed the graveyard. "He said he remained proud of the honor."

"And so? Does that make this place special?"

I was embarrassed; I'd heard the pleading in my voice. "Well, it wasn't run of the mill. Partly because it was a resort and partly because of the tradition of seafaring, the navigational school, Lussino had sophistication despite its size."

"Not anymore," Marco said.

"It's not easy to judge in a day or so." I was irritated. How can you explain magic to someone who does not sense it? Besides, on this visit, the blue sea, the white houses with red roofs, the walk beneath the pine and oak trees conjured for me not so much magic as the memory of magic.

The last time I had visited, in the early seventies, my two great-aunts had spoken nostalgically of the glorious days before the first war: *you should have seen Lussingrande then*—what fun, the waltzes and the gowns and the officers who bent from the waist and kissed your hand. But in the days of their youth and my mother's infancy, I suspect, their elders already regretted the passing of an earlier time when the island was at its zenith, when its great ships sailed the seven seas.

The last time, I sat in the great-aunts' kitchen, in their tiny three-roomed house on the piazza, and listened to their stories. Zia Cecilia had a straight back and thick white hair pinned up in a roll on her head. She wore dangling gold earrings and silk dresses with lace collars. I remember her with a whisk in her hand, beating the batter for a cake. She made birthday cakes for half the village. I remember Zia Giuditta complaining about her sister's compulsive baking: eggs cost money, the gas costs money. Zia Giuditta was tiny and wizened and wore disproportionately large, black-framed glasses. She had lost four sons: one to a World War I internment camp, one to the sea, one to World War II, and the last to the Communist purges.

I wish I hadn't been so young then, so lost in the fog of self-absorption. I could have asked them so many questions about my grandfather and grandmother, about my mother as a child and a young woman, about Lussino, which was disappearing, becoming Losinj. At least I sat in their kitchen and listened to the stories they did offer. And as I strolled along the sea walk with Marco, I carried my memory of their memories. I carried this time and the visit before and the visit before that (my first time in this place), and my mother's time and my aunt's time, when they were young until they were old, and my grandmother's time and her mother's time.

In the late forties and early fifties, after Tito came to power and sent his henchman to Istria to get rid of the Italians, most of those who were Italian not by blood but by culture fled. The white towns of Istria were left empty, abandoned, until settlers from the interior and from the other states of Yugoslavia arrived. Some of the villages were never repopulated. Visanda, for example, was used as the set for the war movie *The Longest Day*. The film company could blow up houses with impunity.

Now the streets of Veli Losinj looked not deserted but empty. Where were the people? A few vacationers, a few locals, were sitting at the outdoor cafés, carrying grocery bags, tying boats up to the dock. Thirty years ago, the tourists had been everywhere: thronging the cafés, clogging the harbor, covering the beaches with their naked flesh.

"For ten years, there was nobody," a waitress in a pizzeria told us. "Because of the war. Bad, hungry times. Last year, the tourists started to come back. Especially the Germans."

In the 1970s, I'd been intoxicated by the babel of languages and peoples, by the atmosphere of indulgence, sun, sea, and sex—a German youth picking up an Italian girl, a French couple rutting in the park, hippies smoking dope and camping on the beach. I was a girl, staying with relatives, watched over, protected. I remembered that visit as enchanted, transforming. I went out to discos and restaurants in Mali Losinj and even to the striptease club at La Punta, but always with a local group of young people. They knew who I was; they knew my mother's family. Some of us were even distantly related.

Thirty years later, I realized that they were children of the *Rimasti;* in a sense they were themselves *Rimasti.* But then I had never heard the word and had only a vague idea of the exodus. Nor did I realize that the restrictions in Yugoslavia had been loosened and the borders opened only the year before.

We had a good time, I remember, laughing and singing and flirting. I cannot remember all their names and faces. Clara, Giordana, Antonio—we had exchanged letters for a while, the four of us. And I knew that none of them lived here anymore. They had gone to Sweden, Slovenia, and Australia, in search of work, in search of a comfortable future. But the others?

Time was my defensive herb (my moly) that repelled any possible spells and ensured that such enchantment, such carefree happiness, would never possess me again. Thankfully, middle age made the self-absorption and ignorance equally impossible.

Marco and I peered at the archduke's palace and botanical garden through the wrought iron gates. "I'm

sure I walked through last time. It was a hospital then."
That time it had been sloppily maintained, a husk of what
it once was. And now the decay was more advanced: the
garden wild and ragged, the façade patched and stained.

The villas of the sea captains, those masters of the
nineteenth-century sailing ships, looked better kept,
painted bright yellow, orange, or blue, the gardens bloom-
ing but restrained. Still, all the shutters were closed, the
houses seemingly uninhabited.

When I was four, on my first visit with my mother, Zia
Cecilia still had the house that would be taken from her,
along with her paintings and antiques and most of her
land and money. My earliest memories are of that house
and that visit. For years I'd thought they were fragments
from dreams. I carried images of a many-roomed house
with high ceilings and soft, lush carpets, a sea both turquoise blue and transparent, of a dolphin arcing from that
sea through the pastel sky and splashing down close, so
close as I sat in a child-sized canoe alone and unafraid.
I was lying on a small bed in the middle of an immense
dark room. The bed was wrapped in a cascade of shim-
mering white netting, the white holding off the darkness. I
was in the land of fairy tales. I heard a conversation about
wolves in the hills, about danger. Most vividly of all, I saw
my toddler body covered in an eruption of boils, like the
bubbles you make when chewing gum, like white balloons
filled with water.

Over the years, I asked my mother various times: Did
we sleep under mosquito netting in Lussino? Did she
remember any stories about the wolves in the hills? Was I
ill? Was I covered in white boils? No, she always insisted;

no netting, no stories of wolves, and no boils. "I would have remembered something like that. I would have been so worried about you." Each time she convinced me. I was remembering dreams, not reality.

But when I returned to Losinj in the 1970s, my arms and legs erupted into boils again. So much for relying on my mother's memory. I asked Zia Cecilia about her house; she confirmed that the rooms were spacious and high ceilinged and that I'd slept under mosquito netting. I forgot to ask about the wolves. They did still exist in Istria during the fifties. But perhaps I heard a coded conversation. Perhaps the wolves were Tito's secret police, who, in those years, carried people off in the night, never to be seen again. I can't remember who was speaking, but I could sense that person's fear.

Mum no longer remembered either our visit in 1953 or its purpose. (My father might have if I'd asked him when I still had the chance.) But now that I appreciate what was happening in Istria during those years, I find it odd that she brought me then. The border between Yugoslavia and Italy was still closed and in dispute. Allied troops were still in control of Zone A, including Trieste, and much of the rest of Istria. Losinj, in Zone B, was under the military rule of Yugoslavia, which was using expulsions, beatings, imprisonment, and executions to enforce its control. And in this area, *l'esodo,* the great exile, was in full flood; two-thirds of the population of Zone B left in 1953 and 1954.

I can only imagine that since my father was English and, for at least one year after the war, part of the Allied occupation force in Trieste, my mother could cross the border when the rest of her family could not. Perhaps, since she had a British passport, she was the only one in the family who could check on the well-being of the relatives who remained. Although if the border guards had checked that passport, they would have seen that she was born in Lussingrande. Former Istrians were not allowed to return for a holiday until 1970. Perhaps the guards didn't realize that Lussingrande was Veli Losinj. Perhaps they were fooled because the country of birth was falsely shown as Italy.

In 1953 our closest relatives were no longer in Lussino. My cousin Oscar Sambo, who had joined the partisans while still a teenager, avoided the fate of many of the Italian ethnic partisans—execution by their former comrades—by escaping to Italy and then the United States. For despite the propaganda, the Titini (Tito's men) did not only, or even primarily, target former Fascists. According to the exiles I interviewed in Canada, there was no pattern to whom was taken. Nor was there any sort of trial. It was like an epidemic, a plague. The victims were either shot and cast into the *foibe,* the natural karst caves and bottomless ravines that dot the Istrian landscape, or thrown into the *foibe* alive, often manacled to a corpse, which is why the word *foibe* has come to stand for all the violence and suffering of that time in Istria.

As often happens, many of those who had been Fascists under Italian rule not only survived but transformed themselves into Communists after the war—and flourished. Meanwhile, Oscar's father, my uncle Erminio, who had never supported the Fascist regime, had his fishing boat confiscated. After a few ill-advised comments in the local tavern, he'd been jailed and tortured. He was released after a couple of years, but by then he had tuberculosis. In 1950, he and Zia Maricci, two daughters, and a granddaughter, Corinna, whom my parents later adopted, left Lussino and joined the diaspora.

In 1953, they were still living in a metal hut in a refugee camp in Tortona, north of Genoa. The five of them were allotted a space of a few meters square, which they marked off with blankets. There was one bathroom for the entire barracks, no hot water, and not enough food. The only explanation I can imagine for our visiting Lussino instead of Tortona on that trip from England is that the refugee camp was even more impermeable to visitors than Yugoslavia. The exiles may have considered themselves Italian, and the Yugoslavs may have considered them Italian, but the Italian government and the Italian people did not. They were not welcomed but spat upon and ostracized. Like many refugees today, they escaped persecution for another kind of imprisonment and years of waiting to be processed and placed in whatever country would have them.

MARCO AND I easily found Zia Cecilia's great house; it still stood tall overlooking the churchyard. My childhood memories had not misled me as to its size and importance. "See," I said, "she was a lady of means." Marco made a sound to acknowledge that he had heard me. As far as status went, my ancestors couldn't measure up to his: his paternal grandmother was the granddaughter of a king.

"Apparently, it's owned by a company from Zagreb. They use it as conference center and retreat," I told Marco.

"Nice house," he said. He was not so much bored as unimpressed with everything we saw. I knew he was thinking: we could be in Venice.

6

Viva le Foibe

Graffiti on a wall in Trieste in 2002

what remains

WE DROVE TO Mali Losinj to find gifts for the only two relatives left: Armida Baricèvic, eighty-one, from my grandfather's side, and Maria Lettich, ninety-three, from my grandmother's. This bigger town used to be called Lussinpiccolo, little Lussino, and the smaller town (where we were staying) was Lussingrande, big Lussino. Now, in Croatian, the reversal was the same: Mali Losinj means small Losinj and Veli Losinj means big, and big is small and small is big. But in the dialect, *grande* also means oldest, as it does when we say "big brother" in English. I should have been calling both towns by their Croatian names, their present names, their correct names, the manager of the hotel informed me. But I was searching for Lussino, not Losinj, for what and who remained, for shards, traces, echoes, glimmerings.

Unlike Veli Losinj, Mali Losinj was bustling: school-children ran out in front of our car; women with grocery bags stood on corners chatting and gesticulating; the streets were filled with packs of young men, motorbikes, cars, traffic-stopping trucks. The whitewashed buildings with their red roofs spiraled up the hills and down to the port. By the water, an open square with a fountain and a broad esplanade were dotted with empty cafés. And every-where spray-painted slogans and posters that we could not decipher. Marco pointed out the letters HDZ on one poster. "Isn't that the latest incarnation of Tudjman's party? The nationalists? Must be an election."

"The Istrian Democratic Party, which is anti-Zagreb and pro-regional autonomy, usually sweeps this area. See there—IDS."

In the shops, we found little worth buying. Shoes and bags were plastic, clothes cheap and dull. I wanted books, but what was marked as a bookshop on the map was actu-ally a stationery store with one shelf of books, all of which were Croatian translations of American writers like John Grisham and Danielle Steele. Finally, we found a perfume shop, and I bought the classic *Je Reviens* cologne and body lotion for the elderly ladies.

As I sprayed and Marco and I sniffed and finally chose, we chatted with the tall, bearded young man waiting on us. When we'd entered, he'd addressed us in broken Eng-lish; our clothes must have marked us as North Ameri-can. Just as he would have in Venice, Marco answered the young man in Italian, and unlike the salespeople in the other shops, the young man responded. His Italian was almost too correct and unusually formal.

"You speak Italian very well," Marco said. "Did you study it at school?"

"No," the young man said, "We were Italian at home. My mother and father."

It seemed only natural and proper that I shift to dialect. *"Lori i xe i rimasti?"*

Also making the shift, he told me that it was his grandparents who had stayed. When I asked him if they ever explained why, he shrugged; this was their home. They couldn't imagine themselves anywhere else. *Anche se i tempi spussavano.* Even if the times stank.

The Istro-Veneto dialect does not flow as musically as standard Italian. Verbs are truncated; double consonants become single; and hard *g*'s and *z*'s are common. Many words have obviously come from German, Croatian, or Slovenian rather than Italian. And the pronunciation is less sweet and singsong than in Venice. Marco was following the gist of the conversation as I answered the shopkeeper's questions about where we were from and why we were there. He'd been exposed to the dialect through my mother and our many visits to Venice.

In the first years of our marriage, he'd thought that when I spoke Italian, I was making mistakes out of ignorance. He'd point out that I was declining "to be" or "to have" incorrectly or that a word I was using did not exist. Marco's family is from Sicily, but, as is common among those educated under Mussolini's regime, which imposed standard Italian across the country, they never spoke Sicilian. Over the years, I have become more self-conscious: hesitant and careful when I switch to Italian. But still the first words that come to me, the grammatical constructions that feel right to me, are the ones I learned from my mother, before I began to speak English. Although he still corrects me, Marco has learned that, especially when I am tired (or caught up in the moment), I will fall into not broken Italian but correct Istro-Veneto.

"*Vera, Lussignana? Ma de chi ti xe?*" the young man asked. Imagine that, from Lussino. Who do you belong to?

My grandparents' last names, Pagan and Lettich, established that my mother was from Lussingrande and that we were probably distantly related. *Ma mi go parentela Lettich.*

Before we left with the gift-wrapped bottles, Marco asked Guido Stepancic, as I will call him, to recommend a good restaurant. Before the trip, I had tantalized Marco with memories of freshly caught fish, of *brodeto* (fisherman's stew) *con polenta,* giant scampi in tomato sauce, lamb roasted over an open fire, grilled octopus, and white asparagus. But those meals had all been in private homes. Now those relatives and friends were gone, and the food at La Punta and at a couple of restaurants we had tried seemed designed for the elderly German tourists: bland and heavy. The only fish was of indeterminate origin and deep-fried. Nor, perusing posted menus, could I find a place that featured those labor-intensive Istrian specialties my mother used to make: the *palacinke* (crepes) with jam, the *gnocchi* with *žgvacet* (veal) sauce, or best of all, *gnocchi con susini* (plums).

Gianni's and Barracuda, Guido suggested, giving directions. The owner of the first restaurant is one of us, he said. And so is the cook at the second.

In the twentieth century, Istria and thus Lussino changed allegiance six times. It was part of the Austrian Empire until after World War I, when Italy, which had joined the war to redeem what it considered its lost territories, Alto Adige and Istria, imposed its Fascist rule. Then came the Nazi Command, the Allied Command, and Yugoslavia, and now Istria is divided among three countries: Italy, Slovenia, and Croatia.

Once, the Austrians, afraid of Italian irredentism or nationalism, encouraged the Croatian societies and schools. However, Istro-Veneto was allowed to flourish and was accepted as the official language of the Austrian navy.

Then, when Italy ruled, Croatian and Slovenian schools were closed; Slavic names were Italianized. And Italian became the official language of the courts and the government. In the schools, children learned about Italian—meaning not Istrian—civilization, art, and accomplishments. In the small Istro-Venetian–speaking town of Dignano, a mother complained to the school inspector that a new teacher spoke "Slav" and the children could not understand a word. The teacher was actually Neapolitan, but to the people of that town, everything that was foreign was "Slav."

Later, when Yugoslavia ruled, everything was reversed. Italian schools were closed, Italian names were Slavicized, and so on.

The next day, Marco was wiped out by a mysterious stomach ailment: nausea and cramps. We had eaten a light dinner at Barracuda—grilled branzino, arugula, and white country wine. He wondered whether the fault lay with previous meals at La Punta. "Sausage and sauerkraut.

My Italian body's rebelling." So he stayed behind at the hotel, while I continued my search.

Veli Losinj snakes along two narrow, contiguous bays. At the first is the *porticello,* the little port with the Baroque church and the main piazza, the eighteenth-century buildings now arrayed in festive colors: peach, salmon, terra-cotta, purple, an improbable royal blue. And close by—the sixteenth-century tower, with battlements, built to repel Saracen pirates. The proportions of Rovenska, the fishing center on the second bay, are more modest; the buildings and marina are smaller, but it boasts a beach and a long breakwater jetty.

On my solitary walks, I turned away from the familiar, from the sea, to the rest of the town, choosing narrow footpaths that led me up and down hills, past holiday apartments and villas. Each one was surrounded by a walled garden, so as I walked, I caught whiffs of sharp rosemary, sweet broom, the duskiness of laurel, and the fresh tang of juniper. Citrus gave way to roses. Then a cloud of something spicier. I could not see the originating plants, only the second floors of the houses, the top leaves of the trees.

The drystone walls lining the paths reached over my head. And under my feet, the same gray stones, though these were shiny and slippery from use. A looming, overcast sky, stillness, silence. I could hear my heartbeat. And again I was seized with apprehension, a sense of failure, of having forgotten something essential.

Was there anything left for me (and of me) here?

Occasionally, my path would cross a road and give me a view of a facing hill: an expanse of green dotted with white houses, divided, marked, by the rivers of stone. I was going up more than coming down, gaining altitude, approaching (though I didn't know it then) the base of St. Ivan's Mount. A broken wall, then another, a missing gate, then another, fallen stones, gap after gap. At last, I could stop and gaze into the hidden gardens, but here only ruins were on display: deserted houses, abandoned homes with sagging roofs, broken glass, missing doors. I felt as if I were walking through a war zone, as if these outskirts had been bombed or were the site of a battle fought fiercely, house to house. Tall grass grew in what had been a kitchen, bougainvillea in the parlor.

These houses must have been empty a long time; such damage took years. The empty houses closer to the center were also probably the former homes of the exiles, but they had been occupied in between. In Edmonton, a friend originally from Belgrade told me that many of the important Serbian artists and intellectuals had holiday homes in Losinj. Now, like the exiles they had replaced, they could no longer return.

Once, Istria was a borderland between Eastern and Western Europe, a point of contact between Germans, Latins, and Slavs. Because of its position as a crossroads, it was repeatedly devastated by malaria and bubonic plague, its white cities emptied. In 1629, a contemporary historian described Pola as no longer a city "but a cadaver of a city." The Venetian fleet brought settlers from the corners of its empire to repopulate and revive the region. The boats transported Montenegrins, Italians, Slovenians, Albanians, Greeks, Romanians, and Morlacchi—all those fleeing the advance of the Ottoman Turks.

Several times, I lost my way. The paths didn't seem to correspond to those on the map. There were more crossroads, more paths than those shown, and they twisted and turned and changed directions. I tried to ask for directions in Italian. Several people answered in English, and two, a woman wearing a headscarf and a young man, walked past as if I hadn't spoken.

I had read that for years the Communist authorities in Istria viewed the speaking of Italian or Istro-Veneto dialect as a subversive act. In 1997, when a group in Rovinj/Rovigno agitated for official encouragement of bilingualism, Tudjman reacted by calling the Italian ethnics "liars and traitors." By 2001, although many Croatian nationalists remained hostile, the official policy had changed. The towns that used to be ethically Italian, such as Rovinj, were erecting bilingual signs. And the enrollment at Italian schools was rising.

Still, fewer and fewer people spoke Istro-Veneto; it has been placed on the UN list of endangered languages. So switching into dialect became my magic wand. As I'd discovered in the perfume shop, when someone responded in kind, I had found one of the *Rimasti* (or their children or grandchildren). The wand exposed not just their true selves but mine; I was changed from a stranger to a daughter of the exile.

7

I didn't betray you
Even if I had to leave you
An Istrian song about the exile

Da qui suso e soso
From here, up and down
Instructions on the way to Maria Lettich's house

them and us

WHEN I COULDN'T FIND Maria Lettich's house, I stopped and asked a man, crouched with pail and trowel at the base of a stone wall. He couldn't help with directions; he didn't live in Losinj. But he offered to take me to his cousin, who would know the way. As we walked, the wall mender told me that he lived in Trieste. "We went when I was little." Now that he was going to retire, he'd decided to repair the old family home that had been empty since his grandparents died. "I've always wanted to come back, at least part of the year."

"Must be quite a job."

His pale eyes and silver hair were startling against his sun-browned face. "Just imagine—there was even a hole in the roof."

"I thought it was illegal for the exiles or their descendants to own property here."

He shrugged in the Italian way that means *you do what you have to.* "A compliant relative. The right papers."

"You're lucky," I said. "So much waste—all these abandoned houses."

"And untilled fields, desiccated olive trees. The land gone to ruin."

He stopped outside a gate and, without going in, shouted at the house: "Katé, be quick." Then, to me: "One of my brothers went to Australia, uncles and aunts to Canada; their lives are tormented by nostalgia. Like a stone in their hearts. I'm lucky." His cousin, a plump woman in a flowered housedress, had appeared at an upstairs balcony. "Eh, Katé," he yelled up to her: "You know a Maria Lettich around here?"

"Bilga," the woman yelled back. "That's who she wants."

"Ah, Bilga. Of course," the man said. A year later, in the index of a book on Lussingrande, I found Bilga in a list of traditional nicknames. The citizens of the town do not know each other by their legal names but by these nicknames. I also found on the list Magnafumo and Ponaronzo, the names used respectively for my Sambo cousins and my mother's family.

Maria Lettich, hunched over a cane, moved and spoke slowly. I went to her to confirm and fill in some details about my grandmother's family. Unlike my mother's other surviving cousin, Armida Baricèvic, Maria had not been close to either my mother or me. But she welcomed me with a long hug and happily answered my questions.

"Good to have someone to talk to, to tell," she said. "It's been hard the last few years. There are so few of us left. Here, in my Lussino, I've been screamed at, spat upon, an old woman like me. *Italianski,* they yell, as if being Italian is a sin.

"And even the priest hates us Italians. Our cathedral says it's a Croatian Catholic church. For a while I didn't care. I went to confession like always, in Italian. Why should it matter if the priest doesn't understand? God understands. But then the priest said he wouldn't listen; he'd walk out of the confessional. And the entire mass had to be in Croatian. He banned the singing of the Italian hymns, the old ones. So the choir all went on strike."

I was confused, since I had always thought the Lettich side was the Croatian side of the family. But Maria had never learned Croatian. And she insisted that her parents and, certainly, her zia Caterina, my grandmother, spoke only Italian.

"But Lettich is a Croatian name," I said.

"Can't judge by the name. Some Italians had Croatian names and vice versa," she said.

"So why didn't you leave with all the others?"

"My sister was staying, and she needed me. Her husband drank." Maria paused. "I couldn't imagine myself anywhere else."

At ninety-four, Maria Lettich was the oldest person in Veli Losinj, the unofficial historian, and an invaluable source of information, though one that tired easily. After forty minutes or so, her mind began to wander. "I don't know what to tell you."

The second time I went to see her, I asked about Lussino and World War I. I had read that in May and June 1915, the Austrian government evacuated the civilian population of southern Istria, whose loyalty they mistrusted, forcing them to leave their homes and transporting them in cattle cars to internment camps in Bohemia and Moravia. An aunt had told me years ago that our family had been part of these deportations but had been sent to Sicily instead of Czechoslovakia. I thought that Maria Lettich might remember not the events (which had occurred, after all, eight-six years earlier) but the stories of that time. She surprised me; she remembered being in the cattle car and the internment camp. And she confirmed that the camp for the so-called Italian inhabitants of Lussino was in Sicily. Maria described watching her mother give birth to her sister on a scattering of straw in a barn.

ALTHOUGH THIRTY YEARS had passed, I didn't expect to find my mother's other cousin, Armida, so white haired and wrinkled. And from the way she hugged and kissed me and shook her head, I could tell that she too had expected my younger self. Several times as we caught up on family news, on my children and her grandchildren and on all the deaths (the list was long), Armida paused and gave me an appraising look. Finally, she said, "You've put on the pounds and the years. Once, you were a flower."

Her comments on my lost youth bothered me not just because they were true but because I knew she would pass them on to her son, with whom I had once been infatuated (as enchanted with him as I'd been with Lussino). I did not point out how she had changed. I exclaimed over the house, which was no longer a fisherman's cottage but had been renovated and shone from top to bottom. "I didn't need this," Armida said, "Not now, when I'm old, but my son insisted. He comes as much as he can with his family."

"It's hard for me to go to him in Koper. It's another country now. It's Slovenia, there's a border, so it's off the bus and passports, then back on the bus. No, no. I'm too old. My legs." She brought me pictures of the grandsons to admire and a poem the oldest one had written in Italian, a hymn to the rocks and the sea of the island. "He won a prize," she said. "Boruth." Her mouth twisted.

"It took me years to learn how to pronounce it. Not one of our names. And then, I didn't plan it, but I was at the grocer's buying a little coffee—it wasn't so expensive then—he asked me about the new baby, and I said his name was Davide." Armida looked embarrassed. "Then I told everyone Boruth was Davide. Even Mario [her hus-band], may he rest in peace, called him Davide. Till that summer, my daughter-in-law was walking the baby and everyone came out and started making a fuss, calling him Davide. Then they made me call him Boruth—though I think they learned something, because they called the second one Leonardo."

I asked Armida, as I had asked Maria Lettich, on which side her father, my grandfather, had fought in the first war. "Austria," Armida said. "No, Italy. Who knows?" (Maria had not known either.) Armida and I were sitting on her terrace overlooking the inlet of Rovenska, rows of small white boats below us, a stretch of pine woods, then a sandy beach to the right, and ahead the stone jetty built by Archduke Maximilian, who went on to become the emperor of Mexico.

I pointed out that despite her Croatian husband and son, she spoke of them and us. "As far back as I can remember, it has always been them and us," she said. "We called them *Slavi,* and they called us *Chioggiotti.*"

"Surely all the Italians weren't from Chioggia," I said, referring to the town on the edge of the Venetian lagoon.

"Maybe originally, hundreds of years ago."

"And lots didn't fit into them and us—some were Austrians and Hungarians." I had seen the censuses going back to 1880.

"We had separate dance halls." Armida continued. "And every now and then, there would be a big fight."

A rumble, I thought. "You never danced together? How did you start with your husband?"

"You're right. We would talk in the piazza. And then he started coming to our dances. I wasn't the only one. Oh no, there's always been lots of intermarriage."

Hard to keep them and us straight, I would have thought. But I said, "You never learned Croatian?" I tried not to sound disapproving.

"Everyone spoke our language, and by the time they didn't . . ."

"But marrying into a Croatian family?"

"I didn't want to. *Po nase,* their dialect sounded ugly to me. It isn't proper Croatian, you know."

"Neither is our language proper Italian."

"When I went to Rijeka to the clinic, the heart specialist and the nurses, they asked Antonio, how can it be that your mother doesn't speak Croatian? So he had to explain—how it used to be."

Circe was not the only witch associated with Lussino. In classical antiquity, until the Romans dug a canal at Osor, the islands of Cherso and Lussino were one island called Apsertides, for Apsyrtos, the brother of the witch Medea. The myth claimed that Medea killed her brother on this island and scattered his limbs across the sea to save Jason from her father. Medea knew that her father would stop and weep over his son's remains, and Jason and his Argonauts would be able to sail away. The island of Apsertides was where a sister turned against her brother, where blood betrayed blood for a false love.

AS SOON AS he felt better, Marco suggested we cut our trip short and go back to Venice. I was growing tired. Trying to discover the true nature of Losinj was making me feel as if I were a child again, straining to see through a white net and decipher the darkness beyond.

When I returned to Armida's with Marco, she chattered, though in Italian rather than Istro-Veneto, even more than the first time. "What can I offer you?" Fetching coffee and anise-seed cookies, uncorking a bottle of white wine, then one of pear brandy. Drink, eat, drink, drink, she said. "Isn't this a view?"

The three of us sat and stared at the curve of the bay, the blinding blue bordered by pale yellow sand. Beside and below us, on the surface, at least, a model of the fishing-port-turned-holiday-village: a scattering of small yachts, a restaurant awning barely covering the sprawl of tables on the quay, and spruced-up houses, plastered and painted, with green shutters and germanium-filled flower boxes. Armida had sprayed herself with the cologne we had bought her, and I was surrounded by the spicy, floral scent. And she brought out her grandson's poem again, this time so that Marco could read and admire it.

And she talked and talked. I prompted her with questions, but I avoided guiding her or putting words in her mouth. She wandered from memory to memory, doubling back at times, taking sudden turnoffs. The red and yellow sails on her father's boats, the cornmeal diet in the war, her heart condition. My mother when she was young, my grandmother when she was old, and me—what a bossy and articulate toddler I was.

She complained that she couldn't get good coffee in Losinj, that her pension did not arrive for months at a time, that she was alone. Oh, her husband's family checked on her, cooked for her if she wasn't well. Like Maria, she didn't go to church anymore: on Sundays, she stayed home and watched the mass on TV in Italian. Antonio had got her a satellite dish, so she got all the Italian channels.

"I hardly know anyone anymore. The town is full of strangers. Your mother is lucky that she lives with you and that you take care of her."

"I don't think she realizes." I felt a twinge of guilt. I flashed to my mother, who was in respite care at the General Continuing Care Hospital during my absence. I saw her bibbed and belted into her wheelchair, her eyes confused, lost.

Armida flipped back to 1950, when her husband was taken away for three months of forced labor. Everyone had to go. Then the soldiers with the red star on their caps came to her door and told her she had no right to be here. She must be gone in twenty-four hours. She was married, five months pregnant. At least the soldiers didn't come in the night, as they did for some. Some people would say they weren't worried—their consciences were clear—then you'd never see them again. Someone had denounced them. A neighbor who coveted their land, we used to think. Or someone they had crossed maybe years before. It was a time of revenge.

"What did you do?" Marco asked.

"Luckily, my husband's family had some connections who produced the right papers."

"False papers?" I asked.

She shrugged. "I became officially a Croat." (Slavicized, Italianized, people here had been shifting, changing their identities, for at least a hundred years. Your proclaimed nationality depended on convenience or, if times were good, on your vision of yourself.)

"You're sure," she said as I wrote in my notebook, "that no one here will read what I say?" When I had phoned her from Hotel La Punta, when I'd told her I would like her to talk about her life, she'd been surprised: "Why do you want to know?" And now she continued to ask me, "Who will see what you write? Will anyone here know?"

I reassured her yet again. "I'm sure no one here will see it. Here or in Italy." Thinking of the number of books I had sold the previous year: "And not many in North America. I'll change your name if that makes you feel better."

"That won't fool them. They'll know who I am."

I thought she was paranoid, but she had lived her life under Fascism and then Communism, and I had not. Despite her fears, however, she was elated by this chance to tell her story. And her excitement fueled her words.

"What else do you want me to tell you? What else do you want to know?"

What else? I was waiting for a revelation: the meaning of her life in this place. More, I was waiting, wanting, to capture what was hidden behind the stone walls, inside the silent, locked villas, under the crumbling roofs. A dark truth like truffles clustered on the roots of oak trees, like spores infesting the blood-colored earth. A luminous truth like the darting, dancing light of the phosphorescence in Rovenska Bay. The truth now and the truth then. *Once.* The word echoed in my head: *once.*

The mix of wine and bitter coffee left me light-headed. "Mario made lots of money ferrying those who left," Armida was saying. "For months, he sailed to Italy, his boat over-loaded. I was afraid the whole time that he'd capsize. You wouldn't believe what people tried to take with them."

The local representatives of the Yugoslav government would not allow the exiles to take anything deemed of value: money, jewelry, paintings, Turkish rugs, or Chinese porcelain. Nor many objects of emotional worth: books, an accordion, a record player, a demijohn of wine, a drum of olive oil, a plow, a shovel, a scythe, a lantern, a sewing machine, wool-stuffed mattresses, wooden chairs, feather comforters, copper pots, dishes, silver rubbed with dirt and ashes so that it looked like tin, a bicycle. A mountain of things were abandoned on the quay, surrendered because there was no room in the boats.

"Mario took my parents and then each of my brothers to Trieste. Silvio and Miro—I never saw them again." For the first time, Armida sounded old and tremulous.

As the sun set, in that round red ball of a moment, I could feel the fear of those in the boats, the urge to flee, abandoning possessions, homes, family, sailing away from their lives, their language, their ancestors, who had been always with them in the earth under their feet. The past, their past, was gone. On sailboats and fishing boats and ferries, in carts driven by oxen, in the military trucks the Americans had left behind, night after night for months, for years, they fled the towns, the islands, the mainland cities. And those who remained—they too were afraid, walking the deserted streets, stunned and alone. And they too—though they never left their homeland—they too lost it.

> I feel I am a stranger in my own country. . . the wrong kind of Italian.
>
> *An Italian-Istrian poet, Quarantotti Gambini, in an interview*

The next morning, I gave in. We would cut the trip short and leave the following day. I had wanted to check the archives in Mali Losinj for records of my grandparents, but Maria Lettich had explained that the old archives, like those of most of the towns in Istria, had all been burned in a supposedly accidental fire. Both she and Armida insisted that the priest would never let me see the parish records.

We took a final tour of the graveyard behind the church overlooking the sea. Neither of my grandparents was buried there, but I wanted to see the graves of Zia Cecilia and Zia Giuditta. The graveyard was austere: no trees and only one family chapel. A drystone wall marked the circumference. The paths were beaten red earth, the headstones gray marble or white stone. There was a small oval picture of Zia Cecilia on her headstone, hair white but thick, chin up, earrings dangling. On her grave, a circle of white lilies. Again, I wished I had asked her questions when I'd had the chance.

The dates on the stones went back several hundred years. In some graveyards, during the time of the *foibe,* the Italian names were chipped out of the headstones; here they were unmolested. Back and back, a Ragusin married a Gladofich, a Penso married a Siminich, a Lanza and a Baricèvic, a Lettich and a Pagan.

Everyone I had spoken to before I had come to Losinj and since I had been here made clear divisions: exiles and *Rimasti,* Slavs and *Chioggiotti,* real Lussignani and new settlers, Italians, Croats, Serbs, and lately, Bosnians. Them and us—but here in the graveyard one category merged into the next.

The house where my mother was born was across the road from the one where Maria Lettich lived. At the end of my second visit, she and I stood outside the tall green gate and rang the bell. "Once," Maria said, beginning a story I had heard before. "Once, there was an orange tree in your grandparents' garden, and that led to their name in Lussino, Ponaronzo. Those of the orange tree." When no one answered, with Maria's encouragement, I unlatched the gate and stepped into the garden.

The house looked solid, secure and substantial. But it was eclipsed by the magnificent tree that stretched taller than the roof. Nestled in the green shiny leaves were small, bright bitter oranges. Once there was an orange tree? Once? Still. This time the word was still. Even if the family had changed. Or could this be another tree? A replacement or an offspring?

I see children, my aunts and uncles, under the boughs of the tree. Two of the boys wrestle, howling, rolling back and forth over the roots. The oldest girl, Maricci, tries to reprimand them. She has a book open on her lap. Enea— I recognize her immediately; even as a child she has a big nose—Enea dangles a baby on her hip. A toddler is trying to cram an entire unpeeled orange into his mouth.

I look back at the silent, shuttered house. In a bedroom on the second floor, I see my grandmother, her black hair soaked in sweat, her face twisted in pain. The shutters are open; the sunlight pours in across the bloodied sheets, the matrimonial bed. She is laboring to deliver her seventh child. Stoically, her lips are clamped shut, but the midwife talks and the mother-in-law prays. Finally, the baby, who was turned the wrong way, has righted herself and is coming. Now her scream penetrates the window, tosses the leaves and branches. The children stop; each one of them looks up.

This place is where my mother began.

Memories and stories—mine and my mother's and my aunts', the memoirs I have read, the exiles' newsletters, the Internet postings. Memories and stories—two glowing ropes that intertwine and separate, slip by each other and knot over the dark pit, the *foiba* of forgetfulness.

8

We were in paradise,
and we didn't know what we had.

Rita Bertieri, a refugee to Canada from Istria

Those children who live far / regret this
port, this sky / so years seem decades /
and when they return they feel
as if they are swimming in honey

R. Cherconi, 1906, "Hymn to Lussino"

who remembers?

JUNE 1914

Little Rosa is happy when Papa takes her down to the piazza. She is happy he chooses her and not her sister Conda—who is too little, a baby, so there. A crybaby, so there. Chooses her and not her sister Nea, who is too big and has to sit and sew with Mamma. And the boys are in the fields with slingshots and old chestnuts, but they never let her play. They let Toni play, but not her. Even around the house, they won't let her play. Even though she knows how to play *ciaparse,* knows how to lie flat under Mamma and Papa's bed, to scrunch up in the kitchen cupboard or crouch behind the umbrella stand. She shows them. But the boys yell and call her nasty names. Serves them right that Papa chooses her and not them.

He has been away a long time, driving the big boat that takes the people to Trieste, lots and lots of people, drives them there and brings them back. Mamma says he has to, that's his job, it puts bread on the table, though really Rosa has only seen Mamma put bread on the table. Papa goes away, but he always, Mamma says, always comes back.

I see her: Rosa Pia Pagan, Rosina they call her, a little girl in a photograph, but alive and in color: the impudent dark eyes, the pink lips that smile and pout, the light brown bobbed hair. She skips along the polished stone path.

Papa, she says—Papa. And he holds her little hand in his big one. And she grows happier and happier, and Papa calls her his Rosebud, his Rosina, and he sweeps her up and up and onto his shoulders. She holds on to the hair on the sides of his head. And she can see everything. She lays a finger on the shiny spot on the top of the back of his head and giggles. Everything: the bright oranges peeking through the leaves, the little birds perched on the stone walls, the big, big sea and the scary waves. She pretends she is on a magic boat sailing through the sky. Stop leaning like that, Papa says. She tries to cover his eyes. Rascal, he says, I'll drop you. Rosina sees everything: Papa's friends shake his hand, good day *Barba* they say. Who is this little bird they say, pointing at her. Papa is *Barba* because he drives the big boat that doesn't belong to him and another little boat that does. They call her a little bird to tease her. Papa's friend Gianni speaks fast. She can't catch the words. Papa laughs. His shoulders shake, and she digs her fingers into Papa's neck. He starts to pull her down. She shrieks.

Papa's friends have small soft caps or nothing but hair on their heads. The gentlemen wear stiff straw hats, so it's hard to see their eyes. The ladies twirl their lacy umbrellas. Their hats are like big plates with fat bows and long bird feathers. She holds her head like the ladies do, to one side, and pretends she is a princess with a big pink hat. She doesn't care that Papa doesn't like the princesses, the duchesses, because Papa always loves her. Even if she is a princess. He'll buy her a chocolate gelato anyway. He promised.

Eighty years later, my Aunt Giaconda remembered: Papa would take Rosina to the piazza, not me. Eighty years and two world wars later, my aunt was still complaining: your mother was always our father's favorite.

Little Rosa sits on a chair at a table and runs the little silver spoon around and around the bowl till the gelato is soft and mooshy. Papa is beside her and still talking to Gianni, using big words. She holds the spoon out, "Try, Papa," aiming for his mouth. A brown blob drops onto the table. The gelato is cold on her finger and tongue.

Papa says, "war." She hears this one word clearly—"war"—in between the other words, and she knows war is the game the boys play. Santo uses a branch of *spuza* that stinks, *eeugh,* and a smaller chunk of dark *bazak* that he chops with his knife (careful, careful) to make a long gun. He and Ermanno whoop and run, shooting at each other, bang bang. She watches, standing by the well, and Ermanno suddenly turns and shoots at her; the pellets from the juniper bush hit her splat on her chest. And they hurt sharp, then prickly, and dirty her pretty pink dress, red gooey marks down the front.

"Bull's-eye," yells Ermanno.

"Be quiet," Santo says to her as she shrieks. "Stop."

But Mamma has heard and runs out with a broom in her hand. She starts chasing Ermanno, swatting at his legs. "Savages. I told you—not here and not your little sister." Ermanno trips on a pail, and Mamma swipes at him but stops, though Ermanno keeps screeching.

Mamma tells Rosina that she must go into the house quick quick and change. For church, they must be clean and tidy. So Rosina climbs the tall staircase. Maricci, her oldest and favoritest sister, is staring into the mirror, turning one way and looking, then the other and looking, fluffing her brown silk hair. Maricci leans over the bureau until her nose touches the mirror and sighs.

"Mamma says you must change my dress," Rosina says.

"Well, look at you," Maricci laughs. "I heard the boys playing war." But before helping her, Maricci picks up a small pile of leaves from the bureau, crushes them and rubs them all over her hands and neck. "Remember when you are big. Verbena to make you smell good. Now get your other Sunday dress." Maricci undoes the buttons, which are too hard for little Rosa, and pulls the dirty dress off, then the clean one on. And Maricci smells bright and lemony like walking in the garden. She gives Rosina a hug.

They go to church, brothers, sisters, Mamma and Papa. Rosina is tired. The priest talks too long. Mamma shushes her, shushes Conda, who whines. The sun is hot; so is Rosa's Sunday dress. It itches her neck, under her arms. Then the walk home is up the hill, and Papa carries Conda, not Rosina, and Rosina's legs ache. Papa sings *Ciribiribin ch'bel Nasin, chi bel bocchin.* He is smiling at

her, his Rosebud, his Rosina, his teeth shiny white in his
brown face. He is singing to her, *ciribiribin,* so there.

A MOTHER, a father, five daughters, three sons, a home
with a bitter orange tree in the courtyard, thick stone
walls, a terra-cotta tile roof, and spacious rooms. A house
built to last centuries: doesn't it still stand? Dalmatian
lace curtains on the windows, a Persian carpet in the parlor, English china in the dining room, Italian silver on the
sideboard. A Murano glass chandelier. Mum could not
remember these details, but I've based them on the other
homes in Lussingrande—ones I have seen or heard about.

A gold coin was buried under the front doorstep for
luck. This home was cherished. Yearly, the white walls
were repainted and the cistern drained and scrubbed
clean. The rest of the house was washed and polished
continually. The floors shone; the dark wood furniture
glowed. In the kitchen, a woodstove and an open hearth:
the polenta was cooked the old way in a large copper pot
that hung from a bronze rod. The laundry was boiled in
enormous cauldrons.

My imagination, fed by research and interviews, erects
the rooms of the house, as it once was. Were there servants
to clean and scrub, to cook for the eight children? Why
not? A girl from the island of San Pietro, a distant relation
of Rosina's mother, Caterina. And perhaps a woman from
Rovenska, her husband an unskilled or unlucky fisherman,
came in to do the washing or to iron.

Still, there were endless chores. Caterina Lettich
Pagan was always busy. The older girls had their duties,
even Antonietta, who was only seven years old. She set

and cleared the table, made beds, stirred pots, peeled potatoes, or shelled peas. Caterina tried to show Antonietta a basic stitch. She could start to sew; Enea had known at that age, cross-stitch and plain. But Antonietta hated to sit still. Besides, her fingers were clumsy; she always pricked herself. Antonietta acted as if she were a boy, trailing after her brothers, climbing trees, hunting for frogs, fishing off the pier, rolling down hills without a thought to her dress.

She hated having to sit through the multicourse Sunday dinner. She would tear her bread into crumbs, then pile them up. Her legs would twitch with the need to move, a leg would flip out, and you couldn't say that she kicked Rosina—the movement was not that strong—but her foot would make contact with her sister's leg, and Rosina would complain to Maricci: Netta kicked me. Did not; did too.

I can see them one summer day, Antonietta less restless than usual because Mamma has made a special treat, *gnocchi con susini,* balls of potato dough boiled, then rolled in melted butter, bread crumbs, and sugar. Antonia bites through the crisp and sweet, the soft and savory, to the plum at the center, the purple core both sweet and sour.

And at the head of the table, her father, Onorato Pagan, Rosina's beloved Papa. My sources are so limited: a few family stories, but no pictures or memories. I deduce that Renato (as he was called) was shorter and swarthier than most of the other men in Lussino, who had Croatian or Austrian blood. Renato's mother was from Ancona in central Italy, and her shortness is a family legend. He must have had the Pagan nose, which my mother, two aunts, one uncle, and various cousins inherited—an unmistakably Venetian nose, visible in Renaissance portraits, reflected in commedia dell'arte masks—a prominent nose with a bulbous end.

Like many Lussignani, he was a sailor, identified as such on my mother's birth certificate. Considering the number of children he had and the closeness of their ages, he must have worked not on an ocean liner that circled the world but on a passenger ship that sailed the Adriatic. I imagine him as hardworking but impulsive, with a quick temper and a quicker laugh. He often brought home spontaneous gifts: cologne for his wife, a book for Maricci, building blocks for the boys. He enjoyed playing *scopa,* an Italian card game, with his friends, betting small sums of money, only what he could afford to lose.

Mum made him into a hero, which, I suspect, he was not.

A father, a husband, sitting at the head of a dining room table, telling a story about a talking donkey and a peasant. A seven-year-old girl with a trace of buttered crumbs on her cheek, half-listening.

Of all the members of the Pagan family, why do I bring Onorato and Antonia into focus? These two are the farthest away. These two were the first to be lost.

She was a pretty, dark-eyed girl, a lot like her sister Rosa: energetic, willful, happy. That is how I see her—my mother's other self. Again, I have a few family stories but no pictures or direct memories of Antonietta Pagan.

I have one photograph of my mother when she was a child. She stands with, but slightly apart from, her sisters Maricci (Little Maria) and Enea. It must have been taken around 1914; Rosa looks four or five, Enea around twelve, and Maricci a grown-up eighteen. I wonder why Antonietta and Giaconda were not included. Were they placed in another shot? One that is missing (like so much else)?

Maricci is wearing a long skirt, a high-necked lace blouse, a thick chain and pendant, probably gold, and delicate earrings. Her thick, dark hair is tied back at the nape of her neck by a large silk bow in the fashion of the time. Enea is in a dark dress, navy blue or purple, with pin tucks and a semicircular lace collar held by a brooch. Maricci's arm protectively circles Enea's shoulder; they are both slightly turned away from Rosina. Rosina's hair is almost blonde, cut in a short bob and held by a white bow. A grown-up purse dangles from her pudgy hand, and a ring glints on her third finger. Her dress, dropped waist, with a turtleneck and light diagonal stripes, eerily resembles one her granddaughter Antonia wore seventy years later. Rosina's chin is firm, her expression wary. She looks stubborn, already a handful. As long as I knew my mother, one of her eyes wandered. In this picture, both eyes stare straight at the camera.

Mum had forgotten and was forgetting so much. She remembered: *my sisters and brothers around the table.* She remembered: *Mamma* and *we laughed a lot.*

And I see the Pagan family talking and laughing around the dining room table. The white linen tablecloth has a few scattered red wine stains and a smear of brown stew. Caterina Lettich Pagan carries in a golden cone of *pandefigo.* "Ooh." Little Rosa wiggles on her chair. She wants a taste of the dried-fig cake. But she's tired of sitting. She wants to go out to play.

"Be good," her mother says. Which isn't fair, because Netta has already slipped out. Maricci is jiggling Giaconda in her lap, reciting a rhyme in her ear. Maricci is making a show of ignoring her big brother, Giovanni, who is drinking yet another glass of red wine and teasing her about Stefan. "After the orchestra concert," Giovanni says. "Giving him the eye. Answering him in German."

Ermanno angles his head and crosses his hands with an effeminate swagger. He bats his eyelashes and lets out a series of nonsense sounds meant to be mock German. They all laugh—even Maricci, despite herself; even Giaconda who doesn't understand and Rosina who wasn't listening—all together.

9

Mi lasci sola come un cane.
You are leaving me alone, like a dog.

A common complaint of the Italian mother

hide and seek

IN TEN YEARS, in twenty, how will I remember those dark winter months after my father's death? As a jumble? A blur? A marathon of endless circuits from work to home to condo, back to work to home. By writing about that time, I am disrupting the normal process, both freezing and canceling my memory.

And the spectators to this iron woman competition, Marco and the girls? What memories will they keep? Images of an edgy, teary mother? A wife with a flushed and strained face? A faltering runner who trips and sprawls on the track only to pick herself up and continue, shakily.

In the first months of Antonia's life, she suffered from colic. I must have read books, watched TV, cooked meals, cleaned, and chatted with friends; I must have continued my daily life. But what I remember is the feel of her tiny, twisting body as I held her and walked, hour after hour, back and forth at night, in the early morning; the feel of her mouth clamping down as I brought her to my breast, my suppressed shudder, and her slow uncurling, a pink, scented flower. We were alone, and the rest of the world was a blur, family and friends insubstantial, ghostly.

Caring for my mother—wiping her bottom, dressing her, coaxing her to eat, spending days and nights at her apartment—was similar to that time with Antonia in the isolation and physical closeness, though this dependency was as dark and fruitless as the earlier had been dappled and promising.

How long could this symbiosis continue? I had to disentangle us. I had to make a decision about her future. Rosa was sometimes left alone far too long. Although she complained loudly whenever she had to stand and walk, when no one was with her, she could and would move. Each time I was a few minutes late arriving, I would enter her apartment fearful of what I would find. Had she decided to wash the dishes left in the sink and splashed water on the counter, the floor, and herself? Had she fallen, broken a bone, or hit her head? Had she tried but been unable to make it to the toilet?

As I drove up to the apartment building, as I walked through the lobby, my heart would clang, my stomach flip-flop. And various times I did find a tap running, a burner on the stove top glowing red, my mother lying on the floor of the living room, spare bedroom, or bathroom. Each time she was lucky; I was lucky. She didn't flood or burn down the apartment. Despite her osteoporosis, her falls left her with bruises but no broken bones, except once when she chipped a bone in her shoulder. I had left her with the remains of breakfast. I had an appointment at the university, and Mum had refused to move to the easy chair, which was more comfortable and safer. *Leave me alone.* The home-care worker was expected any minute. But by the time she arrived, my mother was on the kitchen floor screaming.

Twice I unlocked the door to an unmistakable stink. Her stomach upset, she hadn't made it to the toilet in time. I found her bare bottomed at the sink, trying to wash herself and her clothes and failing. Her eyes bright with anger and shame. "Where were you? You heartless girl."

One day, when I arrived at the condo in my usual state—late, breathless, and anxious—I didn't find Mum in her chair in the kitchen. I called out as I checked the living room, then each of the bedrooms and bathrooms. Could she have wandered out? I went back to her walker and cane parked in the long entrance hall. She couldn't take more than a few steps without support. Mouth dry, heart pounding, I rechecked each room, adding the laundry/storage room, which I'd missed the first time around. Again, nothing. The third time my search was less cursory; I peered behind the two sofas, between an easy chair and a side table, behind half-opened doors. Could she have got out? I had an image of her lying frozen in the snow. I tested the French doors to the snow-covered terrace. Locked. Besides, I could see through the glass that there were no footprints.

Finally—why hadn't I thought of it before?—behind a closed door, in the walk-in closet between the master bedroom and en suite, I found her. She was not crumpled up or unconscious; she was sitting, laughing up at me.

What on earth are you doing? I heard myself shriek. Didn't you hear me calling? These words and more tumbled out.

She covered her face with her gnarled hands and peeked between the fingers. "I was playing *ciaparse* [hide and seek]." I wanted to shake her. "I fooled you. You couldn't find me."

She was alone too long; I was with her too long—in those claustrophobic rooms, overstuffed with furniture. The mother I knew was gradually disappearing. The connections between her memories and emotions and understanding were tangled or severed. But now and then, like that day she hid in the closet, I caught a glimpse of the little girl still inside the aged body. Rosa Pia Pagan survived in fragments, in flashes of light.

Her situation was dangerous. But for several months after Dad's funeral, I could only think of getting through the next hour or the next day. I felt nauseated whenever I tried to think of where she should live. I was too tired to decide, too tired to think.

We have to decide what to do with Rosa, said Marco.

We're worried about you, said Tatiana.

Other grandmothers aren't this much trouble, pointed out Antonia.

Marco outlined three options: I could arrange for Mum to move to an assisted-living facility, put her name on a waiting list for a bed in a nursing home, or have her come to live with us. But if we chose the last option, we would have to sell our house and buy another with a bedroom and bathroom on the main floor. Or renovate our present home extensively. When I considered any one of the three options, my stomach twisted. I don't know, I said. I can't decide. What's best? What's best?

Mum wanted to stay in her condo—in her house, as she put it—with all the things that represented her fifty-two years of marriage to my father. They hadn't got rid of much when they left either Calgary or Nanaimo. The condo was not disorderly but crammed full, layered with their stuff. Too big a sofa, too long a dining room table, too many little tables, shelves, lamps, vases, and rugs over the broadloom. And on the walls, watercolors of Venice hung next to a copy of Titian's *Assumption;* views of Lussino flanked a four-foot seascape with a fluorescent glow. A collection of blue and white plates. Blown-up photographs of Dad's father, Mum's mother. Framed snapshots of Tatiana and Antonia everywhere.

My things, my sheets, my bowls, my television, my table, my stool, mine, mine, mine, she reminded me whenever I moved or even touched anything of hers—when I tried to reposition a chair to make her way easier or to roll up one of their innumerable throw rugs so that she wouldn't trip. If nothing else, she was clear about what she owned.

She'd be disturbed and disoriented if I moved her. But it was impossible for her to remain in the condo. I couldn't continue to dash back and forth between her place and mine.

Besides, living with all those reminders of her life with Dad, staying in the rooms that she had shared with him, was agitating her, if only on an unconscious level. From the time Dad entered the hospital until about three months after his death, she did not want to sleep in the queen-size bed that they used to share. She would refuse to lie down. Whoever was sleeping at the condo that night, Tatiana or Antonia or I, would beg and plead. Still, she resisted. "You go to bed," she'd say. "I'll sit here until I'm ready."

Her chair was close to her bed. She could have taken the few steps herself. She insisted she would, but she never did. Once she spent the entire night in her chair. In the morning, her feet were frighteningly swollen; her neck and back hurt. Another night, she wandered, waking me up when she dropped a dish in the kitchen. From then on, when she resisted, I would leave her for a while and then almost drag her to bed.

We began halfheartedly looking for a bigger house, with a room for my mother and a study for both Antonia, then in high school, and Tatiana, who was at university. Marco and I also needed some privacy, a space where we would be beyond her reach.

And then I found the right house. While skimming the local real estate ads trying to discover how much a larger house would cost us, I came across an ad for a new, spacious house in an older, established neighborhood, for sale by owner. I'm not sure why I phoned; curiosity, I suppose. I didn't expect it to be suitable. And when Tatiana and I drove up, the place looked unlikely. It was set off from the road, accessed by a back lane, a pink stucco neo-château, dominated by the three-car garage protruding from the front. But inside, it fulfilled our needs. It had a separate mother-in-law suite, not tucked away in a dark basement but up a short flight of (I thought) manageable stairs. There were large windows looking onto a garden and tall trees and a bathroom large enough for a wheel-chair, as well as a step-in shower.

The rest of the house had lots of desirable features that I'd assumed were beyond our means: the carved wood door, the stained-glass window, ceramic and stone tiles, hardwood floors, granite countertops, deep Jacuzzi tubs and gas fireplaces (including one in the master bedroom), the kitchen with copious counter space that opened to a family room—all the latest for the middle-class home. When I'd visited show homes in the suburbs, I'd usually left the tour shaking my head at the pretentiousness and tastelessness. In the neo-château, each detail was pleasing and proportioned. Best of all, there was a secret door and small tower room with a circle of windows, a room built for writing. The house seemed designed for our family.

This was not as extraordinary as it may seem. When I called the number in the paper, I recognized the voice at once. The owner and builder was a younger brother of Nadia, who had been my best friend in elementary school and a close friend through high school and university until her early death. In the early sixties, her family (from the region of Friuli) were the only other Northern Italians, as far as we knew, in our treeless modern suburb of dirt yards and cookie-cutter houses. Certainly, Nadia was the only child of Italian background in the grade 5 class I entered when we moved to Calgary. Previously, I had felt uncertain, awkward, an outsider, having frequently changed countries, cities, and schools. With Nadia, I was comfortable, easy. She became my first proper friend since leaving England.

And our parents became friends, too, even though one of Mum's proverbial truths—repeated with regularity—was that Friulani were infamous for being miserly and stubborn. "But always better than Southerners," she'd add. "Or, heaven forbid, Canadians."

So it did not feel extraordinary that Nadia's brother's house, with its mixture of Italian details and Canadian design, would appeal to me. He had built the extra suite for his widowed mother to encourage her visits from Calgary. In Italy, as in Canada, the extended family is in eclipse, and a growing percentage of mothers and fathers are being placed in nursing homes. Still, among Italians and Italian Canadians, the idea that you should take care of and be close to your aged parents persists. It is your duty to look after them as long as you can, particularly if you are a daughter. An old friend, Graziella, lives next door to her still-able mother, treating her well, acting as chauffeur, companion, and—at times—nurse. She takes her mother along on Caribbean cruises and to Hawaiian resorts. When Graziella's husband booked a seven-week trip to New Zealand and Australia for the two of them, the mother played the tragic victim. Graziella knew that her mother was being unreasonable, knew that she was not deserting her, not leaving her alone like a dog; after all, her two sons would be looking in on their grandmother daily. But Graziella confessed she felt guilty. "If I admitted how I felt to a Canadian friend, she would think I was crazy. Inappropriately attached."

"Tell me about it," I said. My Italian relatives assumed that I would bring Mum to live with us, while my

Canadian friends were either aghast or puzzled that I would consider it.

"Get her into a home, where she belongs," one elderly lady said to me once as I was coaxing my reluctant and complaining mother into the elevator.

The pink stuccoed house would have given us the space we needed. To buy it, we would have to sell both our house and Mum's condo, but it was possible. We could have done it. Possible, but impossible. In practice, I couldn't. Couldn't even suggest the possibility to Marco. Couldn't sell her place without committing myself to looking after her. Once we moved into that house, there would be no going back. I changed my mind day to day, shifting between I can, I will, and I can't, I won't.

10

You won't find money
lying in the street.
Istrian proverb

not at home

MARCO AND I BEGAN to visit various assisted-living centers, places for seniors who needed some help, with the emphasis on *some*. The most pleasant one was a high-rise that looked more chain hotel than hospital: dark wood trim, plush green carpet, a lobby with wing chairs and silk flower arrangements, and a dining room with small tables covered with linen tablecloths. No shabbiness, no linoleum, and no institutional smell. Mum was sensitive to such things. She appreciated the niceties.

Still, the residence was expensive, requiring that you "buy in" with at least a $100,000 deposit and then payments of several thousands of dollars a month for board and other services. If you needed extra help—to be walked down to the dining room, for example—someone would be provided at an extra cost. Laundry, pill dispersal, putting the client to bed, waking up the client—all extra.

"But think of all the amenities," said the manager, a glossy woman in a bright blue suit. "A bus to the mall, a library, a games room, activities."

My mother wouldn't use any of the amenities. She would sit in her room, alone. I would have to be there every day. I began calculating how the week could be divided, with the girls taking their turns. Could Marco be included in the rotation? I couldn't count on him much now—he couldn't deal with her physical care—but perhaps when that was taken care of. . .

"Peace of mind," the manager was saying. Then, a bit later, I heard "superior environment." Marco was nodding. The woman so irritated me that I couldn't look at her solicitous smile or listen to her and her pitch for more than a few seconds at a time. I inspected my nails, twirled my wedding ring, suppressed a scream, an obscenity. This urge was uncharacteristic: I rarely screamed or swore. But during each of our visits to these residences, I found myself suddenly irritated with the person in charge, irritated without just cause.

"Nice people. . . The best families. . . Ladies," the woman was saying. And the old women I had seen in the lobby, the elevator, and the halls did look like sweet, polite ladies. Orderly, quiet, WASP. Not at all like Mum.

As if she were reading my mind, the manager said, "Set up an appointment to bring your mother in. We'll do an evaluation."

"An evaluation? For what?"

"To see if we can meet her needs. We are not, of course, the place for someone who needs a certain level of care. We assist."

"Well, there goes that possibility," Marco said as we got back into our car.

"I don't know. Mum can be coherent. Depends on the day."

"She needs a lot of help."

"She does. But I think once you get in, they keep you. It was the nicest of the places we've seen."

"Agreed. But how long would they keep her?"

I went back to my parents' papers. I couldn't make a decision about my mother's future until I knew how much money was in term deposits and investments and how much she'd be earning in pensions and widow's benefits. And reviewing her finances, making calculations on income and interest, felt as transgressive, as wrong, as looking at her passport and birth certificate.

As in most families, money—how much my father made, how much the two of them saved, what they did with it—was not discussed. When my parents did mention money, it was only to complain about how little they had and how much they needed. They talked constantly about how expensive everything was. About how we couldn't afford it—whatever it was.

Many of my friends heard the same lines. Turn off the water, the light, the heat—we're not made of money. Scrimp, save, can and freeze, darn the socks, mend the hole—we have to make do. My friends' parents were the products of the Canadian Depression, the land blowing away and the men riding the rails. *We were raised knowing the value of a dollar.* And a dime. And proud of it. Yes, sir. For my parents, the thirties had been no dirtier than the dirty twenties, but they knew that the value of a dollar or a lira or a krone could change totally from one day to the next. So they shared the attitude of their generation. And they never disclosed their finances.

My mother never held back on anything else, except her age. When I was growing up, she never censored anything she said. She commented on people's appearance or manners or intelligence to their faces. As if they couldn't understand. Which was sometimes but not always true. Certain words, like *stupido* (snorted at my first boyfriend), translated easily enough, while others, like *sporco* (filthy) didn't. But the sound of the word muttered when she entered a house or a restaurant made her contempt clear. *Terroni*, she muttered at the Southern Italian ladies at church—earth people. Holy Mary, she's fat, she'd announce behind the back of a waddling friend. I would beg her not to say anything, remind her, warn her—Mother, please—but it did no good. She saw herself as being honest. "I have to say it."

"You don't."

"Yes, I do."

Mum was obsessed with everybody's weight except her own. With my father, she was the food police, monitoring everything he ate. It did no good. My father continued to sneak into the kitchen to eat bread and butter on the sly and remained overweight. I was a round child and a slim adolescent. My mother nagged first that I was too fat and then that I was too thin. And now I was too fat again. "Fat, fat, fat," she said to me.

I could imagine her shouting her truths at the nice old ladies in the residence. Too skinny, too fat, ugly as death, mean as a snake.

I soon realized it would not be a problem. Even if she had been accepted, the residence was not a possibility. Despite my parents' frugality, it would cost more than her monthly income and quickly eat up her savings.

Even though I had been apprehensive about becoming Mum's permanent caregiver, Marco and I again began to look at houses up for sale. As we searched in vain for a house with a fair-sized room on the main floor and an attached bathroom, we appreciated the lost pink-stuccoed house even more. Even the most likely houses that we toured would need rooms added and bathrooms renovated. In the layout of houses, you can see how society believes that life should be organized. In my community, aged parents and children over the age of eighteen were not expected to live in the family home.

Having a house designed and built to one's specifications was possible. But that would take a year, maybe more. And for it to be affordable, the house would have to be on land at the edge of town. I had had enough of the barren suburbs as a child.

"We could contact the architect who did our entrance for us. See if he can add a room between the back of the house and the garage," Marco said.

"I suppose." My heart began to pound at the thought. "I'm still confused. I still haven't decided."

"I'm not convinced, either. But let's see what we would be facing."

The day after we set up a meeting with the architect, I regretted the decision. When I arrived at the condo in the late afternoon, I found both Mila and Mum upset. "He hit me," Mila said. (Mila usually reversed her pronouns. A man would be "she," a woman "he.")

"Rosa? *She* hit you?"

Mila nodded, "Yes, he hit me with cane."

I turned to Mum and switched to Italian. "What's happening? Why would you do such a thing? You can't hit those who look after you."

Mum looked defiant. "She's a liar and a fool. She has no idea how to wash a floor. And lazy. I told her you can't use those mops. On your hands and knees. And scrub."

Mum complained about each one of the home-care workers: this one was lazy, that one rude, all of them untrustworthy. But she was most hostile to Mila, whom I relied on the most and who spent the most time with her. I was paying Mila to do some light housekeeping and laundry. These had been my mother's area of expertise; she was scathing in her comments to the patient and capable caregiver.

Mum's English was broken and getting worse all the time; Mila's Filipino accent made her speech hard for even me to understand. So Mum and Mila often misunderstood each other. But the problem was the same with most of the home-care workers, who were often recent immigrants with limited English. I think the mutual incomprehension made my mother often view or interpret their words or actions darkly. At the same time, the women frequently did not understand what she wanted. But although they could not grasp the specifics of her curses and insults, they knew from the tone and the loudness of her voice that they were being berated.

The nurse in charge of my mother's case phoned me

at my office. The supervisor of the home-care agency had called her and complained. "She must be assessed," the nurse said. "We have to know what we're dealing with."

Someone who is determined to complicate my life—I thought, that is who we're dealing with. "You won't stop the home-care visits?" I was so anxious that it was hard to get the words out.

"There has to be a proper evaluation of what is needed."

"More. Much more. More hours. Someone to help us get her to bed in the evening. Oh, and help with more than one shower a week. It isn't nearly enough."

"But if she chases them away?" the nurse said. "The agency will not send their staff if she continues to be abusive."

"She—my mother—" I tried to take a deep, slow breath to calm myself. "It's a problem. Rosa wants to continue to live in her apartment—with me looking after her full-time."

"You think she is trying to drive the workers away?"

"Not consciously. It must be difficult for her having strangers coming in to her home, watching her. I wouldn't like it."

"Have her doctor prescribe something to make her more amenable," the nurse advised. "And make up your mind about what you want to do."

"You're right. I've been to a couple of the private residences already."

"Good. Although they might not be the appropriate placement for your mother. We should be considering an extended-care facility."

"Can you give me a list?"

"You can't pick and choose," the nurse said. "She has to go where there is an opening."

"I've heard some terrible stories." In the newspaper and from friends. Fatal cases of neglect and abuse.

"There are complaints about all the extended-care homes at one time or another." Her voice was matter-of-fact.

"Oh . . . dear." I squeezed the words out.

"I advise you to stay involved, advocate for her. Then she should be OK."

Of course, I thought. As long as I was there. As long as I gave my time and attention. There was no escaping it. And with my luck, Mum'd be sent to a place on the other side of town. So I could spend hours in the car on top of everything else. "Can I turn it down if it's far away? Wait for the next opening?"

"Later, sometimes, we can arrange a transfer. But if a bed opens up and you refuse the placement, your mother would be put back at the bottom of the waiting list."

"So then it would take a long time?"

The woman laughed. "Even if she's at the top of the list, it could take a year. Unless it is an emergency—a senior who had a stroke, say, and who had no one at all to help. That isn't the case here."

"A year." I could feel the panic rising. I had imagined that if I decided on the nursing home, Mum could move in a matter of days. Instead, whichever way I chose, I would be stuck caring for her.

11

Tell me your Central Europe
and I will tell you who you are.

Timothy Garton Ash, "The Puzzle of Central Europe"
(THE NEW YORK REVIEW OF BOOKS, March 18, 1999)

nostalgia

BY THE SPRING, I could not go on. I was
exhausted, and—I see now—clinically depressed. All
day, every day, I fought off the urge to sleep. At the dinner
table, over a book, between one sentence and another, I
dropped off. Several times, I could feel myself succumb-
ing while I was behind the wheel, stopped at a red light. I
took to pinching myself or digging my nails into my palms
to keep myself not alert but conscious.

Then, providentially, I was offered a trip to Italy. I was
invited to speak at a conference called *Palimpsesti Cultur-
ali,* Cultural Palimpsests, whose theme was the reading
of overlapping cultures. It was to be held in Udine, the
capital of Friuli-Venezia Giulia, the northeastern province that borders Slovenia. I wanted to go but thought I
couldn't possibly. I was too tired to go anywhere to lecture

about anything. Besides, I did not belong at the conference. The other invited guests were either academics or Canadian writers of Friulian descent, some who wrote in French and some in English. I was neither.

Nonsense, e-mailed Anna De Luca, the sophisticated and intimidating organizer of the conference. *Veneta, Friulana,* you are close enough. (But not the real thing, I thought. The Italian academics would find no signs of the survival of the peasant Friulian culture in my books.) To cap it all, she was offering to pay. Trip, hotel, everything.

I had been a visiting guest speaker at the university at Udine before and enjoyed the role. But now I couldn't imagine it. The thought of writing and delivering an academic paper nauseated me. My days were dominated by caring for Mum, and I was trying to be a wife, mother, and resident writing mentor at the same time. Trying and barely managing. I had no spare hours to think and develop a coherent opinion.

You don't have to give a paper, the ever-persistent Anna said. Just come, give a reading, and talk to the students.

When I told my mother that I was flying to Italy, she made crying sounds without actually crying. "I want to come. I want to see my people."

"I'm sorry; not this time."

"I want to see everyone—my sisters."

I didn't want to agitate her further by reminding her that three of her four sisters were dead. "I'll go to see them for you."

"Oh, oh, I have such a nostalgia to see my country."

"Mum, you can't walk, you can't . . . Listen, such a long plane trip would be bad for your health. For your heart."

"Soon," she said, "soon, I'll go. Tatiana will take me. She's a good girl."

I'd discovered that most of the nursing homes kept a few of their beds for short-term stays called respite care. (Respite for the caregiver, not the receiver.) So I arranged for my mother to spend ten days at the Gray's hospital, one of the so-called extended-care facilities.

She was not pleased. When the time came to drive her in, she refused to stand up. "Now I see what you are planning," she said. "To shut me away." Marco helped me wrestle her into her coat. For a moment, as I buttoned her up, she stood still. Then she went limp, just like a resistant child.

Luckily, Marco caught her, lowering her back in her chair. "Stop it," he said severely.

Mum looked at me with frightened eyes. "But she's trying to shut me away."

"Be good," he said in the same tone. Then, he slipped his arms under her legs and lifted. Luckily, he had lifted weights all his adult life; he carried her to the car.

"You are an ungrateful daughter," she said during the drive. "I will pray to God that he punishes you for what you are doing to me."

"Mum, I told you. I'm going to Italy for work."

"I want to come."

"Marco and the girls can't look after you while I'm away."

"I don't need looking after. Stupid, I can look after myself."

"Right. Mum, I'll bring you a present. Would you like that?"

She shook her head, her lips tight.

"Well, I'll bring you something anyway."

The room assigned to her was bright and spacious; the nurses and aides seemed kind and cheerful, though condescending. I realized the irony: I resented their talking to her as if she were a child, even though I often did so myself. I warned the head nurse to check frequently that she was still wearing her hearing aid and her teeth. Mum had the habit of wrapping them both in Kleenex, then hiding them in unexpected spots. Some days I felt as if I were spending my life in search of one or the other. (The warning did no good, of course. She came home toothless and deaf.)

"It's not forever. It's a week, that's all." I kissed the top of her head several times. Now that my anger at her being so difficult had faded, I felt guilty. The ward was clean, the floors shiny, but still the place had that old-folks'-home smell of bleach and urine and despair. If I felt this bad about leaving her there for a few days, how was I ever going to do it permanently?

Several of the old women seemed to moan continuously. As I left, one old man yelled, "Get me out, get me out, get me out." "Please, please," repeated another. "Please, please," all day long.

THE CONFERENCE was worth the strain of getting there. The surroundings, the exchange of ideas, the food, and the company—together they broke through the numbness blanketing me. I began to laugh and cry (at a banquet, in front of everyone), to feel and to think again. The entire time, I was aware, as I had not been on my previous visit, that I was close to Istria, almost on its border. (Indeed, the region contains the part of Istria ceded to Italy.) And for the first time, I heard Istria might be reunified, albeit in a larger context.

The idea that old borders and old alliances might be revived was mentioned to me by a local businessman, the owner of a ceramic tile factory and a relative of a friend and fellow Edmonton writer, Joe Pivato. He was giving me a ride back to my hotel and extolling the prosperity of the Friuli region. "And to think that so many of our people had to leave, emigrate. Especially after the two world wars. Both times, this region was on the frontlines. Such destruction. Took a generation or two to recover. But now we are not just the richest in Italy but among the richest in all of Europe."

"I can see that," I said, looking out at the orderly city and its well-dressed citizens on their evening stroll. I had heard such boasts before, each time from a middle-class Northern Italian male. My interest in Italian emigrants seemed to set these types off. They had to impress upon me how much things had changed: no need for emigration now, no sir, look at our money, our opportunity, our style. If it weren't for the South dragging us down. I waited for this businessman to bring up (as the others all had) *La Lega Nord,* the political party dedicated to separating Northern Italy from the more impoverished South. When instead he drove on in silence, I said: "Are the Friulani in favor of independence?"

"Certainly, we would like to leave the rest of Italy. What interest do we share with Naples or Palermo? But not to make a smaller country or to stay with Tuscany or Emilia-Romagna. Understand me, we see ourselves returning to the old *mitteleurope.* Austria, Slovenia, Istria, Alto Adige, and Fruili-Venezia Giulia. That is the natural, the geographic and historical union."

I was surprised by this answer: at the possibility that a century of conflict and war could be forgotten or reversed, that nostalgia existed for the Austro-Hungarian Empire (or at least the western part of it). It took me back to my great-aunt Cecilia's kitchen, so many years before, and her stories of Lussino before the Great War: the balls and princes and royal yachts. She had praised Austrian rule while serving tea in bone-china cups decorated with the two-headed eagle. Her nostalgia had been understandable. She was old, and she longed for the time of her youth, before two world wars and three totalitarian governments.

The businessman was in his early forties. "It makes sense," he said. "A government of common interests. Together we'd have power and economic clout."

"It wouldn't be easy for many," I said, "to forget the past and work together.

He shook his head. "Look at Europe. Who would have thought sixty years ago? France and Germany? It's the future."

"A little Europe?"

"A new heart of Europe—German, Italian, and Slav. Coming together."

I was later to discover that the idea of a new *mitteleurope* had been around since the mid-eighties, first as an alternative to Soviet-dominated Eastern Europe, then, after the end of the Cold War, as a dream of cooperation and economic strength, a dream fed by nostalgia for the comforts of empire. One can debate whether it is the Austrian Empire or—as some have charged—the Venetian

Empire that is being reassembled. Whatever the template, the yearning is for the heterogeneity of the past, for diversity dominated and ordered. Nationalisms could be subsumed, ethnic differences wiped out.

Imagine: Freshly drawn borders erased. History reversed, improved. It wouldn't be easy, I said to the businessman—from instinct rather than knowledge. Almost all the people I later asked, on either side of what used to be the Italian–Yugoslav border, about the proposed region, western *mitteleurope,* agreed. *That'll be the day. Impossible. Not in this century.* Although they disagreed about the cause of the difficulty—too much memory or not enough.

12

Alzheimer's disease proceeds in stages,
gradually destroying memory.
Early Symptoms: *The sufferer will hide*
an object to keep it safe from thieves
and then forget that she has hidden
the object. Also, she will search without
knowing what she is searching for.

Alzheimer's Symptoms Web site

family photos

BY THE TIME I traveled to the conference in Udine, the urge to know my mother's past had come to dominate me. Before Dad died, I'd had only a mild interest in the facts of her life. But sometime in those dark winter months, while I had been running and gasping and stumbling on the treadmill of responsibility, I'd become infected. Now I felt compelled, as if I had no choice.

Through research, imagination, and a family photograph, I'd felt I could recreate her earliest years, the time in Lussingrande before the Great War. But the next stage, when her father disappeared, was more of a mystery—a gap, a pit. A few days in Venice, on my way home, provided a chance to continue the search, to question my relatives about what they knew.

I started with my zia Enea, mother to Liliana, Lino, Tarquinio, and Mario. Zia Enea lived in a small apartment in Porto Marghera with Liliana and her husband, Gianni. Zia Enea was happy to see me, appreciative that I'd made the effort. "Offer her a coffee," she said to Liliana. "She's come all this way. And use the good cups." She asked about her sister and expressed sorrow at my father's death. "He was a good man, Franco. Rosina has never been easy."

Once we were settled in the living room, Liliana and I with our respective coffee and apricot jam cookie, Zia Enea with a cup of chamomile tea and a digestive biscuit, I asked her about my grandfather and grandmother. "I don't remember," Zia Enea said. The bottom half of her face had collapsed inward, obliterating her lips. Still the crevassed skin trembled, telegraphing her distress. I asked about how and where my grandfather had died, how they had ended up in Italy. "My head," she said, "isn't what it used to be."

"Hasn't she got worse?" Liliana said afterward, as we walked to the bus.

"More confused, sure."

"Worse every day. How long since you saw her last?"

"Three years. She's not so bad, you know. Not compared with my mother." Enea, who was six years older than Mum, was still mobile; she took a walk every day, and she could care for herself.

"No, no. It's her character. Zia Rosina can't possibly be so irritating."

"Wanna bet?" In the past, all of the cousins had agreed that the four surviving sisters were equally obsessive and anxious and hysterical. But I'd always thought that they were not equal, that Mum was the worst.

"We can't put up with her anymore. We can't. I can't. She's lived with us for ten years. Ten years. Let my brothers try. Gianni is sick of it. He says she has to go. She criticizes everything I do. And she's still sure that she's right about everything."

I nodded. "I know." I was always stupefied by Mum's tenacity. Nobody could change her mind; nobody could make her give in.

"Won't let anything drop. I can't do it." Liliana's eyes were filling with tears.

Next I tried Lino who, as the oldest of my Venetian cousins, I thought most likely to remember some family history. He and his wife, Gina, had invited me to their apartment in the Santa Croce neighborhood for Sunday lunch. The three of us ate at their kitchen table, which was large enough to sit eight and bore enough food to feed twelve. Gina had cooked a feast of antipasti: platters of golden *fritto misto,* poached crayfish and pale pink *cannochie* lined in alternate rows, grilled red peppers, eggplant, mushrooms and zucchini, roasted tomatoes stuffed with garlic and bread crumbs, and a bowl of pasta with mussels.

"Try this," Gina said, over and over. "And this. You must."

"Enough," I said. "I can't." They were taking smaller portions than they were giving me, but I was still struck by the mystery of how they both stayed so slim. Lino was thin and limber, habitually wore jeans, and had about as many wrinkles as I did. He did not look twenty years my senior.

"That's it," I said. "Lino, I've been meaning to ask you. Do you know how our grandfather died?" Mum had always insisted that he'd drowned in a submarine during

World War 1, but this explanation seemed so unlikely that I'd dismissed it as one of her tales, part of the myth she had created for herself. Now that I was reading up on Italy in the Great War, I was not so sure.

"Submarine!" Lino laughed. "What submarine? Makes him sound important. He died of hunger. That's our history, that's our family legacy: hunger." *Miseria.*

What he said felt true, though odd with so much food before us. "You may be right, Lino. Mum's always felt she was deprived, cheated out of what should have been hers." And always acted as if she had to fight for her share. "Do you know where our grandfather's grave is? Or our grandmother's?"

Lino shrugged. "They weren't the kind of people who left granite monuments and sarcophagi. *Miseria nera.* So a hole in the ground, a pile of dirt. Or their bones dumped in a communal grave. And nobody remembers where or when."

"What about where our grandfather was born?" Everyone in the family agreed that my grandmother was from Lussino, but I'd heard conflicting stories about my grandfather.

"Lussino," Lino said.

"My mother always insisted that he was from here, Venezia, from a titled family."

"What a load of crap. They were nobodies, I tell you. Poor bastards."

"She said that the family, some ancestor of ours, lost all the money through gambling and dissipation. And he was forced to sell the title." I was trying it out, not really believing it. It was a story Mum repeated to comfort herself. The

Venetian history I'd read made half her story possible, half impossible. During the late eighteenth century, the noble class of the city was ruined en masse by gambling and general dissipation. But there were no titles to sell. Venice had been a republic ever since refugees fleeing the invading barbarians had founded the city right up until Napoleon conquered it. Although there was a class of nobles, titles were forbidden. The rich were banned from even dressing their servants in livery. The titles of count and countess were introduced by the Austrians during their nineteenth-century rule.

"But Mum always insisted our grandfather was born on the Calle delle Rasse. You know, it runs up from Riva dei Schiavoni, parallel to Piazza San Marco. I mean, why would she make up the street?"

"What does it matter? Who knows what goes on in your mother's mind or in my mother's?"

"There must be records. In the archives," I said. "You'd be surprised what some of my friends have turned up, especially on the Internet. They've traced their family back two centuries or so. Discovered relatives they didn't know existed. Theologians, artists, thieves. Fascinating."

"Records? What records?" Lino stretched his good arm out so that he could refill the wineglasses with prosecco. "Where? In which country? Austria? Italy? Yugoslavia?" He paused for emphasis and a long, appreciative sip. "They were nobodies. There are no records of nobodies. When you're poor, you're invisible—then and now. No one cares. No one remembers. Your life's an endless round of work and worry. Let's not forget disappointment. You hang on, you hang on, then boom, it's done, and your life has meant nothing and you leave nothing. No trace you were ever here."

Lino's outburst expressed the way he judged his own life. At age twenty, he had been hit by a tram on the Lido, the island that holds the sea back from Venice. His shoulder had been crushed and his arm broken. When he finally healed, his left shoulder was higher than his right and he had lost control of his arm. His brothers moved up, Tarquinio through immigration and Mario through education. Lino was stuck working first as a hotel clerk, then as an office boy. Favoring his left arm, he would remind you of his bad luck, as if it were worse than anyone else's. He would remind you that he was born poor and never had the chances his brothers did to get ahead. He was the oldest; he helped the others. Look at them; look at him.

But when I did look at him now in his retirement, at his two children, happily married, both with their own homes in the historic center of Venice; when I considered his apartment, not much light but roomy, and his days playing *bocce,* or taking excursions to the mainland to stock up on provisions from farms that grew the best vegetables or made the best cheese, or sitting at the bar with his friends telling stories and drinking another *ombra* (glass of red wine); when I looked at the feast of food on the table and at Gina, petite, with red, weather-roughened cheeks and an ironic eye—I thought that Lino had been unusually lucky. And it occurred to me that his pronouncement that our grandfather had died of hunger, like his view of his life, might be, if not wrong, then flawed.

The next evening, another lavish dinner—this one with Lino's brother Mario and his wife, Paola. An architectural draftsman turned interior designer, Mario was the most educated of the siblings, and he married up—Paola's family was middle-class and had the right connections. She also brought to the marriage her sharp mind, a "good" job (insurance agent), and an apartment. Part of a fourteenth-century house in the district of Cannaregio in Venice, it had fifteen-foot ceilings, one with a fresco of nymphs and floral garlands. But Mario did not apply his professional skills here: the apartment was stuffed with a mixture of antique and contemporary furniture and was overflowing with books, rolls of blueprints, and navigational maps, so it felt cramped and small.

Sitting at the dining table, which was squeezed into a corner of the living room, I asked Mario, "Did you ever know how our grandfather Onorato died?"

"I never thought to ask." Mario was uncorking a vin santo. Unlike Lino, who bought his wine in the country and thought the fresher, the more natural the wine, the better, Mario was a connoisseur and served bottles of vintage wine. Fragolino, recioto. "Try this one. Just a hint of sweetness, but the taste has depth. I always heard that Nonno died in the first war. He was born here, if I remember right."

"Right." I repeated the story of the noble family and the gambling debts.

"You see"—Mario glanced across the embroidered tablecloth, across the sterling silver and the crystal, at his wife—"my family may turn out to be more Venetian than yours, Paola. How about that?"

She looked displeased. "You have no proof." My aunt Enea had told me that Paola claimed that the entire family, Mario included, were not real Italians. "You can make up any story you want when there's no proof."

"Pagan is an old Venetian name," I said.

"But Onorato isn't. It's a name they use down South."

"In Lussino, they were a good family," Mario said. He turned to the sideboard behind him and picked up a framed picture. It was the one I also had of the three Pagan girls: his mother, Enea; my mother, Rosa; and our aunt Maricci. Most of us in the next generation prized this photograph, the only one that survived their childhood. I suspect we all loved seeing our mothers young, pretty, and self-possessed. Before their eyes became filled with anxiety and panic.

Mario passed the picture to Paola, "You can see they weren't poor."

"Umm," Paola said. "Your mother had that tight, disapproving mouth, even then."

"But beautiful cheekbones," I said.

"And that big nose . . ."

"They were comfortably off," Mario said. "It's obvious." And it was. Their leather boots and woolen dresses looked expensive, and all three of them had a fussed-over, pampered air.

"This must have been taken in Lussino before Grandfather died," Mario said. "Look at the size of that plant." He pointed to a giant yucca.

I shifted my focus to the backdrop. Up until then, if I'd been asked to describe the picture without having it before me, I would have said that it had been taken in a photographer's studio and that the background was dark and painted. Now I wondered at my memory. I must have mentally superimposed the backdrop of scores of sepia-toned portraits of other people's grandparents and great-grandparents onto this one.

In fact, the girls had been photographed outdoors but in a spot so picturesque that it looked unreal. They were posed on a path of light-colored dirt framed by two boulders. Behind them was a curving coastline and a placid sea sprinkled with sailboats. "Lussino is so beautiful," I said to Paola. I pointed at the path, then the boulders. "Red earth . . . white and pink Istrian stone."

"No doubt. For sure," Paola said. "If you go in for seaside towns. German tourists and nude beaches from what I hear."

"Well, it isn't Venice. But then, where else is?"

Mario took back the picture. "The change from pampered girls to orphans of war must have been a great shock to them. Forced to go to work when they were still so young. And before that, the exile and the camp in Sicily. No wonder . . ."

"Sicily?" I'd heard about cattle cars and a camp in Sicily once—thirty years ago. "So that story's true? I wasn't sure if I remembered correctly—"

"As far as I know."

"Or if Aunt Maricci was confused—"

"That's what my mother said, anyway. How hungry they were. How frightened."

"But their being sent to Sicily doesn't correspond with the historical facts—"

"Oh dear God," Paola interrupted. "They wouldn't be the first to suffer a few setbacks. What happened justifies nothing. Playing the victim. Poor, poor me. Other people have adjusted, gone on."

"Wait a minute. Neither my mother nor Zia Rosina has ever used her life to justify anything."

"They don't see a need to justify themselves," I added.

"I am just trying to understand my mother," Mario said to Paola. "I think that time had a significant effect on her."

"You told me that she barely remembered those years. A few images."

"Well, not even those anymore," Mario shrugged.

"It was almost a century ago. Certainly irrelevant now." Paola motioned to Mario to pass her the dirty plates. "Another peach, Caterina?"

"Try soaking a few pieces of peach in the wine. It's wonderful," Mario said.

"I know. I've had peaches and wine before."

"Vin santo? In Canada?"

"You'd be surprised what we manage to get in the wild west." How typical, I thought. Both of them were Venetian snobs.

Paola was back, carrying, with a silver tray, a bone-china cup of tea and two demitasse cups of espresso. The conversation returned to Aunt Enea.

"Your mother has an ugly disposition," Paola said. "That's what you have to understand. It's a truth that doesn't change."

"Wait a minute. That's unfair. She has her faults—I know that as well as anyone," Mario said.

"I wouldn't blame hunger," Paola said. "I bet she was born with that disposition."

"Come on, Paola," Mario said.

"You started it. Her exile, boo hoo." Paola's cheeks were flushed. She had not sat down again but stood across the table from Mario and slightly to my right.

"OK, you two," I said. "I'm sorry, Paola. I'm just trying to get some sense of my mother's past."

"Look at all the old pictures you want. Retell the stories. Reopen the wounds, if you feel the need. But for what?" She paused. "To understand a couple of old women who were not mental giants to start with. And now? They have lost the few brains they had. Excuse me, Caterina. I'm being rude. But you have to admit I'm speaking the truth."

Mario and I exchanged a look. All the children of the Pagan sisters shared a certain nervous energy, but Mario and I had a particular kinship: we were both tense, smart, imaginative, hypersensitive, and self-dramatizing. Both, I think most of our nearest and dearest would say, prone to obsessions, manias, and depressions. On another visit, when our talk had turned to our mothers, Paola had labeled Mario tiresome and me fixated, and she hadn't been wrong. Without needing to put it in words, we both knew that we had to understand our mothers in order, at least partly, to understand, even justify, ourselves.

"I'm starting with this search for my grandfather, birth and death, that's all. I want to know where and when." Since Mario seemed better at recalling details than Lino, I again brought up the submarine story. "I didn't think there were Italian submarines in that war, but then I found out there had been a famous incident . . ."

Mario was looking startled. He saw where I was going. "Of course, Nazario Sauro. His mausoleum is on the Lido."

"The only Italian submarine casualties were Sauro and his men, the sailors of the *Pullino*. Istriani, every one of them. Seamen who chose to fight for Italy though they lived under Austrian rule."

A casual comment to a friend's mother, an Italian lady of the old school about my grandfather dying in a submarine, led to my discovery of Sauro. Along with her eighteenth-century credenzas, antique divans, and oriental carpets, the lady had brought a set of volumes of a 1930s encyclopedia to Edmonton. "Your mother may have been right. There was a famous submarine in World War I. Look," she'd said, passing me an oversized volume with worn leather covers and gilt-edged pages. And in the short entry, illustrated by a tiny, black picture of the *Pullino,* I read a sketchy biography of Nazario Sauro, the hero. Later, wanting to verify or disprove my mother's claim about her father's death, I began to search for a more detailed version of Sauro's story. But everywhere I looked, I found only silence and absence, a silence that partially extended to Istria itself. (Books about the Istro-Veneti and their exile have almost all been written since the mid-1990s. With the end of Yugoslavia and the end to Christian Democrat domination of the Italian government, breaking the silence finally became permissible.)

As Mario and I continued to speculate, Paola began to tease. "A national hero—why not?"

"It could be true," Mario said. "It fits—Grandfather's profession, his loyalties..."

13

O mia patria si bella e perduta
O membranza si cara e fatal.

O my country so beautiful and so lost
O memory so dear and so fatal

"Và Pensiero," Temistocle Solera,
set by Verdi in his opera NABUCCO

Cyclops, you ask my name. And I will tell it...
My name is no one.

Homer, THE ODYSSEY, IX

the cyclops

AUGUST 1916

Captured, arrested, but not yet identified, not yet named, Nazario Sauro huddles on the metal cot in the damp, dark cave of his cell. If the Austrians were sure of his identity, he tells himself, he would already be in front of the war tribunal. Twice the door has clanked open, not to the usual guard but to a confusion of soldiers and officers. Shouts and rough hands pulled him onto his feet. A kerosene lantern was held up to his face. The first time, the glass almost touched his cheek, the heat stung, and the light blinded him. He could not see who stood in the darkness before him. He heard a voice, speaking Venetian. "No, I do not know him."

The next time, a second, smaller lamp outlined two men at the door. Sauro's heart lurched. He knew them both: Zandric and Possetto, fellow mariners and pilots. "This is not the man you are looking for," said Zandric to an officer. "Not him," said Possetto.

Sauro took hope; he could be saved. And his men, if they had not all escaped in the panic after the scramble for shore—if anyone else had been captured—perhaps they too could be saved.

I imagine Sauro hoping, then, in the chill dark, despairing. He mentally composes letters to his wife, to his children. Justifying himself, exhorting and blessing them.

When finally he is escorted from the cramped cave of darkness into the light, he is disoriented. He stumbles. A guard pokes his back with the butt of a rifle. The sun overhead, in his eyes; noon, but of what day? How long has he been in the cell? His bruised buttocks and thighs burn as he takes one stiff step after the other across the courtyard. And the wound on his head throbs. "I am an officer of the Italian navy," he says aloud, preparing himself. His tongue is swollen, heavy. "As a prisoner of war, I have the right..." The guard leading the way lets out a bark of a laugh.

Sauro rasps: "I was born in Venice." He repeats the phrase to himself as he is marched through an archway of white bricks to an open door. "I was born..." He clings to each word, sees them emblazoned on his mind. *In Venice. I am an Italian...*

And then he is in a large, dim room, standing before a table and two men, not navy but military police in dress uniforms: a blond one with a waxed mustache, the other older, with thin gray hair and a scar angled down his right cheek.

Sauro is ragged; the guards took his uniform, left him in prison garb. He stands waiting, his legs trembling. The blond captain writes in a ledger book. The older captain stares straight ahead, as if the prisoner were not standing before him. Sauro tastes his humiliation. He can smell himself: the moldy dirt from the cell floor, his dried sweat, the bitter stink of fear. Still, he manages to keep his back straight, his head up.

The captain, still writing, speaks in German: "August 3, 1916."

It's been only four days, not an eternity. And his body remembers the moment of impact: the pain flaming up over his back, the screech of metal against rock. Black spots eat up the room, and he staggers.

A third man he hadn't noticed brings him a chair. The older captain is making accusations. The prisoner understands the date; he studied German in school. But he can't decipher this rush of language. He can guess from the few words he does catch and from the way the captain's words thump and clang against each other that he is being accused of what he actually did—piloting a submarine into Fiume's harbor, into the Austrian naval base, with the intention of torpedoing an armored cruiser.

How did he miscalculate? He knows this sea, the inlets, the island, the harbor as intimately as he knows the curves of his wife's body. He has spun the voyage over and over in search of the navigational mistake. To run aground on that reef? Was it the fog that misled him? Or chance? A slight turn of the steering wheel and he was finished.

The scarred captain pauses; he has asked a question.

The prisoner shakes his head. He forms the false name he will use: Sambo. "I don't understand German. I am an Italian officer, Tenente Niccolò Sambo, and I claim the right as a prisoner of war not to answer questions." He wants to ask about his men. But what if some of the twenty-two escaped? He would be alerting the Austrians to their presence on what they saw as Austrian territory.

"Do you know others by the name Sambo in the Italian navy?

"No."

"There is a Sambo family living in Lussin."

"I am Venetian born and bred."

Back to the cell. When he is brought again to the room, a sailor named Giovanni Bastianich has joined the three interrogators to act as a translator. There is something familiar about the new man's brown face and light eyes. Has he met him before? Is Bastianich also here to identify him?

There is a difference now in the way the two captains speak to him. They are more formal. They introduce themselves: the wax mustache as Captain Bach, the scar as Von Prica. Bach walks around the cavernous room, the sound of his boot heels echoing. He circles the prisoner on his chair once, twice. Sauro can feel Bach's excitement.

Has he been betrayed? One of his men? No, no, to betray him would be to betray themselves. Istrians every one of them. They knew what they must say. "I am."

"We think you are a traitor who has been attacking both his country's navy and his own people." Bach gloats, smiling, as his words are repeated in Italian. "You planned to enter the harbor and torpedo a docked boat. Such an attack takes knowledge and skill. What naval academy did you attend? Capodistria? Here in Pola?"

"I admit I am the first officer of the submarine, but this was my first mission to these shores. My experience is limited. You saw; we ran aground."

"Look," Von Prica says, "We know who you are. You are an Istrian sailor with an Istrian face."

Bastianich adds to his translation, as if warning him: "You have an Istrian accent. You betray yourself."

"You have been identified," Von Prica says. When? Not in his cell. Had someone watched him as he was marched back and forth to this room?

Despite their insistence, Bach and Von Prica cannot prove who he is. "My family is in Venice," he says truthfully. "At our home—Frezzeria 16–92." But his interrogators are certain that they have the skilled seaman who has been harrying their coastline, striking at their navy for over a year.

Even before his capture, Sauro had been honored with a silver medal of courage from the Italian government for leading sixty missions against the Austrian navy. Did he feel invincible, after so much success? Or, as the *Pullino* motored out of Venice, did he suspect the fate that awaited him on the other side of the Adriatic? On that final trip, two reconnaissance planes caught sight of the *Pullino* soon after it entered Austrian waters. Even before the submarine ran aground, a cruiser was dispatched from Lussino.

Several of the Istrian seamen serving in the Austrian navy who were brought in to identify Sauro claimed they did not know him; others reluctantly identified him. The words of his brother-in-law had the greatest effect. Antonio Steffe pointed out the scar over Sauro's left eye. "It's him—the traitor." Sauro's mother and sister (Antonio's wife), who had also been escorted from Capodistria to Pola, heard Steffe's betrayal but did not waver. When the commander of the military prison, Captain Trevani, told the mother that her son had been condemned to death, she replied that her son was in America.

"We will withdraw," Trevani said. "Signora, you may have a last hour with your boy."

Neither mother nor son showed any emotion; they exchanged a look. She would hold fast. "This man is not my son."

In his last letter to his five children, written on August 10, 1916, just before his execution, Nazario Sauro defined himself as *prima Italiano, poi padre, poi uomo.* First an Italian, then a father, then a man.

THIS TYPE OF patriotism, this primary identification of self with a perceived nationality is alien to me. First a woman, I would say, if asked how I define my identity, then mother, then writer. Wife before friend, western Canadian before Canadian. Roman Catholic? Skeptical Catholic. All labels make me uneasy. If anyone asked Marco, who has three passports, what nationality he was, he would hesitate for a second before answering. As would, I suspect, my sister, Corinna, or her husband, José Carlos, as would many of my friends.

We reflect our times and our world. The word "provenance" comes from the French *provenir,* the Italian *provenire,* "to come forth," and means origin and source, usually of financial profits. "Provenance," or "provenience," is categorized by the *Oxford English Dictionary* as obscure and rarely used, but in the last year or so, it is everywhere, even in gossip magazines. Michael J. Fox's provenance: Edmonton, Canada. Salman Rushdie's provenance: Bombay, India. It is used instead of "nationality," "birthplace," or "homeland."

Nazario Sauro's provenance was Capodistria, Küstenland. He was born in 1880 to an old Istrian family and named after the patron saint of Istria. At his birth, Istria was a province of Austria, and although the idea of Italy stretched back to the medieval era, Italy, as a country, had existed for only nineteen years. Sauro called himself first an Italian even though he was not born in Italy, had never lived in Italy, and grew up during a time when the concept of *Italianità,* being Italian, was still being constructed. The nationalists claimed that Istria, along with Alto Adige and the Dalmatian coast, should be part of Italy, that these territories must be redeemed (which is why their movement was called irredentism). Mounting pressure from the irredentists propelled Italy into entering World War 1 against Austria and Germany, for though the country was relatively new, the claim was old. In *The Divine Comedy,* that classic progenitor of the Italian nation, Dante states that Italy stretches to the Quarnero Gulf, thus including Istria, and Lussino, within its borders.

Verdi's "Và Pensiero," also known as the Chorus of the Hebrew Slaves, in the opera *Nabucco,* expresses longing for both freedom from oppression and the lost homeland. The chorus was taken up as the irredentist anthem. And still today, it remains the alternate Italian anthem, trumpeting not the glory of the beloved country, not patriotism and loyalty, but nostalgia for the past, for all that has been lost. *O memory so dear and so fatal.* In the diaspora of Italian Istrians, at demonstrations and days of remembrance in Rome or Trieste, in Istrian clubs from Australia to Sweden, "Và Pensiero" is still sung with tears and intensity.

I mention the chorus because although today Italian irredentism and nationalism seem suspect and intimately connected to Fascism, when these interlinked movements began, they were dedicated to ending feudalism and tyranny and to throwing off the oppression of foreign rulers.

In 1905, Sauro went to Albania to help free the country from the Turkish oppressors. He called one daughter Albania and another Istria. One son was Libero (Free), another Italo. Their names were seals, he told his children, dedicating them to the goal of freedom.

The Fascists ignored Sauro's beliefs; they used him as an icon of Italian heroism and superiority. And his son, Italo Sauro, did take a leading position in the Fascist party. In 1939, Italo wrote the infamous "Report for Mussolini" (*Appunto per il Duce*) on how to deal with the "Slavs" of the province of Venezia Giulia (now Friuli-Venezia Giulia), which included Trieste and part of Istria. Italo argued that there were too many "Slavs" to send them all into exile; such a move would lead to economic devastation. He suggested instead that the current policy of denationalization, which had been implemented in Istria and Dalmatia since the mid-1920s, should be intensified and expanded.

Slavic intellectuals and political leaders were exiled and Slavic names Italianized; Slavic schools and newspapers were closed. The Croatian and Slovenian languages were banned in government offices. Also, where possible, teachers for the Italian schools and priests and nuns for the Catholic parishes were not native Italian speakers but citizens of the mother nation. The literature and history taught in the schools was never local, never Istrian, but always the culture of central Italy, just as in those years, British culture was the curriculum of the schools of the empire from Jamaica to Canada to India. To be fair, Fascism imposed standard Italian not just on the Istro-Venetians and Istro-Slavs but also on the Friulians, the Sicilians, the Sardinians, and so on. The mother nation was an imaginary construct emanating from and imposed by Rome.

In 1943, Italo Sauro changed his mind about the impossibility (and wisdom) of getting rid of the "Slavs" of Venezia Giulia. He met with German SS officers to persuade them to deport this ethnic group to Germany. But the tide of the war changed before his plan could be executed.

And inevitably the efforts of the Italian Fascists to denationalize the "Slavs," because of the resentment and rage the Fascists sparked, at least partly led to the denationalizing of the Istro-Veneti. In Yugoslavia, *Italianità*, and the desire to retain an Italian identity, was equated with Fascist ideology; this tenuous connection was emphasized by the Communists to justify their persecution and even execution of the Italian ethnics. As Claudio Magris says in *Trieste, Un Identità di Frontiera* (*Trieste: A Frontier Identity*): "Fascism weakened *Italianità* and liquidated it in Istria." He goes on to say that history ripped Istria away from not just Fascism but also Italy, "who disregarded her

[Istria], not knowing her and losing her without regret and without perceiving her tragedy."

After World War II, because Nazario Sauro's life was appropriated by Fascism, he was no longer held up as a hero. The Italian navy named a class of submarines in his honor, and his name has remained on streets and on a right-wing political party Web site. But on the whole, he has been willfully forgotten by the country whose name he shouted as the noose was fitted around his neck. His story vanished from the history books, from the classroom, and from the shared knowledge of the culture.

In the same way, the stories of his people, the later, more significant tragedies of the mass executions by Tito's Communists (the *foibe*), and the subsequent forced exile of 350,000 Istrians have been erased from collective memory, the events minimized, denied, or negated. In 1947, the exiles from Pola, who had to leave their homes and belongings behind, nonetheless took Nazario's body with them. It was transported on the overloaded passenger ship *Toscana* to the port of Venice, where longshoremen, influenced by their Communist union, refused to unload the coffin. Likewise, when the trains full of exiles on their way to refugee camps in the South stopped in Bologna, the station workers did not allow them to step off the train and denied them food and water. All over Italy, the exiles were spat at and called "dirty Slavs" and "Fascists." They were unwanted—an embarrassment.

DID MY GRANDMOTHER tell my mother and her siblings their father had gone away to fight the war on a submarine? Or had that detail come later? Perhaps a ship was mentioned, or the navy, and after many years—after my grandmother was gone—the ship turned into a submarine. Memories can be open to suggestion. When my mother was young, between the wars, monuments were raised and paeans written to Nazario Sauro; streets and schools were named for him. Did she connect Onorato Pagan to Sauro as a way of bathing him in reflected glory, a way to make her beloved Papa a bona fide hero? Yet she never mentioned Sauro. If you are going to invent an important role for your father, why not go so far as to say he was on the *Pullino?*

I don't believe my mother consciously lied. Besides, the link to Sauro was metaphorically true. The facts—where and when—of my grandfather's end may remain unknown. He may or may not have been on the *Pullino,* but there is little doubt that he died because of his allegiance to Italy.

Like most of the men of Lussino, like my three uncles, Onorato was a sailor. That fact is written beside his name on my mother's birth certificate: *Marinaio.* So he *could* have been one of the twenty-two anonymous Istrian crewmen on the submarine, one of the six captured and hanged. I imagine him cramped, constrained, in the tiny engine room, in the heat and the racket and the closeness—a subaltern who followed orders and kept the engines stoked. A nameless sailor whose fate was insignificant and thus unrecorded. A man who left almost no trace.

My grandfather was amorphous to me, a patch of fog on the horizon, until I read that entry in the encyclopedia and saw a way to reach him, to differentiate his features, to arrive at Onorato Pagan. On this voyage, I had to first visit Nazario Sauro, to face the icon.

I pieced together the facts of Sauro's end from a couple of leaflets published by exile groups. Perhaps it would be more accurate to say that I distilled the facts, boiling off the excessive language and melodrama. Later, in Trieste, I was given a longer biography, *Nazario Sauro, Il Garibaldi dell'Istria*. It did not contradict my vision of his imprisonment and trial. But again, the language seemed too emotive and, in describing the man, too laudatory.

In trying to interpret Sauro's story, I studied the two photos I could find. In one, he wore his navy cap and cloak; in the other, a head shot—his nose was large and broad, his hairline receding. In neither could I see the scar that cut from eyebrow to tip of the eyelid, the record of an accident that impaired his sight. In both photos, he looked solid, stubborn, immovable. Wrongheaded? Patriotic? Traitorous? Heroic? Villainous? Nazario cannot be blamed for the racism of his son Italo. But patriotism gives birth to imperialism and ultranationalism. Under Mussolini, "First an Italian" led to "Italians first."

Italo Sauro was larger than life—a man, myth, and monster. He was a cyclops, whose vision was partial, limited by his nationalism. In his day, though certainly not now, Istria was a multicultural and multilingual society. In choosing one identity from a confusion of identities and clinging to it until death, he betrayed not his country but himself.

Would I have felt the same about my grandfather? I will never know.

Two of his three sons joined the Fascist party during the thirties. My mother explained this move as opportunistic, *to get ahead,* and foolish, *following the herd.* But perhaps my half-Croatian uncles were inspired by a father who died for Italy or, at least, for being Italian. Perhaps they were seduced by the idea of the *strong* mother nation.

On my voyage, Sauro is both a necessary and a dangerous way station. As I search out the memories so dear and so fatal of the exiles and *Rimasti*, I cannot let myself be eaten up by rage and bitterness for what has been done. I cannot divide all I encounter into them and us. To vanquish the cyclops of nationalism, my narrative must be not one but multiple. And at this stop on my journey, like Ulysses, I must become no one. In European eyes, I am already anonymous, with no claim to the quarrel: a marginal writer from the northern edge of the world.

14

*This type of dementia proceeds
in stages, gradually destroying
memory, reason, judgment,
language, and eventually the ability
to carry out the simplest of tasks.*

Anne Brown Rodgers, ALZHEIMER'S
DISEASE: UNRAVELING THE MYSTERY

tests

I WAS EMERGING from a long numbness; on
my return from Udine and Venice, I told Marco that we
should go ahead with the extension to our house. We
would bring Mum to live with us. I should care for her; it
was right and just.

I actually made the decision when Tatiana and I went
to pick Mum up from the Gray's hospital, eleventh floor.
The other residents were scattered throughout the large
central room, most of them staring into space, a few
watching the big-screen television; Mum was the last one
at a table, her breakfast congealing in front of her. She
was wearing bright pink pants, an orange knit top, and,
around her neck, a large, terry-cloth bib. Her shoulders
looked impossibly narrow and vulnerable. "Mum," I said.
She continued to stare straight ahead, her eyes blank.

"Nonna," Tatiana said. "We're taking you home." She began to pull the wheelchair away from the table.

Mum looked up, and when she saw me, a switch flipped on. Her face lit up; she let out a long *ooh* of joy and threw an arm around my neck. And a corresponding switch within me clicked on. I gave in; I shouldered my charge.

As I was signing the various discharge papers, the care manager—a tall woman with yellow hair—informed us that my mother had eaten practically nothing. "And she refused to participate in any of the activities," the woman said in a disapproving tone.

"Of course Nonna didn't eat," Tatiana said, after the woman left us to the packing. "The food here is disgusting. I was here twice at suppertime, which is around four thirty for some dumb reason. I wouldn't eat it, either." We were shoving Mum's things into the suitcase, rushing to get out. "I hate it here," Tatiana said, making a face.

My residency at the local university was over. I finally had the time and the energy to take Mum to a series of appointments to evaluate her health and her mental state. First our family doctor referred us to a psychiatrist at a rehabilitative hospital. Two appointments, two tests; I had to stay in the waiting room while she took them. The third test was administered by a psychiatric nurse at Mum's condo. This time, I was asked to attend because of "the language problem."

I had been translating for Mum for years. One of my great-aunts from the English side of the family had told me that when I was two years old, I already went out with Mum to the shops and acted as her translator. "I can see you," she said, "a little wee thing at the sweet shop. Your mum—she was trying to tell Emily Jones about your vacation. Mountains, mountains, she was yelling. And you so serious—you say, 'She means we are going to Wales.' "

"WHAT DAY IS it today?"

"Sunday," Mum said. We were sitting around the kitchen table: the nurse, Mum, and I.

"Do you know the date today?" The nurse smiled and nodded encouragingly. "What year?" She was radiant in her bright summer dress, radiant with youth, prettiness, and health.

"Nineteen eighty-two," my mother said. The nurse smiled and nodded again, as if the answer were the right one. Mum smiled back.

"Mrs. Edwards, what month is it? Can you tell me the month?"

My mother turned her face to me. I translated the nurse's words into Italian.

"November," she said in a confident voice. "November," I translated, suppressing the urge to supply the right answer.

"Can you tell me who the prime minister of Canada is?"

"You pretty," Mum said.

"Thank you . . . The prime minister? At the moment?"

"That stupid idiot."

"Your address, Mrs. Edwards?"

Mum shook her head. "Tell the woman she must know my address. She found me." I translated. She then answered the next two questions, what country and city, correctly, adding, "We used to live in Nanaimo."

"Do you know your telephone number?"

"I don't need to telephone myself," Mum said to me. The nurse smiled, bent her head, and wrote in her book. Obviously, my mother was failing the test. Wait, I wanted to say, she knows how much she paid for this tablecloth twenty years ago. It is not so simple, so clear-cut. You cannot label someone by a few questions. She knows the exact age of my children in each of their childhood pictures. She knows more than you think. Although sometimes I did prompt her; remember, I would say, and drop an appropriate hint.

Remember, please.

Then the test was over. I felt the numbness creeping back, deadening my fingers and my mouth. I dreaded what the young nurse was about to say to me. From the moment the test began, I knew the diagnosis: Alzheimer's. But she surprised me. She didn't express an opinion. She assumed a concerned and caring expression; she touched my hand. She had a pile of leaflets from the Coping with Caring office in front of her: "How to Allay Anxiety." "How to Minimize Disorientation and Delusion." Tips on feeding, bathing, toileting. What a terrible word—"toileting."

In a moment, I would stand and walk the nurse to the door. I would continue coping. Mum was chatting freely now, throwing out a mixture of Italian and English words. The nurse kept smiling. "Oh, yes," she said. Usually I stepped in, adding a little order and meaning, acting as an intermediary between Mum and the world.

But I was exhausted. I could not move or talk. As my eyelids drooped, I saw the three of us at the table, an illustration of the phases of womanhood, with me confused, somewhere in the middle between confident youth and tremulous age, between sun and shadow. The nurse glowed; Mum's eyes were opaque, her body shrunken. She soaked up my light, pulled me to her darkness. I felt myself growing old second by second.

Of course, the psychiatrist's job was to categorize Mum and fix the label. When we returned to his office, he had a folder full of assessment results. "Your mother has Alzheimer's," he said as if she were not in the room. "Or some sort of dementia. The result is the same."

I couldn't speak. I was glad to see Mum was not paying attention. She was staring at a painting of a sailboat on the wall. "Of course, we can only be sure afterward, if we perform an autopsy." His voice and expression were indifferent, which was a relief after the sugary concern we'd received from the other health professionals. "But we are as certain as we can be," he said. "She had a low score on the MMSE."

"Excuse me?"

"The Mini-Mental State Examination. The standard one. Measures her sense of orientation, of placement in the world. A patient with Alzheimer's loses her ability to be at home anywhere. She is disconnected and disoriented."

Mum had lived in Canada for forty-two years, but she had always refused to make it her home. She remained resolutely closed, impervious to this country in both her attitudes and her skills. She'd never learned to write a check, to drive a car, or to speak more than rudimentary English. It did not seem odd to her, or even to me, that she did not know her address or phone number. Part of her never knew where she was.

"On the clock test, she reproduced a clock by putting all the numbers on one side. And when she tried to reproduce a drawing of two intersecting pentagons, she left half of each one off."

"What is he saying?" Mum asked in Italian.

"What does that mean?" I asked the doctor.

"What did he say? I don't like his eyes. Sneaky eyes."

The doctor shrugged his narrow, pointy shoulders. "Could be infarctal dementia, which would mean that she has suffered from a number of small strokes and literally sees only half of things." He stood up, came around his desk, and put his hand on Mum's shoulder. "How are you feeling, Rosa?"

"Bad," she said in English. "I lose my husband."

"Notice how she keeps one eye closed much of the time," the doctor said to me.

I was about to tell him that Rosa Edwards had always kept one eye closed. But I hesitated. I could no longer remember whether this was true or not. Had the squinting started recently? In my memory, I saw her with a permanent squint, but perhaps I was imposing the Rosa of the last few years onto earlier scenes.

I never paid much attention to my mother, especially to her outward appearance. For so many years, she had been my background, my uncomfortable past. I did know that she'd long had a wandering right eye. You could see it in her wedding pictures: a shoulder-length veil, a poised smile, a chin at just the right angle, sparkling eyes, but one of them staring slightly off, away from the camera. In the picture of the Pagan girls in Lussino, both of her eyes were focused. So the change must have occurred between her leaving Lussino as a little girl and meeting my father in Venice.

The psychiatrist wrote a letter to our family doctor, to Capital Health Care, and to Home Care declaring that Rosa Edwards was suffering from Alzheimer's disease.

She was classified and certified. I believed it and didn't believe it. Could it not be the hypoparathyroidism? Depression? I read an article by Dr. Michael Silberfeld and Arthur Fish of the Baycrest Centre for Geriatic Care in Toronto. "All that tests [Alzheimer's] measure is the presence or absence of a set of abilities, but questions of competency cannot be reduced to that level," it said. The tests did seem an inadequate and imprecise method of measuring who my mother was. Besides, I was convinced that she had some responsibility for her state. I kept think-ing that if she had tried harder, if she had just paid atten-tion, she would have done better. Now I was supposed to accept that all her words and actions were the result of a physical illness, a death of cells, the order of the brain dis-solving into chaos.

15

Memory is the only way home.

Terry Tempest Williams, REFUGE

you'll never become a woman

MY MOTHER WAS losing her mind. And the joke was on me. For years, when she was in full control of her faculties, I'd thought she was mentally ill. Now that she had, so to speak, been certified, I couldn't accept it.

Particularly during my teen years, I was sure that no one was oppressed as I was. Some of my friends were also waging wars of independence against their parents, but I discounted their battles. The rules my mother imposed made no sense. No lipstick, no dating, no fashionable clothes, no sports ("They're bad for you"), no ballet lessons, no hanging out, straight home after school, no nasty friends, no, no, no. No life, I thought. I may as well be dead, I thought. She's insane, I thought.

She taught me to starch linen tablecloths, to iron sheets, to polish silver, and although I was all thumbs, to embroider. She sent unmusical me to years of piano lessons. She bought me a hope chest that she expected, dreamed, we would fill with Murano glass and sheets and cloths that I had embroidered.

She said: never place a hat on the bed, never open an umbrella in the house, never eat meat on Friday, never put the bread plate on the right—that's where the wineglass goes. She said: never go out without a vest, never let a man touch you—until you're married—they all want one thing. She said: never drink juice cold from the fridge, never go to bed with damp hair, never wash your hair while you are having a period. Each rule was of equal weight and importance. I insisted—truthfully—that none of the other girls had to follow such rules. "Janice," I would say, "showers during her period all the time. And nothing happens. She's healthier than I am."

Mum would shake her head gloomily. "So far," she would say and then add her favorite rhetorical question: "If all the other girls threw themselves into the canal, would you?"

Into the canal: that should have been my clue. Mum's frame of reference was Venezia in the twenties and thirties, the time when she was growing up. But then, I persisted in judging the rules as irrational, examples of Mum's delusional vision of the world.

"Why are you wearing that undershirt thing?" Janice once asked as we changed for gym class.

I gave my usual answer: "It's my mother. She's crazy."

Janice's response was also habitual. "She is odd. Really odd."

At sixteen, despite the odds, while I was at a girls' convent school, I did meet a boy. Wilfred was intelligent and earnest, a nerd in today's terms, but a tall, broad-shouldered, and handsome nerd, well-meaning and harm-less. Mum treated him as if he were Casanova, bent on plucking my most precious flower. At first, my parents let me see him. I was allowed to attend his high school grad-uation dance. Mum even sewed me a pale-green brocade dress. But as he kept turning up on our doorstep or on the end of the phone, she panicked. She forbade me to see or talk to him. "You're a baby. Like my mother used to say, you're barely out of diapers. You still have shit on your nightie."

I begged. I asked Dad to intervene. No luck. "*Ragazze per bene,*" Mum said. "Nice girls don't date." Of course, I snuck out to see him. He came over to where I was babysitting or met me at Janice's. She was quite happy to cover for us. Whenever I felt a twinge of guilt, I reminded myself that my mother was insane.

Wilfred broke off the relationship. One day he was gone. I tried phoning, but according to his sister, he was never in. I was as brokenhearted as a sixteen-year-old could be. Ironically, Wilfred told me several years later that it was his Austrian parents who insisted that he have nothing more to do with me. They forbade him to even speak to me. His mother was convinced that my parents would not let him see me because of an elaborate plan set up to trap him into marriage. "I know how those Italians work. It's a trap. She leads you on until they can claim you have wronged her and demand restitution. You can't trust any of them."

As the years passed, my mother had to give in on many of her rules. My father pressured her. And then I left home for university, two hundred miles away. She could no longer stop me from wearing pale and shiny lipstick, heavy eye makeup, miniskirts, and tight tops. She had not completely stopped me before. I waited until I left the house and then layered on the black eyeliner and rolled up my waistband. But now I could be more open. "Cool it, Mother." I no longer had to date on the sly. Mum had to limit herself to calling me a *puttana* and comparing the young man to a piece of *baccalà* (dried codfish).

But the undershirt—that fight went on and on. Mum would not budge. I had to wear an undershirt—woolen in winter, cotton in summer—or I would catch pneumonia. In this damned climate, it was a matter of life and death. I told her I was willing to take the risk. "Only grandfathers wear them," I said, echoing the all-knowing Janice. "None of the girls do."

"If they want to throw themselves in the canal . . ."

"You can't even buy those things here."

Mum had the woolen undershirts for herself, my father, and me sent from Italy. They were of a fine, soft wool and were close fitting. But I found them chafing, itchy, humiliating. I was always worried a bit might show at a loose neckline or through a too-sheer blouse. Even if it didn't show, I knew it was there, next to my skin, marking me as different.

It was then that I providentially developed my allergy to wool. Mum added to my pile of sleeveless cotton undershirts. They were less obvious but still irritating. It was the sixties; the look was sleek, modern, and minimal. Three sets of straps from bra, undershirt, and slip were too much.

No way: when I went to university, I dropped all three layers. Burn the bra and the undershirt. We argued on each of my trips home. It wasn't decent, not wearing an undershirt or a slip.

In Mum's eyes, I had grown into someone alien, unrecognizable. When things between us were at their worst, I unexpectedly started spending more time in Italy. And I quickly discovered that what I had thought were Mum's private obsessions were national myths. Undershirts, for example, were almost universal. And cold drinks? Don't even think of it: the dangers were too great.

I also realized that the woman she wanted me to be was not just her particular fantasy. I found the prototype in nineteenth-century novels—the lady, modest, sheltered, and accomplished, who knew how to run a household, who knew how to command servants, who could entertain the dinner guests with a turn at the piano, who could exchange witty conversation with her head bent becomingly over an embroidery ring. A lady fulfilled by her service to her husband, her children, and her aged parents.

"Cucir, Ricamar, Le Facende di Casa Sbrigar" was the title of an aria in the operetta La Gran Piazza, written and performed in Lussinpiccolo in 1913. Sewing, embroidering, household duties, a summary of what a girl needed to learn to be a worthwhile woman. According, I bet, to the heroine's mother. I can imagine the song sung by a contralto—buxom, dark curls, and flashing eyes. Her voice would be insistent, authoritative on the words of the chorus: Cucir, ricamar, le facende di casa sbrigar. The daughter would have a refined manner, her hair—why not—was red, long, and loose. She would be petulant, turning away, her hands covering her ears. Until she, too, begins to sing, not with her mother—this is no duet—but contrapuntally, her soprano voice singing her own words to a different melody. And they would not be facing each other; no, both would be singing their hearts out to the audience.

La Gran Piazza was a parody of a popular Italian operetta, *La Gran Via*, the Great Way. So I presume the message of the song was being ridiculed. Even in Lussino at the beginning of the last century, girls needed to know more. *Le Lussignane,* the women of the island, were famously tough and strong willed. During the time of the great sailing ships, the wives of the sea captains accompanied them on their long ocean voyages. They were not there to serve their husbands but to divide the command. When the husband slept or relaxed, the wife captained the ship.

Yet the song's title spoke to me of my mother. *Le facende di casa sbrigar.* The phrase suggests not just the necessary feminine skills but also the manner in which they are to be employed. *Sbrigar:* to work quickly, with no dawdling. How often did I hear it—*sbrigati,* hurry up, get a move on. For quickness was part of the essence of the mother I remember. Quick, competent, efficient: she cleaned, she sewed, she cooked and canned, a whirlwind. On weekends, she entertained: dinner for twelve—give her a couple of hours. On weekdays, she cleaned the houses and (when I was in high school) the offices of others after scouring her own. No disorder, no dust or dirt or dinginess could resist her.

Now she resisted moving. "I'm tired," she said. "Leave me alone." Getting up out of the chair and walking involved effort for both of us. I had learned to stand in front of her, flex my knees, slip my hands into her armpits, and haul her up. Her legs shaky, she managed only tiny, shuffling steps. Sometimes she let go of her walker and clutched onto the doorway or the sideboard. Then she couldn't move forward at all until I guided her hands back to the walker and gave her a nudge. "I'm going to fall."

"No, you're not. I'm right behind you," I said, though she was right to be afraid; she did fall. When I was right behind her, I could catch her. I wasn't strong enough to hold her up, but I'd ease her down to the floor. Then I'd call whoever was around to get her up again.

It took Mum five minutes to cross the few feet between her chair and the bathroom, ten to reach the dining room table. Now I was the impatient one, and although I didn't yell, "*Sbrigati,*" the word lay on my tongue. She sat, she slept, or she watched me. Her legs and hands shook. When I followed the advice of the nurse and gave Mum a task—"Make her feel needed," the nurse said—when I asked her to prepare some green beans for cooking, her fingers were clumsy and slow.

She sat or she slept or she criticized. "You have no idea how to cook a proper meal," she'd say.

"What do you mean by proper?" I'd say.

A year or so later, in a rare book called *Arie di Lussino,* I discovered that mothers on the island used to feel it was their duty to criticize their daughters. The author, Elsa Bragato, writes, as an example, that if she thought she looked nice in a new dress, her mother was bound to remind her that she had bowed legs, because any good mother would want to stop her daughter from having a swelled head or becoming an egotist. Besides sewing and household duties, a girl needed to learn humility. Mum's criticisms, like her rules, were not unique; only the quantity and the intensity were unusual.

"*Buona da niente,*" she used to yell at me. Good for nothing. She was still yelling it so many years later as I tried to help her. She had lost much of her memory and her understanding, but she insulted me in exactly the same way she always had. "You'll never become a woman," continued to be one of her favorite phrases. "Poor me."

Poor Mum.

Offering Mum company if not companionship, I sat with her for at least an hour every evening. Sometimes I would try to prod her memory, asking her questions about her youth or her early years of marriage. Her memories were thin and spotty and varied from day to day. Other evenings, I would bring out photo albums to see which faces she still recognized and to try to remind her, to stimulate a connection. "Look, it's one of my wedding pictures. Do you remember? No? We're in your backyard in Calgary. Yes, the fence Dad built. Don't I look young? And Marco?" I was testing her, without being aware of what I was doing.

She liked watching television and was usually able to grasp the general idea of a program. I often found myself watching her rather than the TV. I imagined the dense deposits the doctor called plaques coating the outside of the nerve cells in her brain. Like an early, sticky snow clinging to a still-flowering shrub, disguising a fruit-bearing tomato plant, or muffling the sound of a footstep. Some neurons die; some lose connections with other neurons, the doctor said. We don't know why.

As we were sitting together on the sofa, as the minute hand crept around the ornate antique clock, the plaque was settling, silently settling. And inside the cells, the strands of protein that used to be straight, long, and parallel like railway tracks or telephone wires, delivering messages, carrying nutrients—these strands called microtubules were collapsing, twisting and tangling around each other.

"We don't know why it happens," the doctor said. "Or how. But afterward, if we look at the brain, we can see that it has happened."

Jennifer, the psychiatric nurse, returned to check on how Mum and I were, as she put it, managing. Although the day was gray and cool, she wore an orange linen shirt that left her arms bare. She told me she was visiting to ensure that I understood the implications of what the doctor had told me. I looked at her tanned, toned arms and sighed inwardly. Would I ever have the time to exercise again? Not that I could ever banish the cellulite and the slackness. Jennifer asked Mum how she was feeling, and Mum beamed. She loved being surrounded by pretty young faces. "Better than yesterday," Mum said. Then added, as if she had just remembered, "I lose my husband."

"You must miss him very much," Jennifer said.

"The best man . . . *nel mondo.*" Mum shook her head.

I explained. "She is trying to say that her husband was a good man." I spoke a bit louder. "Right, Mum? Dad was a good man?"

"They kill him. Assassins. *Nell' ospedale. Lo hanno fatto morire.*" Mum refused to accept that Dad had had a massive heart attack. She insisted several times a day that

Dad had entered the hospital a healthy man, only to fall victim to the doctors and their machines.

Jennifer looked at me, expecting me to translate. I didn't. She asked if I had read the leaflets. "And you are considering the options?"

Suddenly, I was complaining to Jennifer. I felt petty and guilty but couldn't stop myself. All my peeves poured out. When I had to take my mother out for a doctor's appointment or to the hairdresser's, she stalled and whined. A few times, she was so agitated that she flailed at me, landing a few ineffectual punches. What I did not tell Jennifer was that once instead of distracting Mum, as the brochures counseled, I caught her wrist in my hand and held her arm still. "I am stronger than you," I reminded her.

Jennifer shook her head. "You must look at things from her point of view. And allow her to make her own independent decisions."

The intensity of Mum's rage had always been unusual, surprising. From childhood on, I was determined not to be like her. I trained myself to suppress anger, to control actions and words. My ideal was Canadian: easy does it, don't make a fuss, relax, kick back, play it as it lays. What goes around comes around.

When I was in therapy, dealing with, as the psychologist put it, "issues with your mother," I was encouraged to "face your anger" by hitting a pillow with a tennis racket. I tried. I really tried, but I never could do it. It felt too silly, too foreign.

In those spring and summer months before Mum moved in with us, I was startled not by my mother's anger but by my own. She stalled, she refused, and I found myself shrieking and jumping with rage. Like a cartoon character, up, up, I was jet-propelled, down, thump, and up. I was ashamed and exhilarated. And eventually amused.

You can take the undershirt off, rip it up before you toss it away. But you can't really get rid of it. It stays with you—that sensation of itchy wool—no longer over but under the skin.

When I confessed my tantrums to the nurse, she was reassuring, "It's natural. It's very common." Then, with a professional, concerned look. "You don't have to do this, you know. There are alternatives."

"I have to try," I said. "It's the way I was raised." As if I hadn't spent my life resisting that way.

16

Circe answered me: "I am not going
to keep you in my house against your wishes.
But before I can send you home you have
to make a journey of a very different kind
and find your way to the hall of Hades."

Homer, THE ODYSSEY, X

care calling care

ANOTHER HUSBAND might have protested at
the disruption to our lives, the tearing apart of our house
to accommodate my ailing mother. Marco had always
found Mum an ordeal; still, he never questioned my decision. He had walked this path before, and I'd followed
him down, down, to the border between life and death.

Years earlier, when I'd first brought him home to meet
my parents, I'd thought Mum would be pleased that I'd
chosen an Italian after a couple of Anglo-Canadian boy-
friends. She wasn't. "A Sicilian!" she said ominously. "Does
he carry a knife?"

"Don't be silly, Mum."

"*Teste dure,* hard heads those people, stubborn."

"He mostly grew up in the States. California."

"Worse and worse. The land of the crazies." It was the early seventies, and she still associated California with Charles Manson and other degenerates.

"He's the opposite of all that," I said. "He's a pacifist. He left America because of the Vietnam War."

Now my father shook his head. "One of those draft dodgers?"

Marco's parents were equally horrified by me, though their enmity was not due to my place of birth or where I grew up. Their dislike was personal. From the moment I was introduced as the bride-to-be, there was tension, unease. "Why can't you just live together like everyone else does?" my future mother-in-law asked.

Her husband was too much the old-fashioned Sicilian gentleman to suggest something so improper. "Marriage is forever," he told Marco. "Marriage lasts beyond death." His eyes, his hands, the tone of his voice added: so you must not choose her, not her. There is a telling picture of Marco's parents at our wedding. They are a striking couple, elegant in pose and dress. They have refused to smile for the camera. Their expressions say, "All this is beneath us." Yet, in a letter to their son a few months later, they accused me of being "a princess in a tower, a prickly, haughty girl." I was not what my father-in-law thought I should be: innocent, sweet, subservient.

"Like Christ to his Church," the wife of one of Marco's cousins instructed me, "so must a husband be to his wife: the head, the ruler."

Obviously, my in-laws had been complaining about me to whomever would listen. "Patriarchal shit," I said to the woman. I'd been a child during the fifties. I had absorbed the injunctions about a woman's role from magazines, TV, and the movies, and later from the teachers at my Catholic high school and the university professors extolling those sixties' literary heroes: D.H. Lawrence and Norman Mailer. So the idea of subservience was still too close and threatening.

However, I knew that practice didn't always follow doctrine. Mum had tried to mold me into a perfect housewife, *cucir, ricamar, le facende di casa sbrigar,* but she ruled the household. Marco's father, Manuele, had been thirty-two, Rosabianca a sheltered eighteen when they married, but by the time I entered the family, she had a mind and a will of her own.

In 1974, Marco lived out his beliefs by returning to the United States, entering the military, and then declaring himself a conscientious objector. I am embarrassed to admit I was against his doing so. I was young and selfish and couldn't see the point of his moral gesture. Besides, I liked having a border that Marco couldn't cross between us and his domineering parents. Still, for the first two months that Marco was in Fort Ord in Monterey, I took a leave from my job at a college in Edmonton and joined him in California. I could see him only during the day on weekends. During the week, when he was not allowed off base, I stayed with my in-laws, 190 miles away, in Carmichael, a suburb on the outskirts of Sacramento.

At that time, my mother-in-law's parents, Ernesto and Santa Tuzzo, had recently arrived from Italy so that Rosabianca could care for them in their old age and infirmity. Years earlier, when they'd previously come to live with the family, Manuele and Marco had built an extension on the house, a true in-law suite, for them. So they had their own space, and a woman, Anna, came in to help with them. I rarely saw or thought of them. I did notice that they were demanding of my mother-in-law's time and attention. Rosabianca was then a professor and head of the Romance Languages department at California State University, Sacramento. When she arrived home after a long day of work, she began her second job looking after them.

At the time, the situation seemed unusual, even eccentric, to me. I didn't know any other family that had an older generation living with them. Old people lived either in "homes" or on their own, often on the other side of Canada or in a different country completely. And I never knew my grandparents: three of them had died before I was born; my English grandmother, several years afterward.

My father-in-law, Manuele, who had been forced into early retirement, was as idle as Rosabianca was busy. Their home, a large, sprawling bungalow, looked worn around the edges; it could have used a new paint job, inside and out. Door hinges needed oiling; a couple of windows, resealing. When I lay in bed at night, I heard scampering and rustling in the walls: I didn't let myself contemplate what could be making the sound. (Rats, Marco told me several years later—rats, rats, rats.)

The garden covered 1½ acres and included sixty olive trees, as well as an orchard of lemon, orange, plum, cherry, persimmon, and white and black fig trees. It was more neglected than the house: overgrown trees, tall grasses, and ragged paths. For some time now, at least a couple of years, fruits had ripened and dropped ungathered to the ground, where they cracked, rotted, then shriveled or were consumed by bugs and passing animals. So beneath each tree lay a carpet of pits, stones, and desiccated fruit flesh.

Manuele played tennis; he ran the odd errand. He smoked and read and wandered through the many-roomed house. Above all, he waited each day for his wife's return. He'd be standing at the door when she came in. Often he was already angry, already complaining. Rosabianca would have barely put her briefcase down, hung up her coat, and checked the stove top (Anna cooked dinner during the week) when her mother would scream for her, the cry cutting through rooms and walls.

When I let him, Manuele talked to me about his life (never mine), his theories, his philosophy—the wisdom of a lifetime he called it, though he was only middle-aged. He lectured me on the crassness of American culture, the richness of Italian, his student years in Genoa, his war years in the Italian navy, man's basic brutality, stupidity, and venality. The inscrutability of God.

I lived for weekends and the long bus ride to Monterey; the rest of the time I felt cut off from anyone and anything that I valued. Through January, then February, northern California's version of winter—a little rain, the slightest of chills, and sudden impenetrable fogs—the outside world would disappear from view, the house precipitously swaddled in white mist.

As with the first months after Antonia's birth and the year after my father's death, I have two different methods of remembering these months in Carmichael. The first is rational and deductive—a narrative built from flashes of scenes and the reports of others. The second is emotional and impressionistic—a story that evolves into a personal myth. I know that Manuele and I were not alone in that house, but I remember—I can still feel—the isolation and loneliness. And I still hear his voice, talking at me.

He only touched obliquely on his years of top secret work on rocket engines. When commenting, for example, on America's shortcomings, he might say, "We were all foreigners: a German, a Chinese, me, all the top theorists at the company." Otherwise, he never boasted, never mentioned he'd helped design first the Polaris missile and then the engine of *Apollo 11*, the first manned spaceship to land on the moon. Nor did he ever complain that Marco's decision to evade the draft had cost him his security clearance and his job. Even then, when I was insulated by the walls of my resentment, I admired him for never pressuring Marco, as other men who worked for the company had pressured their sons, into compromising. He didn't even mention to Marco the connection between the son's going to Canada and the father's being fired.

But I asked Manuele, and he confirmed my supposition. "It wasn't a time of cutbacks or layoffs. The head of our division was intent on keeping me." He shrugged his exaggerated Sicilian shrug. "No way."

In a sense, it didn't matter that much to Manuele. Unlike his wife, his work had not been his passion; it was more of a nasty necessity he could have avoided if he had been born in another century. When I finally read Lampedusa's *Il Gattopardo*, I recognized his prototype. Manuele wished to be another Prince of Salaparuta: pessimistic and wise, an amateur yet serious thinker and scientist.

Most of all, respected, both listened and catered to. If not by a fiefdom, by his family.

During those two months I stayed with my in-laws, I audited a course at the university given by Kate Millett, who was then a celebrated feminist leader and author. If I happened to leave one of the texts anywhere except my bedroom, Manuele pounced. Checking out the pictures on the back covers, he made nasty comments about the looks of the writers. Flipping open a page, he would read a random sentence aloud and sneer. Or he lectured, trotting out the standard (male) Sicilian line. Women were too powerful already. (*How many times did I hear it?*) They were stronger than men, both better and worse than men, and therefore had certain duties, certain responsibilities. Feminism was unnatural and unnecessary. I could not listen to this in the same patient way that I listened to the rest of his pronouncements. I argued back.

After those months, Manuele never again shared his theories and stories, but our argument continued. One Christmas at my parents' home, he and I started bickering about whether a man should be expected—as I expected Marco—to do some of the household chores. He shouted; I burst into tears. He grabbed my arm. "You see," he said, "You women don't play fair. You're sneaky and manipulative."

His anger at me and my refusal to bend, to serve, was a projection of his anger at his wife. And she, in turn, projected her unhappiness, her sense of entrapment, onto Marco's and my marriage. A year later, Rosabianca divorced Manuele and had Marco's brother, Stefano, take her parents back to Sicily. The land, the house, and all its contents were sold. Manuele had already lost one son to the frozen wastes of Canada and a chilly wife. Now Stefano was trying to make it as an actor in Los Angeles and had little time for him. Manuele's most precious possession, his family, was no longer his.

Over the years, I grew close to my mother-in-law. But not even two beautiful granddaughters improved the relationship between Manuele and me. He seemed to make a point of favoring his other son's wife, pointedly embracing her, not me, at family gatherings. I could see why he did; she knew how to humor him, teasing him about his need to control.

In 1986, when he was seventy-two, during a Thanksgiving dinner at the house of a friend, Manuele had a stroke. He was left unable to speak, paralyzed on his right side. He needed full-time care. His wife and sons had pulled away, going off in different directions, but now all three of them turned back and pulled together. None of them—not Rosabianca, Marco, Stefano, or his wife, Mary, who is a true-blue American and thus free of Sicilian cultural imperatives, hesitated or dithered as I later did over the care of my mother. Stefano and Mary, who were then struggling actors living in a tiny apartment on the Upper West Side of Manhattan, agreed to take Manuele first, but they needed time, several months, to reorganize themselves, find a larger apartment, and move. So when Manuele was released from the hospital, his ex-wife took him in.

During the summer after his stroke—by this time he was living with his son and wife in Hoboken—Manuele grew sicker and weaker. He was diagnosed with gall-bladder cancer and operated on. Even a minimal level of recovery was slow, and after a resident doctor dropped a catheter on the floor, picked it up, and inserted it without sterilization, Manuele developed a life-threatening infection. When he came out of Mount Sinai Hospital, six weeks later, whether because of the operation, the infection, or a further undetected stroke, Manuele could no longer swallow. He had to be fed through a tube to his stomach. His mouth had to be cleaned, and gag-producing mucus had to be removed. Stefano and Mary managed all of it—all the tubes and physio and cleaning. And this was on top of auditions and off-off Broadway plays and working at legal offices all night as proofreaders. They were matter-of-fact and cheerful, examples of what could be done and (though I didn't know it then) should be done.

Finding trustworthy help in California and New York was a constant problem. Women were hired; proved incompetent, nasty, or even mentally ill; and were fired. Stefano and Mary grew desperate; they were willing to pay well for what they knew to be difficult work. They tried newspaper ads and employment agencies until finally they found a Jamaican woman, Lynette, who was patient, polite, and strong enough to move a stroke patient.

Marco went to help out when Manuele had the cancer operation. And we spent that Christmas in Hoboken so that Stefano and Mary could have a break. I was comfortable providing backup care, but more was required. After a year with Stefano and Mary, Manuele was to come to us.

As the date of the handover drew near, we searched for another house, and Marco looked into the necessary papers and visas for his father to come to Canada. It could not be done, at least not in a timely manner. We would have to apply for a special Minister's Permission, and that—if it was granted at all—could take years.

Providentially, Marco was given a sabbatical. Again, Rosabianca moved into a bigger apartment, with three bedrooms. Manuele, Marco, our daughters, then five and nine, and I all moved in with her. I felt as if I were the victim of a cruel and unusual punishment.

A few months earlier, after a treatment of gold injections, my arthritic disease had gone into remission, but I was still recovering from the exhaustion and the pain. And adjusting to caring for Manuele was a shock. His lifetime savings were disappearing rapidly; full-time help was no longer affordable. We did hire three of Rosabianca's students, two pretty and accommodating girls and an indolent young man, to help out here and there. And although the doctors in New York had insisted Manuele would never recover his ability to swallow, he was eating normally again.

Marco managed most of the care—the washing, feeding, and exercising. But I was at the apartment with Manuele more than Marco. I had found after several attempts and an anxiety attack that I could not drive on the freeway; Marco had to chauffeur the girls and run most of the errands. So I soon learned the care routines.

In the first few months, both Marco and I learned patience: to be on call twenty-four hours, to follow a strict time schedule (Manuele's), to order things exactly as he wanted them, to soothe his cries of rage and frustration, to stay in, to stay close, to put ourselves third after Manuele, after the girls. Outside, the heat was another blow, week after week, one hundred degrees Fahrenheit and higher: hot, parched, merciless. Encircling Sacramento, a ring of forest fires. We watched the acres burn on TV. We inhaled and choked on the smoke and ash.

At a mall, I found a T-shirt that expressed how I felt. Across the front in medieval script was written the opening lines of Dante's *Inferno*. The T-shirt was half-price. "They just didn't sell," the salesclerk said. One day, as I was massaging cream into the dried, broken skin of his paralyzed hand, I noticed Manuele staring fixedly at my chest. I pointed and read aloud. *Nel mezzo del cammin della nostra vita / Mi ritrouvai per un selva oscura . . .* In the middle of the journey of my life / I found myself in a dark woods . . .

He laughed and I laughed. It was the first time we had laughed together. No one else had appreciated the absurdity of my wearing the stanza on my chest. But he was lost in the darkest of woods and understood.

Was that the moment things changed between us? No, but it was when I became aware that the change had occurred. It had happened gradually as I cared for him: care calling care. I ministered to his ruined flesh, uncurling his fingers, moving the dead weight of his arm through the range of motion exercises, and lifting him off the toilet (though my rheumatologist had warned against heavy weights). I had always been finicky, not at all the nursing type. Now I was surprised at what I could do and never automatically or mechanically. Still, taking him to the toilet, giving him his sponge baths, or bringing him his plastic urinal and then waiting for him to finish—that did embarrass me. I could not make myself wash his genitals. It felt too wrong, like breaking a primitive taboo.

Care calling care. Manuele could not speak, but he made himself understood. At least to me. Often when he had trouble getting through to Marco, he turned his eyes to me, expecting that I would know. And I would.

I began to sit with him to watch *Jeopardy* and *Wheel of Fortune,* programs that bored me but pleased him. I began to cook what I thought would tempt him to eat. As month followed month, he ate less and less. He could swallow, but he would stop after a few bites. Marco and I tried to coax him. Be firm with him, said the social worker who visited to check up on us. He seems a willful type. Don't let him run you, she said. And I thought, what do you know? We sensed the cancer was back, but the doctor did not believe us. No sign, he said. The flu, he said. But we felt Manuele was breaking down.

And then suddenly, there was more than a sign; there were too many signs. His bowels loosened; his stomach refused any food. We changed and washed both Manuele and the sheets, over and over. His temperature shot up, and we were awoken every hour of the night. Manuele broke apart into blood and nerves, flesh and innards, a heart, lungs gasping for air. But his will hung on. At home and then in the hospital, the weeks passed. In a preview of what would happen with my father, he was placed on the respirator and taken off. Stefano and Mary arrived, and the four of us divided up the day and night so that Manuele was never alone. Rosabianca came every day. His skin turned dark yellow; his legs swelled; the air rattled in his throat. Still he hung on, fighting that last dissolution from flesh into matter.

I could smell death radiating from his mouth. And I was afraid. But I made myself lean over into the stink of decay and touch his face and hand. "You can let go now," I said. "Because you got what you wanted. You and your Sicilian ideas. You've won. How many have sons like yours? They gave up everything when you needed them. And look at me: I served you. I bet you liked that. Being waited on hand and foot. All of us serving you, even your wife. Loving you—all of us. So you can let go, give in. You've won."

When Manuele called me a princess in a tower, he wasn't entirely wrong. My tower was built of books and theories, none of which were wrong or false. But caring for him, I fell out, fell to earth, was grounded.

I watched Manuele's two sons clean and dress him in preparation for burial. I helped shift and lift his stiffening body. Before the coffin lid was closed, I bent and kissed his forehead.

{ **17** }

To live is to remember
and to remember is to live.

Samuel Butler, THE NOTE-BOOKS
OF SAMUEL BUTLER

strangers

I EXPECTED GRATITUDE. I told my mother
she would be moving in with us. She did not need to
worry; I would look after her. "We'll all be together," I said,
thinking it would please her. "And you'll see your granddaughters every day—Tatiana and Antonia."

"I'm not going anywhere," Mum said. "I'm staying here
in my house."

I reminded myself how upsetting the idea of change
must be for her. "You can't stay alone."

"I can look after myself."

And pigs can fly. "We'll take some of your furniture—
whatever fits. And your pictures and things. A few of them,
anyway."

"I'm staying here."

While the renovation was being done, we had this conversation day after day with only slight variations. Each time, I expected, I hoped, that she would come to some sense of her situation. I craved her acknowledgment that I was doing the right thing.

With the architect, we had designed an addition to the house. Mum would have what I had not found in the new and old houses we'd looked at: a large, light-filled room on the main floor with an attached bathroom and a gas fireplace. There would be windows overlooking the garden and space for distinct sleeping and living areas and hardwood floors for easy cleaning. In the bathroom, the shower would be large enough for a chair and a pole (for her to hang on to), and the toilet would be elevated for easy access. There would also be handrails and a cork floor, which would be softer than ceramic if she fell. Unfortunately, a gulf of months yawned between the planning and the execution. Inevitably, the project grew. We decided we might as well replace the worn flooring in the dining room. And since the new bathroom and part of the bedroom was where our study had been, the addition should have a second story with a new study and—why not?—a new bathroom for Marco and me.

So, on top of everything else, we had to endure months of chaos and strain. For the first month, when the house was being ripped apart, we escaped, flying to Sicily for a family holiday that we had been planning for over a year. Mum went back into the General's respite care. This time, she did not accuse us of trying to shut her away but seemed to trust that we would return and release her. Still, she insisted that she did not need to go to *that place* with the vulgar, lower-class people. "They never use table-cloths," she said. "And there is no one you can talk to." As well as, repeatedly: "I can take care of myself."

Mum had even more trouble than usual communicating when she was at the General. Some of the other patients could no longer speak; others did not seem to want to, hiding out in their rooms or scowling in response to a question. Inevitably, in such low-paying jobs, most of the staff was foreign-born, and Mum had trouble deciphering their various accents, as they did hers. Tatiana and I were still unpacking Mum's clothes when a sweet-natured woman from Calabria, who usually cleaned on another floor, came in with the unit supervisor. "Look, Rosa, a friend to talk to. Isn't that nice? Gemma. Another Italian lady," the head nurse said in the smarmy voice commonly used for talking to the old.

Gemma had a large smile full of crooked teeth; her language was a dense Calabrian dialect. "I don't under-stand this one," Mum said to me in her habitual Venetian. "What does she want?"

"She's asking how long you are staying," I guessed. "And commenting on how lucky you are to have such a lovely granddaughter." I was using standard Italian, hoping Gemma and Mum would follow.

"One night—me," Mum answered in her version of English.

I asked Gemma how long she had worked at the hospital, whether she had a family—the usual. She replied in English with as heavy an accent as Mum's.

Mum's isolation was not helped by her habit of taking out her hearing aid. Later, I discovered that at some point it had ceased to fit properly, exacerbating its tendency to emit a high-pitched squeal.

To ease my guilt at leaving Mum for a month, I hired Mila to visit her three times a week, to do her laundry, to make sure she was eating, to give her some care and company. (At least Mila's face would be familiar. I didn't expect that they would actually talk.) I also arranged visits from a couple of my close friends and Severina Bolzon, who had been my parents' friend since they had moved to Edmonton in the late fifties.

I told myself that it made sense for us to go away; we all needed respite. A holiday from responsibility and sadness. The tenseness that was holding me together, impelling me on through those last months, did melt under the heat of the Sicilian sun. We went to the beach for the girls and to the historical sites for us, to the beauties of Erice and Taormina for all of us. We visited relatives in Palermo and friends on the island of Vulcano. We laughed together and squabbled, as we had before—before Dad had been struck down. But while we hiked and ate and swam, while we climbed a volcano and sailed around the Aeolian Islands, the winds that buffeted me were internal ones: anxiety, euphoria, and resentment. I was always aware that my enjoyment was bought at my mother's expense.

WE RETURNED to find that Mum's hearing aid no longer worked and her teeth had disappeared (again). She blamed both on a nurse's aide—a large black woman with dreadlocks. "She's ugly and she's bad," Mum said. "A devil."

"Shush," I said, thrusting her things into the suitcase as fast as I could. I didn't want anyone to hear her. "I talked to the supervisor. I filled out a form. Maybe they'll find your teeth. They could have got mixed in with sheets—sent to the laundry." Fat chance. Mum tended to take out her teeth at the end of a meal, wrap them in a napkin, and lay them by her dish. Ten to one, they had been thrown away.

"She stole my teeth—that one."

"Why would she steal your teeth? They aren't like a sweater. They're made to fit you, your mouth."

(Poorly, roughly. She did need a new pair, but still.)

"She did it to hurt me. She did."

"You have to think about what you're doing, where you're putting your things."

"The black one—"

"We'll have to see if they can fix the hearing aid. This is going to be expensive."

"*Ze stregà*. It's bewitched. She did it."

I wondered by what process Mum came to her conviction that the woman had stolen her teeth and cast the evil eye on the hearing aid. Had it been an instinctive response? She feared the woman as Other? Or had the woman mistreated my mother? She or one of her coworkers? I had seen the headlines in the newspaper, seen the commercials for the exposé documentaries: elder abuse, the shame of nursing homes. I could never read the entire article or watch the TV program; I grew too agitated. But I knew. I knew it could happen.

When we got back to the condominium, while Tatiana fixed Mum a cup of coffee the way she liked it—dark roast, lots of milk and three sugars—I used an excuse to change her clothes. "I have to do a load of wash right now." I checked her arms and legs, her chest and back. No bruises. Purple spider veins, moles, a long scratch below one elbow, several scabs above the other wrist, a hard red spot on her back, some cracked skin on her legs and on the bottom of her feet. No bruises. Only the ravages of age—soft, helpless flesh.

"Your skin is so dry," I said, grabbing her best bottle of body lotion.

"Terrible," Mum said, and then, seeing Tatiana with the tray. "My beauty, my treasure—"

Tatiana was the good granddaughter, the angel; Antonia, the bad or, at least the spoiled one. Corinna's daughters, Cristina and Michelle, were also divided into the good one and the bad, as were the young girls who lived next door to my parents in Calgary and the sons of a friend in Nanaimo who was originally from Lussingrande. Mum hadn't used to classify others so absolutely. At least, I don't remember her doing so. She had split Tatiana and Antonia into favorite and not, good and bad, since they were little. But earlier the roles were not so fixed; she would switch them from one category to the other, depending on which one was being cooperative, which one independent.

Only in the last few years did Mum's response to some people become extreme, even paranoid. If a person were not young and pretty, Mum labeled that person not just as bad but as a demon. And this immoderate, irrational hostility began to erupt into hallucinations or delusions. As she had with the missing teeth at the General, she blamed any mistake she might have made on a handy scapegoat. And if no one was handy, she created one. A tall man with dark eyes had entered her home in the night and stolen her gold necklace. The same dark man had turned on a burner on the stove and left it on, endangering her and the condo. Although I say "created," which implies intent, she obviously did not consciously make the dark man up. She believed in his existence.

Did he spring from a shadow, a black flutter, a disturbance of her old eyes? Or did she see him clearly? Standing before her, a long, thin streak of a face, a purplish line of a mouth, and eyes with the dull, impersonal gleam of an empty bottle. "The man came and stood by my bed," she would tell me.

"Don't be silly, Mum. Nobody could have entered the apartment. I was in the other bedroom, remember?"

"I was terrified. He was going to take me away."

"I would have heard something."

"He wanted to rape me."

I was suddenly curious. "How did you know?"

"I knew. I yelled and you came and he went."

"It was a dream."

"No, it wasn't."

"No one can get in without my hearing. It was a bad dream."

"No. No. Why don't you believe me? Why?"

Although disbelieving, I wanted to understand her delusions. I was convinced that they must have some hidden meaning, some significance beyond the death of brain cells. I could not list her symptoms of mental disturbance as a doctor or a scientist would. I had my own fears and suspicions, my own hallucinations, both aural and visual. We were simply at different points on a continuum; I could still evaluate and classify phantoms as night terrors or hallucinations.

"Don't worry," I would tell Mum. "No one will get in without my knowing. The doors are locked. There are no strange men here."

I could never reassure her. Whether it was a bar of soap from her drawer or her red Merino sweater that was misplaced, she was sure it had been stolen. "Thieves, thieves," she'd yell. "One of those bad people has robbed me."

Ironically—or is it inevitably—she and my father *had* been deceived, defrauded, in effect robbed, not by a stranger or by someone she'd called bad or a devil but by one of her angels. A family of angels, the Donnellys— devout, earnest, and dull was how I pictured them (having never met them). They became friends with my parents through a church in Nanaimo that declared itself Roman Catholic but was an anti-ecumenical, breakaway sect. Mum and Dad began to attend because the mass was pre-Vatican II, in Latin, with much incense and genuflection; Holy Communion was taken by mouth, women kept their heads covered, and the sermons were all about the hell that was the modern world. Nostalgia brought them to that church, and the welcome they were given by the tiny congregation drew them back. They must have been lonely in that new place. Retired, old, and lonely.

As long as I remembered, Dad had only gone to church because he had to drive Mum. He'd been raised as an Anglican, but I never heard him express any religious sentiments one way or another. I suspected he was a skeptic. Mum wanted him to convert, but uncharacteristically, she did not nag or insist. She would mention to me, from time to time, that she wished he would convert so that they could be buried side by side in a Catholic cemetery. Then one day, about two years after they moved to Nanaimo, he announced during a weekly phone call that he had become an initiate, studying to prepare himself for "baptism into the faith."

After that, the Donnellys often came up in our phone calls. They knew how to raise their children (unlike Marco and me). Their girls weren't always out with their friends. They didn't wear lipstick or dangly earrings or jeans, ever. "No pants," Mum said. "Carol says women must be women. No pants." Carol homeschooled all six children until high school. "The Donnellys say there's too much corruption, too many bad influences in schools, even Catholic schools."

"Drugs, sex, and rock 'n' roll?"

"Terrible, these days; terrible." The oldest children were sent away to special convent schools. "Strict. Very strict."

After my parents moved back to Edmonton, my father told me that he'd guaranteed a line of credit for Mr. Donnelly's home-repair business "They are good people, religious people," Dad explained. "No need for you to worry."

It broke Dad's heart—both the loss of the thirty thousand dollars and the personal betrayal. Mum and Dad had been so careful all their lives, then a lump sum was gone with no warning. It happened just before his heart attack and contributed to it, I'm sure, along with the burden of caring for Rosa. He didn't want to tell her, I remember, knowing how it would agitate her. And, although we could have used that money now, I was not so cruel as to bring up the loss or to expose the true nature of her angels, her second family. "Don't worry about the dark man," I said instead.

Getting her to bed each night was an invariable ordeal. I couldn't wait for the extension to be finished. On weekends, when she was at our house, we had to get her up the stairs. And at her condo, she still did not want to go to bed. She would scream if I started undressing her. She did not want to get into the large bed she had shared with Dad. Memories, ghost, the dark man? She was afraid. "Sleep here," she would say, "with me. Look how much room."

But I couldn't. "I won't sleep," I said.

Then she'd insist she could manage on her own. "You go to bed," she'd say. "Don't worry about me." But I would worry that she'd fall; she was so weak. And if, worn out, I did give up and go to bed, I'd inevitably wake up in the middle of the night to find her slumped over, asleep in an armchair. In the morning, she would have swollen feet and a sore back.

The days, weeks, and months dragged on, coated in plaster dust and filled with the sounds of hammers, electric saws, and staple guns. The study was gone, books and files all in boxes, and I could not find a quiet corner or one safe from workmen, cheerful strangers in the kitchen and the bedroom.

18

For a moment I thought Istria
would be one more forgotten world
like Tlon, Uqbar or Orbis Tertius.

Martin Bassani, founder of Istria-talks

istria talks

THE YEAR MY FATHER died and I had to
begin looking after my mother, I was a writer-in-residence
at the university. When the residency ended, I had to find
a job. Since I'd committed myself to caring for my mother,
I couldn't continue to work as a sessional lecturer, as I had
for the last fifteen years or so, teaching writing and literature. I couldn't leave her for long stretches of time, not
in good conscience. So I started working for a distance-
learning university, teaching by phone and Internet from
home, freed from the need to appear dressed up and prepared in a classroom.

Of course, I now had fewer excuses to get out, to get
away.

I missed chitchatting with colleagues and students or
kvetching with an office mate. I'd liked being able to drop

in on a lecture or a reading that was conveniently sched-
uled in a room one floor away or to wander through the
stacks of the library, pulling out a book that caught my
eye, skimming the latest literary magazines. I'd stayed
home with each of my daughters during their first year of
life, but those times had felt different. I knew they were
going to end. They didn't stretch on indefinitely. Besides,
babies are portable: you can bundle them up and take
them with you.

I hoped I would get back to my writing, but I didn't
have the space, time, or even the mental concentration I
needed. My days were filled with people: workmen, family, home-care workers, and Mum. But I felt disconnected
from a wider world, isolated, and trapped at home.

I escaped through the Internet, in particular a discussion forum dedicated to Istria. In 1996, a year before my
father had his heart attack, I'd begun looking for information on Lussino—in particular, a history of the area.
I wanted to know whether my grandfather had been on
Nazario Sauro's submarine and whether his family had
really been exiled from their home during World War I
and sent to a camp in Sicily. I didn't expect to find the
answers neatly typed up and waiting for me. But I thought
I could learn enough to understand the times and the context and thus work out what was probable and possible.

Moreover, I found I was developing an authentic interest in the place where my mother was born. Foolishly, I
thought it would be simple: learning the history, uncover-
ing the truth. After all, I didn't need an excess of details
or specifics. No articles titled "The Roman Missal in
Glagolitic Script in Istria of the Seventeenth Century" or

"The Thirteenth-Century Plague Epidemics in Pula and Motuvan" for me. I wanted the Istrian equivalent of *A History of Venice* by John Julius Norwich, a book for the lay audience in English or Italian. Through a mutual friend, I asked Dr. Fulvio Salimbeni, a respected historian of Istria and professor at the University of Trieste, to recommend a good, general history of Istria. He answered, "There is no such book."

Perhaps his criteria are too restrictive, I thought. Probably he is too critical. I tried the online catalogue at the university, which has an extensive library judged to be one of the top three in Canada. I was prepared to read anything I could find about the area. There were a few books in languages that I didn't know: German, Slovenian, and Croatian. Nothing in Italian. In English, a nineteenth-century travel guide and an eighteenth-century memoir of a trip down the Istrian and Dalmatian coasts; in both, English gentlemen described the natural beauty and the picturesque Balkan tribes. I found two history books about the struggle for Trieste after World War II. One was a PhD thesis, which argued that the city was unjustly taken from Yugoslavia; the other, a memoir by the American general who helped run postwar Trieste. Otherwise— nothing, only an absence, a gap, a *foiba* they would call it in Istria, a sinkhole, a dark pit into which garbage, history, and people are cast and disappear.

Frustrated by the lack of books, I turned to the Internet. At first, it too offered little, until I found and joined Istria-talks. The discussion forum had been started and was run by Martin Bassani, a computing engineer who lived in Pennsylvania but was born in Vines, Istria, of a distinguished Istrian family. The membership was small, around fifty, I think, though the active members, the ones who posted comments, were about twenty, all male, ranging from a Croatian nationalist to the mouthpiece of an underground Istrian independence group. No one in this forum could answer my questions, but I remained a member, becoming ever more interested in the debates about the identity of Istria—*L'Istria xe Mia o Tua?* (Is Istria mine or yours?)—and in the nature of past events and the possibilities or probabilities of Istria's future.

My involvement grew after I took on Mum's care and was more often at home. Whenever I had a few minutes—three, four, five times a day—I logged on. The computer was in the corner of a tiny upstairs bedroom, filled with the contents of our former study. Walled in by boxes of books, I sat at the keyboard, eagerly reading Martin's latest reminiscence of his school days or Vladimir's description of the beauties of Lake Vrana, "Jack's" manifesto for the liberation of Istria, or Davor's translation of a news story about the beating death of an Italian tourist in Rovigno.

In November 1998, when the renovation of our home was finally done and Mum was moving in permanently, Martin Bassani closed down Istria.com. With a new business and a new baby, he could not continue to spend endless time and money on the Web site. Before I began to suffer from full-blown withdrawal, a new site was formed, Istrianet.org, with many of the former participants. The new Webmaster was the feisty Marisa Ciceran, who had almost no financial support and no training in computers or Web design. She did have several important qualities: an Istro-Romanian ethnic background that kept her from being swept into either the Italian or the Slavic camp, a polished writing style in English, Italian, and Istro-Veneto, a broad and varied education, intellectual curiosity, precision, patience, energy, and dedication.

Martin had begun the forum because of his feeling that the Istria that was his homeland was vanishing, being sucked into a black hole. Marisa rescued the Web site because she felt an even more bitter sense of loss. The Istro-Romanians and their language were on the edge of extinction. Over the next few years, with a few far-flung volunteers, she would build the Web site into an encyclopedia of a culture that (it could be argued) no longer exists except in stories and memories.

I was ever more drawn to Istrianet.org and its discussion forum, Istria-talks. It dominated my thoughts and conversation even when I was not at the computer. ("One of these days," Marco would say, "you're going to tell me that Jesus was from Istria.") It was giving me what I needed—a link to the outside, to people and ideas beyond my very limited reach. I was comfortable, at home, with many of the participants. I felt I knew them—the regulars. Marisa, who lived on the Upper West Side of Manhattan and was also stuck at home, looking after her aged mother. Giancarlo de Angelini, in Rome, a poet who wrote in Rovignese dialect. Piero Grimalda, in Arizona, a retired Air Force master sergeant. Franco Alitalia, another poet and irredentist. Mario Demetlica, in Australia, who tended to post pages of books rather than messages, and Guido Villa, also in Australia, who played devil's advocate or the voice of reason on the forum. Ed, Al, Bruno, Ondina, Franko P., and Frank T.

The purpose of the site and the forum was, in Marisa's words, "to celebrate and thus preserve" multicultural Istria. But the need for this celebration and preservation, the reason why the process was more archeological investigation—excavation, extraction, interpretation—than reportage, was the post–World War II migration from Yugoslavia, the great exile.

Many wrote to bear witness.

I remember. . . I saw. . . I heard. . .

My uncle was taken in the night, and we never saw him again.

And my cousin—a partisan—taken/imprisoned/killed.

A young woman tortured/a young man executed. Innocents—

Says who?

She did no harm—

It was war. Excesses happen.

We lost our homes, our language, our lives.

But who cares, no one cares, who cares, no one cares.

Whiners. Get over it. Life's like that (in the twentieth century).

I was ashamed to realize that my aunts, uncles, and cousins, and my sister, Corinna, had all been refugees, all spent years in refugee camps, yet I'd been only vaguely aware of what had happened. And my ignorance was typical. A people had been uprooted, cities had been emptied, a culture that went back a thousand years had been obliterated, and the reaction of the world was indifference and silence. Even in Italy, in schools and universities, the great exodus was not and is not taught.

In contrast, in the forum, the shadow of the exodus was inescapable. This topic that was not talked about elsewhere, that even in 2004 in Italy I was told should not, could not, be talked about, ignited rancorous and endless debate.

How many had left? Estimates varied from 20,000 to 350,000.

What is verifiable? People began to leave Rijeka in 1945, soon after the Yugoslav army gained control of the region from the Nazis and before any official agreement about the future of the area had been reached. On May 1, Tito's men entered Trieste, and during the following forty days, people disappeared, were executed by firing squads, and thrown into *foibe*. New Zealand and American soldiers witnessed some of these acts, but the Allied troops were forbidden to stop them. (In 1992, Fred McRae, who served in the 88th Infantry Division of the American army, described how one of his first duties in Trieste in 1945 was to take 2½ tons of lime and pour it into "a bottomless pit"—a mass grave.) Churchill does not explain why in his memoir *The Second World War* but comments that "in Venezia Giulia our men were forced to watch, with no possibility of intervening, deeds that offended their sense of justice and they felt this was tacit acquiescence to the misdeed."

On June 12, Tito handed Trieste, Pola, and Gorizia back to the Allied forces. A new accord, meant to be temporary, was written by Generals Morgan and Jovanovic in Belgrade. It divided the contested area into two zones of occupation: Zone A, which included Trieste and the immediate area, was to be under the command of the Anglo-American forces and Zone B, a strip of the Istrian coast, would be under the command of the Yugoslav military. The rest of Istria (and all the Quarnero islands) would be governed by the civil government of Yugoslavia.

At the ratification of the Paris Peace Treaty of 1947, the exodus became a flood. Pola was about to be transferred to Tito, and its citizens panicked. In February 1947 alone, twelve boatloads of around a thousand people each were transported to Venice or Ancona.

The exodus, from all the "Italian" cities and villages, continued through the signing of the Memorandum of Intent in 1954, when Trieste was returned to Italy and the border between the two countries was officially drawn. During this last stage, which lasted until April 1956, it was the farmers, those most connected to their land, who *opted* to leave. The middle-class workers and fisherman had gone long before.

Did this population jump, or were they pushed? Were they exiles or immigrants? Inadvertent casualties of war or ethnic targets? Was it class warfare? Ideological sorting? Or ethnic cleansing? And those cast into the *foibe*—were they slaughtered in reprisal or simply because they were Italians?

Who belonged in Istria anyway? The Italians? The Croatians? Were there any Italians left? And if there were, were they traitors or patriots? And the Romanians, the Austrians, the Hungarians, the Serbs, and the latest, the Bosnians? Who belonged? Who was first?

We were—since the Romans. And Venice ruled Kres and Losinj from 1145 onwards. (Except for 1358 to 1409, when Hungary dominated.)

No, no, we were. The Veneti were a Slavic tribe. We were there before you.

Often the words of the individual postings crackled with anger, fear, or hatred. Insults were used to categorize a member as "other." Fascist, Communist, bourgeois, rabble, crybaby, liar, idiot, devil. (Night phantoms, dark strangers, black flutters in the eye.)

Your group was worse than mine.

No, your people raped/murdered/tortured more than mine.

If only someone had kept a ledger, death by death, atrocity by atrocity. Then I could blame you still more loudly.

We are good; you are bad.

19

When writing about the onset of
Alzheimer's, it is difficult to remember
a sequence of events—what happens
when, in what order. The condition
seems to get into the narrative,
producing repetition and preoccupied
query, naming its own state.

John Bayley, ELEGY FOR IRIS

who belongs?

ONCE THE EXTENSION was finished and we moved Mum into our home, life became easier for me and harder for the rest of the family. To my surprise, since change is upsetting to people with dementia, Mum seemed pleased with the move, calmer. At least for the time being.

Her new room was bright and full of light. We'd brought over her favorite pieces of furniture, a TV, most of her clothes, a few of the framed photographs, her jewelry box, a couple of Murano glass mementos of trips to Venice, and her two fur coats. We'd hung a mounted gold-framed lace fan, woven by her sister Enea, over the fireplace and a watercolor of the church of Santa Maria della Salute on a wall.

I no longer had to race back and forth between condo and house. I could work in the study and still be on call. And Marco and the girls, at least on weekends, were more likely to be around, available as support and backup. Of course, that was the difficulty for them. Whenever they were home, they had to deal with, accept, her presence. She could not be ignored. And interactions with her were numbingly repetitive.

Each suppertime, we went through the wine ritual. Marco would usually pour a glass for him and me. "I would like some wine," she would say. "Why didn't you give me any?"

One of the girls would answer: "Nonna, you don't like wine."

"I've drunk wine all my life. My mother used to buy bottles fresh from the country." She'd look indignant. We were trying to cheat her. I'd fetch an extra glass and pour a small amount.

"Is that all? So little?" She was sure now that we were conspiring against her.

"Just try it." She would smile, raise the glass, and drink. Her face would instantly contract in a spasm of distaste. "*Que terrible.*" We would all laugh. Antonia sometimes rolled her eyes. "You like this *scifo?* Impossible. You played a trick; you switched the bottle."

At first, Marco would try to add water or 7-UP. For years when they were in Calgary, Dad had made his own wine, and they'd grown used to cutting the foxy home-made taste with pop. Our table wine needed no alteration, and 7-UP made no difference. Mum never drank more than a sip or two.

Mum had lost her appetite. A year earlier, when Dad had fallen ill, she'd been—as she had been most of her married life—not obese, but overweight. Now the pounds were melting away; her skirts didn't stay up, and her sweaters fell off her shoulders. The new clothes I bought were not what she would have ever bought herself. She did not approve of slacks for women, unless it was minus thirty degrees, and even then only grudgingly.

"That's why the world is going to hell," she would say, observing my jeans. "Women trying to be men," quoting the priest of their Nanaimo church. But now that she could not dress herself, I discouraged skirts, for they meant the ordeal of getting her into pantyhose. I bought her jogging suits in bright colors and soft fabrics, tops that didn't have to go over her head, and slacks that were easy to pull on and off and to wash (no ironing).

As Mum got smaller, I was getting bigger, seized by sudden and intense bouts of hunger. Although often confused and disoriented, Mum remained aware enough to remind me (several times a day) that I was too fat and had an enormous backside. The only food she wanted was sweet and soft things that would slide down her throat, yet she continued to be interested in what everyone else at the table was eating. She was convinced that Antonia and Tatiana were starving themselves and that Marco was taking more than his share. He was fit and in shape, but each time he served himself, Mum would shoot me a significant look, then shake her head. "Whatever he is paying you, it is not enough," she said, as if he were a boarder. "You won't get any profit out of him."

When Marco placed a portion on her plate, always more than she would eat, she complained: "Could there be a smaller piece?" If the serving dish was close enough, she leaned over to spear herself another piece of chicken or spoonful of potatoes, often knocking over glasses or dishes that lay in between. She was always alert to the possibility that she was being shortchanged and was ready to fight for her fair share. Once she had the extra piece of meat and the mound of potatoes, she did not eat them. My waste-not-want-not mother would poke and push her supper around, then leave it to be thrown away.

She now had new dentures to replace the ones lost at the General. (Lost on the second visit. The first time they were found in the laundry.) At some point, who knows how long ago, the old ones had become useless; she'd been unable to chew. The teeth were effectively a decoration. My father had noticed that Mum was taking her teeth out more frequently, but perhaps he thought it was part of her general decline. So did I, until we went to get a new pair. It took several visits to the office and several adjustments before the denturist assured me that this pair fit properly. At least, the upper plate did. Her bottom gum had shrunk to the point that the bottom dentures had little to anchor on. She still pulled them out.

Whoever brought her to the table had to make sure that she was wearing her hearing aid and to locate her teeth and have her insert them. When we began to eat, she would chew—for a moment or two. "This meat is tough. The butcher cheated you. The vegetables are raw. Why can't you cook them longer? This pasta is hard. You never learned how to cook properly," she'd say to me. The teeth would come out and be wrapped in Kleenex or perched on the edge of her plate. The next few bites were gummed.

"Gross." This was from Antonia, who—at her own insistence—sat at the corner of the table farthest away from her grandmother. She usually avoided looking at Mum while she was eating, but now and then her attention would be caught and she would stare, horrified. If I reminded her that she was being rude, she forced herself to look away, cutting off peripheral vision with her hand. She had turned sixteen the November Mum moved in with us and was at the peak of teen fastidiousness. Her once omnipresent friends rarely came to the house now and never joined us for dinner. Later Mum sometimes used her teeth as an implement to guide food onto a fork, eliciting a shriek of "Nonna!" from Antonia and an equally loud "Mum!" from me.

I soon realized that I had to cook separate food for Mum: blenderized vegetable soups, scrambled eggs, quiches, mooshy pasta, and puddings. And she would eat more of this soft food. But she still wanted to have on her dish whatever we had on ours. What about me? she'd say. Why don't I get any? Getting Mum to drink was harder than getting her to eat. She refused all water—filtered, bottled, or tap. *Que terrible.* And all juice except apple, served at room temperature in a small glass and with a straw. She would take tiny sips, managing about a glass a day. I was afraid she was chronically dehydrated.

She was prone to bladder infections; she had had urinary tract problems for years. But they were hard to detect. She no longer suffered from any of the usual symptoms, including pain. I would guess she had an infection whenever she seemed weaker and more disoriented than usual or when she suffered sudden incontinence. And I'd be right. Unfortunately, producing a urine sample for testing involved me and her and juice boxes and running water and coaxing and at least half an hour in the bathroom at the lab.

Plenty of fluids, doctors ordered for Mum, no matter what the illness. *Plenty of fluids,* looking straight at me. I'd have liked to have seen one of them try.

Every time Tatiana and I would go into her room, we'd encourage and beg. You must drink. The doctor says. Let me hold the glass. Come on, that's right.

I must drink, she would agree, I must drink, and she'd take one sip.

To get her to take the large antibiotic pills, I crushed and mixed them into chocolate pudding. Then Tatiana, who has a sweet yet firm manner, would spoon-feed her.

The appointments for the new dentures were part of a blitz of medically related consultations. In the first six months that Mum lived with us, I took her to the denturist, a dentist, an ophthalmologist, an audiologist, a neurologist, a cardiologist, a gerontologist, and—repeatedly—the family doctor. I couldn't make up for her loss of Dad, but I could drive her to the appointments he either had not thought necessary or had not had the strength to face. I was trying to make her life more comfortable, better. But as Dad had known too well, getting Mum into a car was an undertaking that called for patience and planning. She did not want to go anywhere, or, rather, she both did and didn't want to go. So even with the appointments she requested, such as with the podiatrist and the hair-dresser, and church, where she wanted to go, she was balky, slow. She wanted to get ready on her own, comb her own hair, put on lipstick and perfume, choose a hat and scarf. But if I left her to do it, when I returned she wouldn't have started. So I had to stay with her and prod. We'll be late. We'll be late. I was nagging her as much as she used to nag me. She also serves, I'd tell myself, who only stands and waits and waits.

Were the appointments worth the hassle? I did develop a clearer picture of Mum's health, her chronic heart failure and progressive dementia. Her medication was adjusted, and our family doctor put her (and me) on antidepressants. Zoloft seemed to calm her. She remained difficult but was less subject to rages. In the next year, she never physically attacked a home-care worker. And the new, stronger hear-ing aid was an improvement over the ancient one. She could hear more of what was said, even if she wouldn't fol-low a long conversation. And this aid was smaller and fit better, which meant less of the high-pitched whistle that had annoyed both her and us.

Six months after that flurry of appointments, Mum developed a new physical problem, which added to Anto-nia's (and all of our) distress, especially at mealtimes. Mum made chewing motions with her mouth all day long. The chewing was accompanied by odd facial grimaces and an excess of mucus that she couldn't seem to swallow but would eventually spit out into a Kleenex.

Swallow. Can't you swallow, I would hiss at her, par-ticularly when we were out in public.

It chokes me, poor Mum would say. I can't.

Although tardive dyskinesia is not a listed side effect of antidepressants, our GP stopped the Zoloft, just in case, and the grimaces stopped. The excess mucus did not. Months later, the problem took us back to the Glenrose Rehab hospital, where Mum had been tested for Alzheimer's. There a video X-ray was taken while she drank a quarter-cup of juice and then ate small portions of food of different texture and density. And I was able to see in black and white and gray, see the skull and jaw and esophagus moving like a primitive cartoon or an early National Film Board short. And I expected, at any second, to hear a joke or to see the anatomical sections fly apart, circle in a bone dance, then reform into a bird.

Mum was having difficulty with the mechanics of eating and drinking. Some of the necessary muscles were malfunctioning; food was not being propelled efficiently to the back of her mouth, and her swallowing reflex was impaired. When liquids hit the back of her throat, she felt as if she were drowning. And any quantity more than a trickle, even of saliva, would choke her.

When we had looked after Marco's father, Manuele, he had to be fed by a tube to the stomach because he could not swallow. Marco had routinely cleaned the recesses of his father's mouth with an aspirating wand. You would think we would have recognized the signs over the previous months, instead of ascribing Mum's behavior to her too-familiar stubbornness.

I had accepted that our roles had reversed—that I was now the parent who must protect and care for my mother. But my emotional climate was not exactly serene, stable, and mature. I was subjected to the squalls of adolescence and the torpor of old age and frequently overwhelmed by irritation, boredom, queasiness, affection, guilt, and pity. Too often I shouted at her; too often I was as embarrassed as if I were thirteen or sixteen. In the waiting rooms of medical offices, Mum would stare at anyone with different-colored skin. She'd suddenly switch to English. (She usually spoke Venetian dialect to me.) Too many of these people, too many immigrants. She'd speak loudly. I'd try to distract her; shushing didn't work. I hoped no one understood.

In the examining rooms, to the doctor or nurse, she said, "I been fifty years in this country."

"Forty-three," I said, as if it made any difference.

"Me Canadian." She had never identified herself that way. She'd always said *these Canadians*. She'd always said: *cold, cold, cold*. Now she was telling the doctors and nurses that no matter what they thought, she belonged here. She had a right to attention and care. She deserved it.

"You don't have to tell them how long you've been here," I told her. "You're getting the best care."

She shook her head. "They always ask me where I'm from. I don't like it."

"Maybe they're interested."

"And what am I going to say?"

"Italy," I suggested. "Venice. That's what you used to say when people asked."

"Eeehhh," she said in irritation. And I remembered that the questioners always looked surprised if she mentioned Venice. As if no one ever came from that fabulous city.

And, of course, it wasn't exactly true. But how to answer? Austria, Italy, Yugoslavia, Croatia? No one had heard of Istria. No one was asking for a history lesson.

In March 2000, the nurse supervisor at home care in charge of Mum's case announced that her needs would have to be re-evaluated and her competence retested. From early on, home-care workers had been coming to the house four mornings a week to awaken, wash, and dress Mum. The job included making breakfast and getting Mum to take her pills and eat. I requested more time; I wanted Mum to have two showers a week instead of one. Also, since I was still having a dreadful time getting her to bed, I asked for short visits five evenings a week. I didn't expect the worker to get her into bed; that was asking for the impossible. But Mum refused to take her medication if I was the one giving it to her and refused to have her nightgown put on if I was the one holding it. Tatiana managed all this whenever she was home, but she was twenty-one years old by that point and had university, a multitude of friends, and a boyfriend to keep her busy.

My weight and my blood pressure were rising. I'd developed a constant eye tremor and mouth sores. I thought (and our doctor agreed) that I would feel calmer without the nightly battle of wills.

Mum's evaluation took place during a four-hour-long appointment at the gerontology clinic of the nearby university hospital. As on other visits to other clinics and other hospitals, blood was taken, many vials, and an ascending order of medical personnel—nurse, resident, psychologist, and specialist—took turns questioning her.

I had to translate—not everything, but enough. And I had to interpret, explain each side to the other.

Mostly, we waited. Mum dozed off, and I read the *New Yorker.* Then I heard an arrival in the curtained cubicle next door. Voices on the other side of the curtain speaking a language I couldn't understand. Slavic, probably—two women, one older, one middle-aged. Another mother and daughter. Mum may have seen immigrants and newcomers crowding the waiting rooms we frequented; I saw aged mothers and their burdened, graying daughters.

"You're speaking Ukrainian?" the nurse said to them. I might have jumped to the same conclusion. Edmonton has a large population of Ukrainian-Canadians.

"Slovenian."

"Your mother doesn't speak English?" A hint of disapproval in the tone.

"She speaks Slovenian, Italian, and French." Aha, I thought, Istriani.

I waited for a few minutes after the nurse left. Then, since I couldn't knock, I stood at the opening of their curtain. "Excuse me."

They were indeed Istriani, from a village across the Slovenian border from Gorizia. They had left in the early fifties, during the time of the great migration. They'd traveled through several refugee camps, lived for over ten years in Belgium, and finally come to Canada. The daughter was a bleached blonde in a snug, gray knit dress. The mother—let us call her Mirjana—was in her nineties, her face as spotted and desiccated as an old apple. She had lost a leg below the knee because of diabetes, but she had a welcoming, yellow-toothed smile.

My mother is a *Lussignana,* I said. Didn't grow up there but went back a lot—summers.

"Caterina." A panicky call through the curtain.

"Bring her in," the daughter said. "They'll talk."

Why not? I plopped Mum into a nearby wheelchair and pushed her next to Mirjana's bed. A few minutes of confusion followed as we daughters introduced the mothers to each other and explained (in different languages) their connection.

The two older women looked each other over. Mirjana spoke first. "I went to Lussino on vacation once." She used the Venetian dialect. Mum's face cleared; she connected, and they began chatting away. The other daughter and I exchanged stories, though not names. The father had died a few years ago. The mother lived in a French-speaking seniors' lodge. The daughter, an only child, lived with her family in Montreal.

"Must be tough. Do you worry?"

"It's tough whatever you do. I worry. I fly back and forth."

Mum was angled forward in the armchair, her arms resting on the bed. Mirjana took both of her hands and began to sing: *Ancora un litro de quel bon* (Another liter of the good wine). Mum joined in on the repeating lines.

"She was getting along fine, had lots of friends; she visited in their rooms. She still seems fine to me most of the time."

Po andremo a casa. Then we'll go home.

"But the nurse at the lodge called me because she was having spells of agitation, complaining a man was coming into her room, disturbing her things."

No go le chiave del porton. I don't have the key to the door.

"Tell me about it. First of all my mother had a dark man taking things. Lately he's started to molest her."

"Oh no. Is that next? She's already so afraid."

"Ah yes, fear, paranoia—" I paused as I looked at the two old women. They still clasped their hands like little girls. "Your mother looks easier than mine. More with it."

Pe'ndar a casa. So I can't go home.

"She has her moments. I may be thousands of miles away, but she still thinks it is her duty to tell me what to do."

"Never a positive word? I know. I know."

Mirjana was singing *Che bel che iera / co'erimo giovani.* How beautiful it was when we were young.

Mum was shaking her head. "*Non lo so.*" I don't know it. But her eyes were still awake. She was almost smiling.

Mirjana lifted a hand to mark a switch, a new song.

Vola colomba bianca vola. Fly white dove fly.

"I don't believe it," Mirjana's daughter said.

"All the old chestnuts."

The two cracked, tremulous voices could not manage that lyrical song so connected to the time of exile. They hummed bits and missed notes. Mirjana sang many of the lines in what I took to be Slovenian. Yet they hung on to each other.

Diglielo tu, che tornero. Tell them I will return.

20

The starting point of critical
elaboration is the consciousness
of what one really is, as a product
of a historical process to date,
which has deposited in you an infinity
of traces, without leaving an inventory.
Therefore, it is imperative at the
outset to compile such an inventory.

Antonio Gramsci, LETTERS FROM PRISON

archives

I WENT TO THE archives of the city of Venice, hoping to find my grandfather in the ledgers of the once Serene Republic. For years, I had believed my mother's story that Onorato Pagan was a true-born Venetian, because it felt true, emotionally true. Each time I returned to Venice, I felt as if I were arriving home. Walking the city's labyrinthine streets, I was at home. But was her story true, or was it a comforting construction?

My grandfather's name, for example, Onorato—as Paola had claimed—was indigenous to Southern Italy and not to Veneto or Istria. (Just as the name Salvatore—as the new son of a Venetian friend and his African wife was called—was labeled *not one of our names* by another cousin. *So Southern, poor child.*) The southernism was easy to explain, as I'd always heard that Onorato's mother, Serafina, was from near Ancona, on the Adriatic coast. But when I was growing up, my mother had always told me that her father's name was Renato. She would say, "When I was expecting, your father and I decided the baby would be named after my mother, Caterina, if it was a girl, and after my father, Renato, if it was a boy." Renato could have been my grandfather's nickname: Onorato and Renato sound similar. Still, the names have different meanings. Onorato is the honored one; Renato, the reborn. So I don't know if my grandfather was ever known as Renato or if he acquired that name only in my mother's memories.

My visit to the archives of Venice occurred in May 2001, three years after I suggested to my cousins Lino and Mario that our grandfather was Venetian born. Like most lives, mine is one of detours and interruptions. This particular research had been put on hold during the years of grinding, daily responsibility for my mother—years in which I witnessed the continuing erosion of her mind and self. The older generation was going, going, gone. During this time, Aunt Giaconda was placed in a *casa di riposo,* a house of rest, as such places are called in Italy; a few months later she was dead. Aunt Enea was put in a grayer, grimmer nursing home and collapsed into dementia. On this trip, as always, I went to see her. She no longer knew who I was. Then Marco and I left for Croatia and, in Losinj, discovered that the archives were gone and the church records unavailable.

I became more determined to find something concrete, something I could label real. On our return from Losinj, I went to the archives of Venice, searching for physical proof of my connection to the city. Since no one could give me a date or year of birth for my grandfather, I was prepared to examine as many records as was necessary.

Marco and I began at a building behind the Church of the Frairi, which had been pointed out to me as the home of the archives. I filled out a form stating the years of interest and my purpose—"family history." Only after I handed in the form did the woman at the reception desk explain that the archives were split up according to different eras and stored in libraries all over the city. The building we were in housed records from the time of Napoleon: 1806–1815. Some of the archives between 1815 and 1870 were spread out in the individual parishes, but most from 1820 to 1880—the ones I was interested in— were in a library close to the Celestia vaporetto stop. Since Celestia was at the opposite end of the city, we couldn't get there before closing time.

So on a rainy May morning, we set out again. Dodging puddles, we ran for the *motoscafo*. We sat inside in the forward section, straining to see through the dirt- and water-smeared windows. Marco and I were the only passengers to get off at Celestia. The quay and the streets were deserted. Through the rain, the buildings were blurred, the colors darkened. We were a world away from the elegance and glitter of tourist-choked St. Mark's Square. The fierce rain and the wind off the lagoon made holding an umbrella open and upright a struggle. From the knees down, our slacks were soaking wet. "Damn rain," Marco said.

"It must be here somewhere." We reached a *campo* (a square), but I could see no sign, no official-looking entrance, and no passersby to ask for directions. One side of the *campo* consisted of a long, blank brick wall. Half-way along the wall was a green wooden door with a small metal plaque beside it. The plaque did not say *Archivio di Stato—Venezia*, but *Campo Celeste*. "It has to be . . ." I said, pressing the doorbell. We heard nothing, but after a long minute, the door creaked open.

"Open sesame," Marco said.

And past the gray stone entrance, we did discover my version of a cave full of gold and jewels: a library of books about Venice or by Venetians, a large, warm, brightly lit room, with wooden tables and a scattering of young men and women, their heads bent over documents and manuscripts. Scholars, I thought, and I envied the life I instantly imagined for them: the silence, the order, their industriousness, and their access to the intellectual treasures on the shelves. I hesitated a moment until one wall of books and a dozen titles began to glow seductively, asking to be pulled out and examined. I did not need to come to this library to find books on Venice. The city is a favored and seemingly infinite subject.

But books on Istria were neither in this library nor in the ones at home. Istria was ignored, denied, forgotten, misunderstood—dark. The continuous and complete records of the once Serene Republic endured because the city was a center of power. Istria was the hinterland, the frontier, the resource base. The near-thousand years of Venetian domination left its mark on the cities and towns of the Istrian coast, on their design and layout, on the architecture of the palaces, churches, and houses. Venice is still visible in the shape of windows, audible in the rhythms of speech and the proverbs, perceptable in the art

and the music and the food. And although in the post–
World War II period, a percentage of the stone lions of San
Marco, symbols of the potency of Venice, were crowbarred
off the façade of Istrian arches and doorways and smashed
to bits, winged lions still survey many a town square.

In turn, Istria survives in Venice but less ostenta-
tiously, less symbolically. Istria is underwater, in the for-
ests of trees driven into the sand and mud to sustain and
anchor the city, and under our feet in the *fondamente,* the
pavements. Istria is both out of sight, on the horizon, in
the *murazzi,* the fortifications that hold off the sea, and
before our eyes in the bridges, palace fronts, church walls.
The stones of Venice are Istrian stones, invisible in their
ubiquity.

I could hardly believe how easy it was. I asked for the
book of records and volumes were brought to me. The
young man in charge carried two piles of books to the table
where I waited. "Here—1870 to 1880, PA to PE," he said.
"If you don't find anything, we'll try something else." The
archival books were large, at least twenty-four inches wide
and thirty-six long, with black cloth covers. They were
heavy, substantial; I felt as if I held history in my arms.

Pagan was a common Venetian name, and the births
of dozens of Pagans were recorded here. My eyes ached
skimming the handwritten lists of names. For the books
were not strictly alphabetical; there was a page of Padovani, then one and a half of Pagan and two lines of Pagan-
nini, followed by another half-page of Pagan, this time
followed by Padovani and then Pagano. Either Marco or
I checked each page. But of all the Pagans born between

1865 and 1880, not one was called Onorato Pagan. "Do you *know* he was born between 1865 and 1880?" said Marco.

"It's a calculation based on his first child being born around 1897. If he was young enough to go to war in 1914..."

"But you don't even know that for sure. He disappeared sometime during the war. That's all you know."

We carried the books back to the librarian's desk. Prompted by the young man's sympathetic face, I said, "I thought... I was always told my grandfather was born on Calle delle Rasse, but..."

Part of me expected the librarian, despite his pleasant expression, to dismiss me with a shrug of the shoulders or a superior tone. My accent exposed my foreignness. How could I have dared to think I had a claim, let alone a blood tie, to the city? But he continued to take my search seriously. "He could have been born outside the time frame. I'll bring you the earlier archives and the *Schede Famiglia*, families registered by their residences. Look through the relevant district. You can.cross-reference. Who knows?"

He brought us another tower of black books. Then another. I gave up hope of finding anything. The story of my grandfather's Venetian birth was another one of my mother's myths. Still, I opened the next book and inhaled the dry-dust smell. I turned the fragile pages, skimming the lists of names. Page after page, book after book. Marco rubbed his eyes; I wished I'd brought eye drops.

I was back in the 1820s, about to give up, when I found a Vincenzo Pagan, born September 17, 1822, and married to Serafina (Angelucci). (In Losinj, my mother's cousin

Armida had confirmed that Onorato's father's name was Vincenzo; his mother's Serafina.) Of course, this Vincenzo Pagan was not necessarily the right one, but the dates were probable.

I switched to the registration of residencies. In Venice, addresses do not include the names of streets or squares. The city is divided into six districts, and addresses consist of the district and a number: Cannaregio 1260/b, Santa Croce 723. Calle delle Rasse was in Castello, so I focused on that area. I found no Onorato, but a Vincenzo Pagan had lived at a location (according to my calculations) not far from St. Mark's Square, thus possibly Calle delle Rasse, which is close to the square. There was a phrase scrunched into the box opposite his name. To read it, I had to take off my glasses and lean over until the tip of my nose almost touched the page. *Emigrato Chioggia*: immigrated to Chioggia. I'd been told in Losinj that the Italians were called *Chioggiotti*. And my mother and her family had ended up in Chioggia at the end of World War 1. So there had to have been a previous connection. This must be him, my great-grandfather.

I was bemused at the thought that a move to a place twenty kilometers away and still on the Venetian lagoon had been recorded as an emigration. And since the phrase appeared in the box where a date of death was usually inscribed, it seemed to dismiss Vincenzo Pagan, to sever the tie between him and the city.

As we handed the books back to the librarian, I said: "My great-grandfather seems to have moved to Chioggia."

"Chioggia!" The pleasant young man startled me with a laugh. "Chioggia. Well, you'll have to go to the archives there. I can't help you, can I? Chioggia." His tone implied the very name of the city was ridiculous.

We couldn't make the trip to Chioggia. We were leaving the next day, flying back to Edmonton. But I accepted (even without proof) that my grandfather had been born in Chioggia. But where and when had he died? To me that detail was more important. If I knew that, perhaps I could understand why Rosina Pagan had lost her father and her home, why she had been cast out, exiled from the garden that was the Lussino of her infancy.

When Marco and I visited in 2001, Losinj was out of the way and isolated. During World War I, Istria had been central, part of the disputed territory and battleground between Italy and Austria. When Italy entered the war against the Austro-Hungarian Empire in May 1915, it was with the promise set out in the Treaty of London that if the Allies were victorious, Italy would be granted Alto Adige and Istria. And throughout the war, the Italian air force repeatedly bombed the cities of Trieste, Pola, and Fiume; all three were strategic centers for the Austrians.

So what did Onorato do in 1915 and beyond? Had he died in battle? Or as a prisoner? And what happened to his family? Why had they left Lussino?

My search for Onorato Pagan was a way station on the odyssey to find my mother.

{ 21 }

Power destroys the past, the past
with its treasures of alternative ideals
that stand in judgment on the present.

Simone Weil, GRAVITY AND GRACE

who remembers?

JUNE 1915

The knock, finally, the pounding at the door.

Rosina is already awake, her heart beating hard and fast. Her sister Antonia has pulled back the curtains. She is standing at the window, looking out, a shadow in the early light.

Did Antonia call out? Did she see the two soldiers on the path, then outside the gate? Did she cry *Mamma?* And wake up Rosina?

Conda is still asleep, her thumb in her wet pink mouth. Her chubby legs are angled into Rosina's space, a foot nudging Rosina's ribs. Rosina shoves Conda away. "Get off me." And at that moment, the first knock, fist on wood.

Since Papa and then their oldest brother, Giovanni, left, they have waited and waited. For a letter, for news, for—Rosina doesn't know what, but she feels that something more, something big and important is hovering, about to happen. And her chest hurts and her tummy flip-flops and she is scared.

The war, her mamma answers, the war, each time Rosina asks why. The war, her nonna Pagan and big sister Maricci and the nonni Lettich say, the war; they say it a hundred times a day. The war is why they eat polenta every day and Mamma doesn't smile anymore but frowns or screams over the teeniest mistake. The war is why Papa is gone and brother Giovanni. And Stefan, who used to bring Maricci bouquets of yellow flowers. The war is why all the grown men are gone. Only the bent, white-haired ones are left.

Ermanno and Santo, who are big now, say they are going, too, going to fight. But Mamma says no, their job is to fish and to help feed the family. Although the boys aren't very good at their job, and there aren't many fish.

The war, Rosina decides, must be in a big, big place with room for lots of people. But Mamma says that it is not one place but many—on the mainland, in the mountains. And Ermanno points at the waves of the bay and says that the war is on the sea and under the sea too. But far away, Rosina asks, Papa had to go far away? And Mamma and Maricci yell at her for pestering them again.

Then one morning, as she and Antonia were drinking their *caffelatte,* they heard loud bangs. And when they ran outside, they saw red and orange flames in the sky. And no one had to tell Rosina that the war is not far away but here, falling to the ground like rain.

Today, when the pounding on the door starts, she pulls the covers over her head. Her heart beats louder and louder. Friends or family would not knock that way, so stridently. Soldiers. Their voices interweave with her mother's voice. Who do they want this time?

The door to the room opens. *Girls,* Maricci calls them, but Rosina stays covered, clutching Giaconda, who has started to whimper. *Quickly,* Maria says. *It's not a game.* Flipping the sheet and blanket off them. Her face is odd, her cheeks red. And she is in her nightie with no dressing gown on top. *Quickly.*

This time it is all of them. *They must all go.*

They are given an hour to pack, an hour to prepare themselves and then assemble at the little port. There are only two suitcases in the house. Nonna Lettich, who was classified as Slav and is not leaving, is called upon; she delivers every bag she owns. Each one of them (except Giaconda) is too busy and too shocked to cry.

Enea looks after her own and Conda's things. Maricci directs Antonia and Rosina to pack all their clothes, even the warm ones. Who knows how long they will be gone? Or even where they are going? Rosina wants to take Papa's last gift: a china doll with the bright blue eyes that open and close. Mamma makes her leave Elenora on the bureau. "She'll be too heavy," she says. Maricci manages to take a note from Stefan; Santo, a ball; Enea, three silk ribbons for her hair. Mamma carries documents, two photographs, a pair of gold and crystal earrings, and every coin she or her parents have left.

They leave behind clothes hanging in the closets, a crucifix on the wall, a pot drying by the sink, a skipping rope and spinning top in the courtyard, a house full of their daily lives and daily things, ten bottles of olive oil, fifteen of country wine, one of rue-infused grappa, two salamis, a sack of cornmeal, a package of flour, salt and coffee.

The piazza is as crowded as on St. Anthony's feast day, but there's no town band or visitors, only Lussignani—women, children, older men—and the soldiers shepherding them into straggly lines. Mamma yells when she sees Nonna Pagan with her big green suitcase. Nonna is praying aloud. *Santa Maria, madre di dio.* The talk back and forth buzzes like a thousand bees around the hive. An Austrian captain checks off names. The colonel watches from the stairs of the church. Unlike the other soldiers, he is known. He owns a villa on the edge of the village and used to come with his family each spring. He addresses the crowd in a German-accented Venetian dialect. "You have been identified," he tells them, "as citizens of an enemy power." He tells them that they are lucky. He knows that they are not bad people, so they are being treated with mercy. "You are going home," he says.

A few in the crowd misunderstand and send up a cheer. The colonel shouts, "Italy. You are being sent back to your Italy."

THEY WERE LEAVING, not going home. Italy was not theirs, particularly not Sicily, where they were apparently being sent. I can still make no sense of what happened to the Pagan family in 1915. I can't decipher a coherent story from the few facts I have gathered.

My mother said she did not remember the ordeal. She was, I believe, five. (Enea, who was eleven years old in 1915, also did not remember anything about the camp in Sicily.) And it was not just those years that were wiped out.

Mum's whole childhood was an area of darkness, unre-lieved by any flashes of recall, even before she began to lose her past, before brain cells collapsed and neurofibers tangled. "I was too young," she would say if I asked her about her childhood. "Who remembers?" And although I was not certain how old she had been, I did know that at the time of the uprooting, she was no longer a toddler. (I am now at the age Mum was when I began asking her about her early years, and although I have a sense that I have forgotten more than most, I still have strong visual memories of Lussino, Venice, and the England of my childhood.)

In his book *On the Natural History of Destruction,* W.G. Sebald writes about Germans' lack of reaction to the devastating Allied bombing of their cities toward the end of World War II. "Obviously in the shocks of what these people had experienced, their ability to remember was suspended, or else, in compensation, it worked to an arbi-trary pattern."

All of the sisters, except the oldest one, lost their abil-ity to remember this exile. And the pattern of Maricci's memories was arbitrary and incomplete. But it was she who had given me my first clue as to what had happened. I had never heard a word about the family's being forced to leave their home during World War I. But in 1969, I was twenty years old and visiting Corinna, who was liv-ing again with her grandparents, my zia Maricci and zio Erminio, this time in Astoria, New York. Zia Maricci and I were standing side by side in her tiny kitchen, peeling the skins of cooked potatoes, the second step in the pro-duction of gnocchi. I don't remember Corinna as part of the scene; she was probably at her job with an Italian firm in Manhattan. "We were so hungry," Zia said, "I had to beg the soldiers for the peel from their potatoes. Otherwise we would have starved."

"How horrible." The potato peel was scorching my fingertips.

Zia went on to explain how during World War I they had been sent to a camp near Catania. "We were loaded onto a train, in a cattle car, squeezed in together. No light. My sister Antonia—your mother has told you that she had a sister Antonia, who died? At least that? Good. Well, she got sick. Your mother too, the fever. By the time we arrived in Sicily, on that long, long train ride, Antonia was dead. In my mother's arms."

Before I could ask Zia for more details, her husband, Erminio, staggered in. "Where's the slivovitz?" he yelled. "I left it in the dining room. At least half a bottle."

"There's no bottle." And just like that, Zia Maricci was caught up again in one of their endless fights. She berated him, and he yelled and swore, and she pretended to pull at her hair and pray, all as if I weren't there. And although we did eat pillowy gnocchi in ragu that night, we never got back to the camp in Sicily and their hunger.

The story of the camp surprised and interested me, which was why I remember the scene so vividly. How could my mother never mention such an important experience? When I questioned her about the exile, she seemed to confirm Maricci's version. But only because it was the story she had been told. "We caught the fever, and it killed Antonietta." And now as I write these words, I remember what I'd forgotten when I discussed her lazy left eye with the doctor. My mother had told me, that day or another, that the fever had affected her eye. Or so she had been told by her mother; it was why she had the lazy eye.

"Why did the Austrians send you away—women and children?"

"My father was Venetian. And he was in the Italian navy. I told you, on a submarine."

"But then why Sicily? So odd."

"*Boh,*" she shrugged. "It was a long time ago. Who remembers?"

If my grandmother Lettich was from a Croatian family, if she was, as I was told, San Pierina—that is, born on the island of San Pietro in Volta, just south of Lussino— if her children were all born in Lussino, why would they be evacuated to Italy? Well, it would make sense if (as claimed) my grandfather had joined the Italian navy; his family would be under suspicion. But why, then, would Italy place the family of one of their men, perhaps even one of their heroes, in a camp in Sicily?

Then, I didn't try to find out what actually happened to my mother's family; I was young, careless with the past. Still, the uprooting explained not everything about my mother but something—the hysteria that lurked under the surface of her daily manner and felt so dark and bottomless. And I held on to the knowledge of what had happened to her and tried to remind myself to be patient. Not that the reminder worked; I'm ashamed to admit that I was rarely patient with her.

An Arab proverb says, "The death of an old man is equal to the destruction of a library." By the time I wanted to know more, by the time I was hungry for any morsel of my mother's early years, my best source, Zia Maricci, was dead. The possibility of finding out any more seemed blocked off to me, since the only impressions of the time and the internments were in the fading and about to be obliterated—memories of the very old. My mother's story was bound to her people's history, which had been judged too insignificant, too inconvenient, to remember or record.

Actual libraries (at least the North American ones I consulted) were no help. For several years, I skimmed books about World War I, looking for any mention of internment and finding nothing, nothing, nothing. The search was contemporaneous with and linked to my search for Nazario Sauro, but at least Sauro still had streets and squares named after him—even if his story had been expunged.

It was my online friends at Istrianet who gave me the first confirmation that people had been interned, that it was not a Pagan family fantasy. Several participants had heard stories from parents and grandparents; others had seen references in unpublished memoirs. Finally, a search on the Web turned up a PhD thesis written by Mara Manzin in 1998 at the University of Padova.

A few days after Italy entered the war in May 1915, the Austro-Hungarian army began to deport the population of southern Istria to internment camps in Austria, Czechoslovakia, and Hungary. The empire did not trust the allegiance of its Istrian citizens and feared some might give aid to its enemy. Pola was both the headquarters of the Austrian navy and its arsenal and had to be protected. The coast was depopulated, the white cities emptied.

The testimonies that I got through Istrianet were rough outlines, susceptible to the unreliability and imprecision of memory. But together they reinforced each other; themes and details recurred. The deportation came suddenly, leaving the Istriani shocked and surprised. They were transported to the internment camps by train in cattle cars, crowded in together, almost on top of each other, with no straw to lie on, no bread, and no water, no way to get down at stations to buy food. The camps, which had been built in advance, consisted of wooden barracks, organized with Austrian order into small towns of straight roads, work areas, dormitories, schools, and halls. Nevertheless, what came through in the secondhand, retold stories were three years of hunger and misery, when the young and the weak died. "A way of the cross," a man who became a priest wrote in a letter. "They treated us like animals" was the summary passed down through generations.

A more direct and textured account came from a spry and alert ninety-five-year-old in Edmonton. I visited Rita Bertieri in her studio apartment in a seniors' lodge, planning to interview her about her experience as a refugee to Canada after World War II. That Rita had vivid memories of World War I was a surprise, and a useful one.

Before the Great War, Rita's father owned a restaurant in the Istrian city of Rovigno. Once the war began, he and her oldest brother went off to fight for Austria. Still, in 1915, the rest of the family, along with almost everyone else in the city, was interned. With her mother, two brothers, and a sister, she was sent first to Hungary for three months, then to Wagna, in Austria, for the remaining years. She remembered that the barrack they lived in was number 22, that they slept on sacks of hay, that they were often hungry, that they had nothing to wash with, that they had lice in their clothes and on their hair. She remembered that one night, as they slept, rats attacked her mother's hair and fingers. She went to school in Wagna, but the school had no books, pencils, or paper. Her baby brother died. Another family, friends from Rovigno, lost all four of their children.

"We had been comfortable," she said as I was leaving. "Our house had been full of everything. When we came back from the camp, there was nothing left. They took everything but the walls."

And then, after World War II, again everything was seized. "The Yugoslav soldiers took our savings, our gold coins. This time they took the walls, too."

But these were camps inside the Austro-Hungarian Empire. Periodically, I would ask on Istria-talks if anyone had ever heard of refugee camps in Sicily during World War I. New people were joining Istria-talks all the time: Bruno Clapci, a real estate agent in Vancouver; Alberto Cernaz, a radio host in Koper; Davor Sisevic, a deputy minister of energy in Zagreb; a special needs teacher in the Bronx; and so on. But no one answered my question. I was at the point of wondering whether the family had actually been sent to Austria or whether Maricci had somehow been confused. Then Mario Majarich in Australia, Will Gladofich in Virginia, and Etty Simicich in Seattle—all three with strong roots in Lussino—joined Istria-talks.

Etty, who had left Istria as a young girl, confirmed that my aunt's story was accurate, that the Italian citizens of

Losinj had been sent back to Italy and had ended up in a camp in Caltagirone, near Catania. She also made me realize that I had misunderstood part of that long-past conversation in my aunt's kitchen; I'd missed a transition. Etty insisted that the begging for potato peels happened during World War II, when the Germans controlled Losinj. That was the time of great hunger. Zia Maricci had been telling me about two separate traumas.

In Istria, one historical event often echoes another—with slight variations. Once, they took everything but the walls; the next time, they seized the walls, too. The people were taken or sent away once, twice, three times? The white cities were emptied once, twice, ten times? The rulers, the assigned nationalities, changed once, twice, six times in the twentieth century.

The deportation of the Italian citizens and their relatives from Losinj differed from the mass deportation of the southern Istrians in scale and import. The Lussignani went to a refugee camp in what was their "mother country." The other Istrians were sent to internment camps in the far reaches of the Austro-Hungarian Empire; they were considered potential traitors. Did the Italian government also consider the Lussignani untrustworthy? The transportation by cattle car, the crowding, the illness, the displacement, the fear, the lack of food and water and beds, the details and the effects echo each other, with only minor variations.

Etty sent me the phrases she remembered from a song, "Caltagirone," that was routinely sung in the taverns over glasses of wine. Based on a song from the nineteenth century, it boasted of how the Lussignani survived the dislocation. *Abbiam dormito sul duro terreno / paglia . . . fieno . . . / dove le bestie andavano a riposar:* "We slept on the hard ground / then with hay and straw / where the animals rested."

During Marco's and my trip to Losinj in 2001, I was able to ask the two elderly relatives I visited, Maria Lettich and Armida Baricèvic, about the Pagan family's being sent to Sicily. Maria's family had been allowed to stay in Lussino. "I think they chose by name," she told me. "The Lettich name was Croatian, though we spoke Italian at home and thought of ourselves as Italian. Pagan seemed Italian, though there had been Pagans in Lussino for a couple of hundred years."

Later, I found the Austrian census of 1911. My Lettich great-grandmother was recorded as *Slava,* as were two of her children, Filippo and Antonia. Her daughter Caterina (my grandmother) and her children were registered as Italians. Which may be why Caterina Lettich Pagan and her children went, but her mother, brother, and sister didn't. That and Onorato's treachery in supporting Italy.

Armida was born in the mid-1920s, but she remembered what she had been told about Caltagirone. Her grandmother Serafina (my great-grandmother) died there, died lying on straw. And Armida's mother (my grandfather's sister) was pregnant when they left Lussino. Yes, she'd heard about the cattle cars. All the stresses brought the baby on early. The woman gave birth on the straw, but the baby died.

"I was told that my aunt Antonia and my mother got sick on the train," I said. "Does that sound familiar? They got a fever? Antonia died."

"I don't remember anything about Antonia," Armida said. "But there was typhoid fever in the camp. All the children about four years of age and under died. Remember Zia Giuditta [my great-aunt]? Two of her children died of typhoid in Caltagirone. None of the little ones survived."

22

Youth, youth, springtime of life.

"The Fascist Anthem"

a remengo

I CANNOT BE SURE that the Pagan family spent the three years until the end of the war at the camp in Caltagirone, Sicily. At the time of the deportation to Italy in 1915, not all the Lussignani (Etty Simicich tells me) were sent to the camp. A few were allowed to join relatives in Chioggia, the town where my great-grandfather settled on the southern edge of the Venetian lagoon. And although I am sure that the Pagans went to Sicily and stayed there for at least two years, they may have made the long trip back up the length of the boot before the end of the war, perhaps as early as the spring of 1917. (It wasn't until the winter of 1918 that the Austro-German forces were turned back from the entrances to the lagoon.) I have not been able to uncover any relatives in Chioggia that Caterina Lettich Pagan could have turned to for help, support, or shelter. Still, at the end of the war, the family was living in Chioggia, and unlike the other Lussignani, they did not return to Lussino.

Italy withdrew from the Paris Peace Conference of 1919, when France, Britain, and especially the United States opposed Italy's claim to Alto Adige and Istria, which Italy had been promised in the Treaty of London when it entered the war on the Allied side. (This treaty had also promised Italy the islands and a stretch of the Dalmatian coast, as well as a port in Albania and islands off the coast of Asia Minor, territories where Italians were obviously not in the majority.) The Italians viewed the annexation of the Alto Adige and Istria as a culmination of the unification of the nation that began in the 1860. (Garibaldi, the liberator-hero who began the project of unifying Italy, encouraged and supported the Croatian struggle for independence against the Austro-Hungarian Empire but eventually fell out with Eugen Kvaternik, the Croatian leader, over the sovereignty of Istria.) Italian troops were in Istria, including Lussino, at the end of the war, but the territory was not ceded to Italy until the signing of the Treaty of Rapallo by Italy and Yugoslavia in November 1920.

Was this time of uncertainty, the two-year gap between the end of the war and the transfer of Istria, the reason that my grandmother stayed in a place that must have felt very foreign to her and that was far from her immediate family, her brother and sister? Perhaps Caterina Lettich Pagan had had enough of uncertainty and sudden change. She must also have faced a question of survival, of where, as a widow with seven living children, she could best eke out a living. Perhaps she had taken a job *in servizio,* in service, as they used to say, to some well-off family in Chioggia—a job to make do until the future became clear. Mum never mentioned that her mother had a job, but the possibility could have seemed unreal to her, for Rosina wasn't with her mother in Chioggia.

1919?

Rosina is too short. The bakery's shiny wood counter reaches up to her shoulders. She stretches her neck to peer over the top.

"No, no, this won't do. How can she wait on customers like that?" Signore Bonito peers down at her. He is the tallest man she has ever seen—a narrow black figure topped with a white face.

"I can see fine, no problem." Rosina can tell that neither Signore nor Signora Bonito, both of whom are standing on the other side of the counter, sizing her up, expect her to speak. She is supposed to await their decision.

"Impossible; you look silly," says the Signora. Her eyes, below the edge of her gray cloche hat, are a cold, pale blue. "Her place is upstairs. That's why we took her in."

"No, please," Rosina says. *I can't stand it.* For two weeks, Rosina has worked as an assistant maid in the Bonitos' home in Padua, and she hates it. Sweeping the tiled kitchen floor, waxing the heavy, dark furniture in the dining room, dusting rows of white china figurines, careful, careful, polishing silver cutlery. She hates being shut in the house all day. She hates being under the surveillance and the command of Pina, the other maid: this way, not that way. Hurry up. Don't dawdle. No, no, I told you . . . Careful, careful. You're a clumsy, slow girl.

Pina has been directing her with an air of satisfaction. "You'll be doing heavier work soon enough. Proper work. Floors, laundry, toilets. It's too much for me to do. It's about time I had some help."

And when she caught Rosina sniffing one of the Signora's crystal perfume bottles, Pina was triumphant. "I will tell," she said. "I will tell."

"Tell what?" Rosina said. "That I sniffed?"

Pina snuck up behind her while she was paging through one of the daughter's books and grabbed Rosina by her braid. "Don't you dare touch the Signorina Anita's things." Pulling hard so that her head was angled back. "Don't touch." Which was ridiculous. The Signora had told her that each day after the children left for school, Rosina's job was to make each of their beds, hang up their clothes, pick up their toys, straighten their respective desks. Her job was to keep their rooms tidy. So she had to touch, didn't she? Rosina had been lining up the books, when she'd been tempted, when one opened in her hands.

"No, please," she says to the Bonitos. "I'm good at sums. I'm quick. Test me. I'll make the right change, you'll see."

The Signore smiles, his teeth a white flash beneath his mustache. "I did tell your mother you would be working in one of the shops." *You promised.*

"You agreed she was too young for the wine store," the Signora said.

"I thought it would be inappropriate for her to be pouring wine for workers. And the oil bottles are too heavy for her to be in that shop." *I can lift them; I can.*

"Of course. No, it's a ridiculous idea. A child, here. When she's ready. If she's ever ready. After all, what can we expect? With her background." *And what does that mean? Nothing good.*

The Signore puts a hand on his wife's arm and lowers his voice. Rosina catches enough to know that he is reminding the Signora that—after all—the girl's uncle was a fellow officer in the war. He means her zio Vincenzo, her father's younger brother. If she concentrates hard, she can picture him at their old house in Lussingrande, dark eyed and handsome. Mamma has told her he was wounded at Caporetto in the arm, or was it his leg? And he has gone back to Lussino and his fiancée.

The door behind Rosina, the door to the bakery, opens. One of the bakers carries in a plank of golden, fragrant loaves. The Signore goes to help him unload the bread onto the shelves. "I can stand on a box," Rosina says. "There must be one back there. Then I'll be big enough."

Signora hesitates. "This is serious. You won't be playing store."

Her husband has already brought a box from the back. "Let's see you then."

Rosina climbs up. The counter now reaches to her lower chest. She can survey the shop. See out the window to watch the passersby. She steps down and slides the box—*ooffa,* so heavy and solid—slides it sideways until she is half behind the cash register. She rests her hand on the brass knobs.

"Ada," Signora says, referring to the old woman who waits on the customers. "Ada will explain how things work. She'll be here any minute."

Rosina spends her days climbing on and off the box. But working at the bakeshop is worth it; the hours never drag as they did when she was the Bonitos' assistant maid. All day she can smell the bread and see the light pouring through the windows and the people walking by. And the customers come in and out. They like her and call her *piccina* and *bellezza,* for Rosina is good at her job. She never forgets part of an order halfway through; five *rosette,* four *brioche,* two *cornetti,* one loaf, she calls out as she carefully slips the merchandise into the net bags. And she is quick and accurate in her calculations—better than Ada at figuring out totals and change.

Rosina's nights are harder, especially when she lies in the dark in her bed. She has a recurring dream that she is in a rowboat on a turquoise-blue sea. On the plank opposite is a bearded man at the oars: her father. *My Rosina,* he says. In the dream, she is small, smaller than now, and she realizes that they are back in Lussino. She can see the silver, yellow, and orange fish through the glint of the sun on the water, flashes of color darting by the white rocks. *Look, Papa.* But when she turns back, he is no longer there. She is alone on the water. And the rocks on the bottom are not rocks, she sees, but a green metal face with blank eyes.

She misses the low timbre of her mother's voice singing the staccato rhythms of their dialect, the firmness of her roughened hands braiding her hair, the convex drum of her belly, where Rosina rested her head when she was allowed. *Dai,* Rosina would say, let me. *Dai,* her mother would say, in an irritated tone, stop it. Rosina misses her brothers' joshing and teasing, her sisters' easy gossip and back and forth, their daily concerns, their company surrounding her like the walls of a house. She misses sleeping with Giaconda, her little body pushed up against her,

her soft skin smelling of dust and grass. Despite all their travels and changes, this is the first time Rosina has had to sleep in a bed alone, and she feels cold and exposed.

She wants to cry—the tears prickle her eyelids—but she mustn't give in. Pina will hear her. The older girl's bed is too close, a few steps away; her acrid smell, sweat and sweet talcum powder, permeates the room, marking it as hers.

Ever since Rosina started working in the shop, Pina has pretended to be nice to Rosina, telling the Bonitos that the two of them have become friends—though they are not friends—asking her to go with her on a *passeggiata* or to the movie theater. But behind her back, speaking to the cook, for example, Pina calls Rosina a "dirty little Slav," and Rosina wants to scratch her face and tell everyone that Pina is the one who doesn't wash herself. But she doesn't because it would mean an open battle, and Pina has been with the Bonitos for six years, and the Signora's eyes are still cold, cold, when she looks at Rosina. The Signora would choose Pina, not Rosina, if she ever had to.

Pina admires the lace collar that Rosina's sister has woven. She tries it on much too often. So Rosina writes a letter to Enea, who is training to be a lacemaker, and another one is sent for Pina who acts extravagantly grateful. But Rosina knows that Pina continues to make nasty comments behind her back.

As the months, then the years, pass, the name calling and gossiping grow worse and worse. Rosina gradually stops trying to respond to Pina's periodic spells of manufactured warmth and goodwill. She stops caring about what the older girl thinks or feels. The Signora may be on Pina's side, but the Signorina, Anita, has become Rosina's friend. Anita lends Rosina her *fumetti* (her romance comics) and her magazines. She gives Rosina blouses she has outgrown and on one occasion a pair of good leather boots that hurt her feet. Best of all, Anita persuades her parents that a small room in the attic should be done up so that Rosina can have a room of her own.

And the young masters, Giacomo and Livio, too, seem fond of *La Slava,* treating her as if she were—no, not a sister—but a cousin, perhaps, or a favorite classmate, teasing her one day, ignoring her the next. When the Signori are out, all four of them play *ciaparse,* chasing each other up and down the endless halls and through the extended rooms, giggling and shrieking. Or the boys let Rosina and Anita act as goalies for their soccer games in the cavernous kitchen. And Rosina doesn't even care when Giacomo kicks the ball into her stomach and she can't breathe. He laughs, and after a minute she laughs.

Mean Pina says she will tell, and she does. They have broken a bowl, made a mess. Three or four times she complains to the Signore and the Signora. And each time, Giacomo, Livio, Anita, and Rosina are reprimanded.

Behave like civilized boys and girls. Control yourselves. Be good.

Until the games almost cease. They are leaving childhood behind. The young Bonitos are more often away from home. And Rosina works longer hours, from morning to evening, until her back aches and her feet throb.

Livio advises her to join the *Giovane Italiane* (Italian Girls). Anita belongs. The Signore has joined the Blackshirts; his wife, the *Fascia Femminile.* Livio and Giacomo are members of the Balilla, the Fascist organization for young men. And it is inspiring, Livio says. The badges, the rituals, the physical challenges—*largo ai giovani,* give way to youth. We are marching into a new world, Livio says.

What bullshit, Giacomo says, catching the end of Livio's spiel as he enters the kitchen. Living up to his reputation as the rebel of the family. "We march, but we go nowhere. Like little tin soldiers."

A disgrace, Livio calls his brother—an idiot and an egotist.

You should join the Italian Girls group, Giacomo tells Rosina, no matter what I say. It's useful. That's why I keep going to Balilla, even if it's a bore.

Livio shoves his brother out of the way and takes a step closer. Rosina can feel his breath on her cheek. The Italian Girls group, he concedes, will not be as exciting, as stirring, as the Balilla. How can it be? The female role is subordinate to that of the male. But it will help prepare her to be a modern wife and mother. She will learn first aid, sewing, calisthenics, and discipline.

"I don't need discipline," she says, turning away from him. "I have enough," thinking of how regimented her days already are.

"But you can learn how to dedicate yourself to the greater good, to the family, the community, and the nation."

Livio sings this tune for several months. The other Bonitos stress that the commitment is a necessary step. The Signora says Rosina can have time off to attend. Even her brothers, Ermanno and Santo, she learns in a letter from Enea, have joined the Fascist party. But Rosina does not join. She does not like military uniforms on others. Why would she voluntarily wear one herself? The pretend-soldier uniforms of the youth groups are just as bad as the Signore's actual regalia. They all make her queasy. Her heart beats faster; her mouth grows dry. (She does not remember the expulsion from Lussino, but her body still carries the imprint, the trauma of those Austrian soldiers.)

And although she is a proud Italian, no matter what the Signora or Pina may call her—wasn't her father born in Venice within spitting distance of Piazza San Marco?—the Fascist trumpeting of the glories of the Italian civilization and the Fascist talk of the destiny of the Italian people make her uneasy. Who will decide who is an Italian and who not? She does not understand why, but the mottoes, the salutes, the constant evoking of the love of *la patria* make her shudder.

When the Bonitos ask why she won't join Anita at the *Giovane Italiane,* she makes up an excuse. She can't tell them the truth—that her body won't let her.

23

*People are trapped in history
and history is trapped in them.*

James Baldwin, NOTES OF A NATIVE SON

family history

I HAVEN'T BEEN able to discover exactly how many years Rosa lived with the Bonitos (whose name I have changed) and worked in their bakery. I suspect twelve or thirteen. She was ten years old when her mother sent her to them in Padova, ten when she entered the working world. That was one of those details, like my grandfather's being born in Venice, she told and retold me when I was young. She also said that before going to Padova (and afterward), she lived for a time with a well-off aunt (her father's sister) and her family in Trieste.

Meanwhile, her mother and her other siblings stayed, at least for the time being, in Chioggia. By 1920, they may have found continuing the stopgap arrangements easier than moving back to Lussino and finding new ways *per tirare avanti*, literally "to pull ahead," but meaning to keep going. Life was not easy in Chioggia. It was always Venice's poorer, younger sister, but in those years all of northeastern Italy was devastated from the three years of continual battle. Conditions were no better in Lussino. Italy may have longed for the redemption of Istria, but soon after it took possession, Mussolini and the Fascists took over. The treated Istria as a colony to exploit, particularly for its coal. Croatians and Slovenian Istrians lost their schools and their jobs in the institutions and bureaucracy. The new teachers, the new bureaucrats, were almost always not Italian Istrians but Italians sent from Rome.

Istria was ruled by five empires. The first three— Roman, Venetian, and Austrian—created layers of infrastructure and stimulated and added to what had existed before to create a rich hybrid culture. The last two, Italian and Yugoslav, only sacked and looted. An earlier chapter quotes the Trieste writer Claudio Magris: "the Fascists were responsible for the *liquidation of L'Italianita* of Istria." The mother country that the Italian-Istrians had dreamt of while living *under* Austria, the Italy that Nazario Sauro gave his life for, did not exist. As Rita Bertieri from Rovigno told me when I interviewed her in Edmonton, "We thought we were going to our mother nation, but Italy turned out to be not a mother but a wicked stepmother."

The three boys of the Pagan family became what they would have been if they had stayed in Lussino: men of the sea. Giovanni, the oldest, went to work as a fisherman. He spent the rest of his life in the rough and tough town of Chioggia. (His four daughters are all married to fishermen and live either in Chioggia or on the adjacent Pellestrina, one of the three barrier islands of the lagoon.) Ermanno and Santo sailed out of Trieste, working on the ocean liners of the Lloyd's Triestino line.

What was left of the family was scattering, blown about by the *bora* of need. Of the girls, Maricci was soon married to Erminio Sambo, and together they moved back to Lussino. Enea, who had an artistic eye and talent, did stay in Chioggia, working as a lacemaker, but Giaconda followed Rosa's footsteps, going first to Aunt Maria in Trieste and then, when she was ten, *in servizio* to a family in Padua. Unlike Rosa, Giaconda stayed with this family for many years, up until World War II.

I have just one photograph of my grandmother Caterina: a headshot that must have been taken in Chioggia. Her hair, black without a sign of gray, is pulled back into a bun; her eyebrows are heavy, lips tight. At age forty-five, she looks middle-aged, sad, and severe. Her dark eyes are opaque, without hope. This is a woman who has grimly held on, who has endured.

Mum always spoke of my grandmother as severe. Whenever as a child I was finicky about food, Mum would say, "I once told my mother that I didn't like rice, didn't want to eat it. She made me eat rice every day for a week." Back then, this convinced me that my grandmother was mean, though I did wonder if Mum was telling me about this incident so that I'd be grateful that she was my mother. After all, she never forced me to eat anything I didn't like.

Years later, if either Tatiana or Antonia declined a dish, which happened frequently, since Tatiana can't digest animal fats and Antonia is a vegetarian, Mum would return to the story of the rice. "Mamma would have never allowed it," she would say. Now I wondered at the context. How

could Rosa reject such a staple as rice? It was like a Neapolitan refusing pasta, a much more petulant gesture than
my rejecting calves' liver or Antonia's refusing scallops.
And when did this week of eating rice occur? Mum did
not remember Lussino. Their time in the camp was one
of hunger and want. If they did eat rice for a week, it may
have been because there was nothing else. And if they
were hungry, was it likely that she would have rejected the
rice? So the week of rice must have occurred during the
time in Chioggia. Yet after Sicily, Mum never lived with
her mother for any extended period.

Moreover, although the details of the story Mum told
did not change between my youth and my daughters'
youth, she began to use the incident for a different purpose, mentioning it whenever I served rice. As always, I
interpreted her remark as a comment on how spoiled the
rest of us were. I continued to make risotto (despite the
twenty-two minutes of continuous stirring), thinking the
dish was something she could eat: a tasty, soft, easy-to-eat
combo of starch and vegetables. Then, one evening, as I
was doling out the particularly Venetian *risi e bisi* (risotto
with peas), Mum exploded. She shoved the dish away. "*Va
a malora.* (Go to hell.) You do this to spite me," she said.

"You know I hate rice. You have no consideration, no
respect. You're a wretch, a disgrace. I get better treatment
from a stranger crossing the street. How often do I have to
tell you?"

In these last years, Mum invoked her mother more
and more. When she was in pain, she called out to her,
Mamma, or to the Virgin Mary to help her. Other times,
Mum used her mother as an authority on proper behavior

and child rearing—or, at least, as a mouthpiece for her own opinions. "*Mamma* would never have let you be such a slob," she'd say. Or if a boy dropped in to see Antonia, or Tatiana was away for a few days, out at a lake with friends, "*Mamma,* may she rest in peace, would have thought it a disgrace," she'd say. "*Mamma* would have forbidden it."

Then, one evening: "Franco was so good to Mamma," she said, speaking of my father. "He asked her permission to escort me to the officer's ball before he asked me. He was so respectful. And he brought her flowers, each time he came. Oh, Mamma loved him."

This proclamation was too much for me, pedant that I am. "Mum," I took her hands in mine and looked into her eyes. "Your mother never knew Dad."

"She told me. She said, 'Rosina, he's a good man. Marry him.'"

I had heard that my grandmother died of peritonitis at fifty-six, which must have been in 1930. She went into the hospital for an operation, but her appendix had already burst. As soon as word that she was doing poorly arrived in Padua, Signore Bonito drove Rosa and Giaconda by car the thirty-eight kilometers to Chioggia, but they arrived too late. Their mother, whom they had not seen in months, was dead. "Your mother died a long, long time before you met Dad, long before the war. And you met him toward the end of the war."

Rosa's eyes were suddenly anxious. "I don't know." Her face crumpled, and she let out a series of little cries, culminating in a long "*Mamma.*"

Slippery memories, shifting meanings, alternating realities.

Although I'd accepted that my mother suffered from dementia, I could not treat her words as nonsense, as random sounds. Their meanings might not be obvious, their correspondence to a shared reality absent, but her words signaled what was going on in her mind. And in my long, tortuous voyage on that unmapped sea that was my mother's past, her words and the slippery memories they alluded to were pictograms to be deciphered, rough clues to be interpreted

"How much are you charging him?" she said, meaning Marco. "Isn't it time for him to go home?" she said when he walked into the room. Or if he and I were talking, "What does he want?" Many times I explained that he was not a lodger, that the house was his house as much as mine. He was my husband, father to the girls. No, she said, with an emphatic shake of her head, no. "What about the other one?"

"He's the only husband I've had." I placed two framed wedding pictures on the mantel, one of her and Dad, the other of Marco and me. "He's the one earning most of the money," I emphasized. "And you must be polite to him, or he won't want you to live with us."

"I will tell you the truth," she said at dinner to Tatiana, grasping her by the wrist and giving her a conspiratorial look. "I will tell you who your real father is, later in secret."

"I had two husbands," she said to Jody, the student who provided home care on Saturday mornings. I was carrying in the groceries and nearly dropped a bag. So that is where she's been going, I thought. Her two men. And it took me back to Padua and her time with the Bonitos.

24

> Il passato non esiste: tutto è presente.
> *The past does not exist: all is present.*
>
> Biagio Marin, Istrian poet

cast out

I SEE HER: a girl on the cusp of womanhood, a girl with dark eyes and thick, dark hair, strong cheekbones, and a prominent nose. A pretty girl strolling down the oval path of the Prato della Valle, arm in arm with her pretty friend, the blonde and delicate Anita. Both of them are stylishly dressed, although Anita's outfit is silk rather than cotton and cost three times as much as Rosina's. Both of them are field-testing their first pairs of high heels (*heads up, shoulders down*), taking short, quick steps under the blank eyes of the seventy-eight white statues that encircle the way. (*Don't trip, don't totter.*)

On this sun-filled Sunday afternoon, the young men are out, their hair brilliantined, their shoes shined, not a few of them giving these two, the blonde and the brunette, the eye; a posse of university students follows, a few steps behind, murmuring indecent words to their backs. Neither Rosina nor Anita concedes a glance. Anita half-sings, half-hums the latest song of the summer, *"Non Ti Scordar di Me."* And Rosina feels the laughter bubble up inside her, feels the flip of her skirt, the flash of her slim ankles, and the stares of the students. *Do not forget me.*

Across a wide piazza, down cobblestone streets, *my poor feet,* under the arcades and into the Caffè Pedrocchi. They promenade through the green room, where young and old can sit and read for free, through the map room, to the most elegant—the gold room with the few choice tables and the chandelier as radiant as the sun in the sky. Rosina and Anita lean in, their heads together over the damask tablecloth, chatting.

Rosina wants to talk to Anita of Giacomo, of how things have changed between them, of how her heart beats when she sees him and how his eyes change—soften—when he looks at her. Of how she becomes flushed and clumsy and tongue-tied while he talks as much as he ever did about his classes, about this professor and that one, about his plans to be a leader of men, a forger of the future, but now he repeats words, pauses, loses his concentration. And now when his hand touches hers, or he brushes past her in the hall, it is different, different from when they were children playing. Now she is jolted by his touch.

Anita talks of an upcoming holiday: "I'd rather go with you to Lussino. The Lido is so proper, so stuffy. And every year, it's the same thing."

Giacomo—the name is forming on Rosina's lips; she wants to, needs to, say it. Who else can she tell besides her best friend? "Giacomo. . ." Anita has turned away, her attention caught by a tall young man who is hovering close to their table. He tosses a note that nearly lands in the gelato bowl, bouncing off the rim. Anita laughs, and Rosina catches herself in time.

I SEE HER NOW: young, with her heart in her mouth.

For most of my life I didn't. Despite all the pictures of the young Rosa in my parents' albums. I glanced at those black-and-white or sepia-toned photos, nothing more. Her aging barrel-shaped body was too present, too intrusive, too smothering. I was busy trying to see past her, not into her.

During the time I was taking Mum to doctor after doctor, one of them, a youngish man, said to me, "She must have been beautiful in her youth."

And I was surprised, even shocked. "My mother? I guess she was," I stuttered. The wrinkled and sagging skin of old age blurred the lines of her face. But with all the weight she had lost, the bones of her face were more visible. You could see the delicacy of her features and the strong cheekbones.

"Rosina always had men trailing after her," Aunt Giaconda had said on several of my visits to Venice. Each time her smile was so tight that it shaded into a grimace.

"Rosina had a certain fascination," Armida had said, when I saw her in Losinj. Her eyes searched my face and then looked me up and down. "There's something—" she said.

"Rosina had so many suitors," Anita told me the last time we met, ten years ago. For the two of them remained friends from childhood until first she and then Mum were afflicted with dementia. "We both did. Oh, the flowers and love notes, poems, I remember, serenades. Not like today. We had so much fun together," she said. "We were like sisters. We grew up together. And we were the closest of friends. How the young men courted us! And we were so innocent; we would have none of it. We played tricks on them. Rosina would accept an assignation, and we'd both turn up, or neither of us would. We'd make up names for ourselves and tell false stories. Then, we'd laugh at the silly boys who believed us."

"We told each other everything," Anita said. And again: "We were like sisters." She did not mention her brother Giacomo.

Two years after that sunny May afternoon, Pina announced that she had seen Sior Giacomo come out of Rosina's room. The Bonitos had grown fond of Rosina. "They treated me like another daughter," she told me. She'd proved herself in the bakery. She was now in charge, directing women twice her age. But none of that mattered after Pina had made her accusation. As they say in Italian, *era un fini mondo*; Signora Bonito acted as if "the world were ending." Her screams and tears encouraged Pina to produce more incriminating details: late-night footsteps in the hall, muffled sounds from Rosina's room. And she had seen, oh-so-many times, the Sior whispering in the girl's ear or the two of them laughing at a private joke.

Giacomo was cross-examined, then spirited away to a vacation in Cortina. There was no one to defend Rosina. When she spoke for herself, claiming that the affection between her and Giacomo was true and pure, the Signora launched herself upon the girl (*how dare you*), slapping her face, pulling her hair, and twisting her ear. *Puttana.* Rosina packed her suitcases. She spat at the gloating Pina—*stregona* (big witch)—on her way out.

THE INCIDENT WAS another one of Mum's mysteries. To me, she made a couple of elliptical references. "The other maid spoke ill of me. She made everything seem bad." And: "She spread scandal. I had to leave." That was all. But before I ever heard about her exile from the Bonitos, I'd noticed something I'd never heard before in her voice—a formal, tremulous tone—when she would ask Anita for news of Giacomo. He was her first love; I sensed that without her ever saying so. And when her mind failed and she began to speak of her first husband, I suspected he had also been her first lover. In these last years, she may have forgotten who Giacomo Bonito was, but part of her remembered what he was for her.

I knew I should contact Anita's children to test my vision of Mum's past, but I was reluctant. Pina had remained with the family until she was old and could no longer work; my mother had been cast out. I felt her humiliation. I told myself I would never find them; I had forgotten the daughter's last name. The son had moved house and changed jobs. And they wouldn't know anything anyway. Whyever would their family talk of Rosina and Giacomo? And if they had heard something so unimportant to their lives, whyever would they remember it? After all, the romance I was imagining would have happened more than seventy years ago.

I Googled Anita's son's full name and immediately got his business's Web page. My e-mail, "Are you the Dario

Merrigoli I used to know?" was answered the same day with "How great to hear from you."

Marco and I spent five weeks in Italy during the winter of 2005, so I was able to visit both of Anita's children. Dario and Margerita were welcoming, gracious, and warm—as if Marco and I were long-lost cousins. Dario drove to Venice to pick Marco and me up (though we easily could have taken the train). With his son, he gave us a tour of old Padua, the cobblestone streets and the arcades, where Rosa used to walk. We had a coffee at the Caffè Pedrocchi, the most elegant coffeehouse I have ever seen. "Our mothers used to love to come here," Dario told me. We saw the place where the bakery had been and the two-story family apartment. The Bonitos no longer owned any of it. "My uncle Giacomo was not much of a businessman," Dario said. "He lost most of the family fortune."

Finally, over dinner at Margerita's *Architectural Digest*–worthy villa, in Padua I swallowed my unease and asked.

"Yes," said Margerita. "I did hear that your mother and my uncle Giacomo were in love and wanted to get married. But our grandmother didn't want it. She put a stop to it."

"Mamma said that Pina, your other *donna* [maid], did her some harm—lying about her and the romance."

Dario was refilling the grappa glasses. "*Le donne* always resent each other, always fight."

Maids squabble. The help can never get along. For centuries, there was another commonly held assumption: sex with *le donne* was an old master's right and a young one's opportunity. When Marco's grandparents lived with the family in California in the early sixties, his grandfather had to be reminded repeatedly to stop trying to "feel up" the cleaning lady. Don Ernesto couldn't understand the prohibition. *Le donne* had always been his prey. Even the Italian word for maid had a sexual connotation: *la donna,* the woman. She substituted for the lady of the house in performing the female role, cooking, cleaning, child care, and whatever else she could be bullied into. It was odd hearing my mother referred to by that phrase—*la donna.* And it brought back the old insult she tossed at me when I had done something wrong. *Non diventerai mai donna.* (You will never become a woman.)

Although dalliances were common, although Giacomo was not her boss, although she was not working as one of the Bonito maids, she was the guilty one. Inevitably. "It's up to the woman," she'd warn me during my teen years. "She has to say no." The Bonitos were outraged; they'd treated Rosina like a daughter, and she repaid them by seducing their son. That the two thought they were in love, that it was not a routine fling, made the affair worse. The intensity of the Bonitos' anger ensured that the situation became known beyond the family circle.

Another of my mother's favorite phrases was: "A woman's good name is everything." For years, it made me bristle, because she was referring to sexual reputation, as if it were the only part of a woman that mattered in the public sphere. Now I realize that Mum had suffered the consequences of losing her good name.

For a while after Rosa left their employ and Padua, she alternately visited Maricci in Lussino and Zia Maria in Trieste. Zia Maria was well-off; her husband was the director of the Trieste train station. They had one child—a daughter, Lea. Rosa was a few years older than Lea and was to be a companion and a good influence on the willful only child.

I have a small photo from this time of Mum standing with her aunt and cousin. Unexpectedly, she resembles Zia Maria more than Lea does; aunt and niece are the same height and share the same features and the same bemused facial expression. Also unexpectedly, Rosa stands out as the best dressed of the three. The drape of her dress and her pearl earrings, clutch bag, and brimmed hat, worn on an angle, combine to produce an elegant, polished air.

Lea is wearing a suit that looks too large. She has a large, white, floppy bow on her upper chest. Unlike the other two, Lea is looking not at the camera but at the ground. She is obviously disgruntled. Aunt Maria has taken her daughter by the hand. Perhaps she is trying to reassure Lea or cajole her into a better mood. Their joined hands anchor the center of the picture; they are a couple. Rosa is being edged out of the picture.

Lea was hostile to Rosa from day one. She erupted if her parents gave her cousin any attention. And she resented any male attention that Rosa drew. Rosa's possessions were meager compared with Lea's, yet the spoiled younger girl stole one of Rosa's bead necklaces. She deliberately stained a favorite pink dress. Rosa complained to her aunt, who replied that she must learn to handle Lea. *Fà la contenta.* Give in to her. Make her happy. And Rosa did try. But when Zia Maria bought her a new pair of shoes, because her dress ones had a hole in the sole, Lea cut the straps, ruining them. Rosa left; her aunt's house was not to be even a temporary home.

Rosa somehow found work with a Milanese family; I remember visiting them when I was fourteen. She was hired as personal maid for the lady of the family, and when the husband was made a consul-general in Tunisia, she went with them. She spent two years in Tunis; she told me that a rich Tunisian wanted to marry her. She also said that she worked as a clerk in the consulate, but I wonder since she had so few years of schooling. Not that she ever admitted this; she was always vague about her years of schooling. If she had been at school in the early twenties, as she once claimed, she would have learned to speak proper Italian. The Fascist government was trying to stamp out the dialects, and schools were their prime tool. But Mum only spoke a combination of Istro-Veneto and Venetian. (When I was growing up in Calgary, I remember a British friend of my father often suggested that Mum take a course in the English language. Mum rejected the very idea. And when a friend brought over a book of basic English grammar, Mum waited until the woman left, then threw it into the garbage.)

My impression is that before and after the Milanese family, she worked in Venice, part of that time for a distinguished family that had a palazzo on the Grand Canal. She had many suitors, but she would have none of them. Not until fifteen years passed and she met my father.

For most of the years before she married Frank Edwards, she was on the outer edge of various well-off families, sometimes a poor relation, sometimes a servant. At close quarters, she watched how other girls lived and were educated. She observed other mothers counseling their daughters. And she aspired to an ideal of the refined gentlewoman, the modest chatelaine. The model was Victorian, outmoded by the twenties and thirties but still potent in the middle and upper classes of the Veneto. Over the years and miles, the aspiration intensified into a fixed purpose. She was determined to give me all the guidance and all the rules she never got and to shape me into all that she had wanted to be.

What a disappointment I had been to her: cold and Canadian.

25

All they now wished for was to stay
where they were with the Lotos-eaters,
to browse on the lotos, and to forget
that they had a home to return to.

Homer, THE ODYSSEY, IX

losing it

MY MOTHER WAS always hostile to my passion for reading. "You'll ruin your eyes," she'd say. "You'll ruin your posture," she'd say. "What a waste of time." The words were a chorus through my adolescence. *A waste of time.* For when I was supposed to be practicing the piano or washing the dishes, she would catch me reading. (I'm still compulsive; I have to read, for example, when I'm brushing my teeth, washing my face, or blow-drying my hair.)

"Romances," she'd say, even though that wasn't what I was reading. "*Ti mettono grilli per la testa.*" Books hatched foolish ideas (crickets) in my brain. And although I wasn't given to whims or caprices, for who would ever indulge them, I was a distracted, often dazed teenager. In contrast, Corinna paid attention. She did her chores when she was supposed to. She didn't hide behind or escape into a book. (Although now Corinna is even more of a reader than I am.)

The woman Mum dreamed I would become, the woman she was trying to mold me into—modest, capable, and accomplished, Victorian lady–cum–Venetian Signora—that woman was supposed to be educated and cultured, but to an appropriate degree. She should not be obsessive about reading and writing, and she should not be a writer—a practice Mum judged as frivolous and potentially traitorous. Mum often mentioned a writer she had known in Trieste, always adding that the woman had a wealthy husband and could afford to indulge herself. I wonder now if that writer was Elsa Bragato, who wrote a series of books about Lussino.

My writing was as much of a *waste of time* as my reading. Once I began to have some minor success, if I told her I was invited to another city to give a reading or that I had a new publication, she'd say: "There are too many writers [*true*], too many books [*true*]. No one wants to read *tua roba,* your stuff." *Too true.*

I am embarrassed now to remember how angry I would get, how red faced. "You should be proud of me," I'd say. Or: "I have to. I have no choice." Or: "I need to write."

Mum would look as if she knew better. She would make me admit—again—how little I made from my writing. "One of these days, you'll understand how stupid you have been. Wanting to be a writer."

"I am a writer."

"If you have to work, you should get a proper job teaching. And not a few hours here and there. Earn some good money. You still don't have nice furniture." Then she would expand on the theme of what I needed and didn't have, culminating in a newer, bigger, and better house.

And although I didn't crave a bigger house or a newer car, I did wish I could earn more; I did wish for a few outward signs of success to reassure and justify myself. My mother was so good at giving voice to my fears: "You're not a little girl any more. You're too old for fantasies." And she was right on one level: my compulsion to write, like my addiction to reading, was a holdover from childhood.

Before I could write words down, I told myself stories. *Once upon a time.* My cousins tell me that as a child, I would talk to myself and tune out the world. *In a kingdom far, far away.* A family friend, Lavinia Hall, whom we first met on the ocean liner ss *Scythia,* which brought us to Canada, claims that even at the age of seven I was a writer. "Whenever I saw you, you'd be oblivious to everyone and everything, your lips moving." *At the bottom of a special garden* . . . "If I listened, I caught fragments," Lavinia said. "You were in your own world."

That was why I told stories then: to make a space for myself. To erect a wall against my mother. The impulse was strongest in times of transition. And we moved so often in my early years.

I suspect that my mother unconsciously feared that one day I would write about her, that I would do what I am doing—exposing her secrets to the world. She'd be enraged if she were still her old self, enraged at the inevitable betrayal. She'd let out a high-pitched, wordless scream, throw a dish, land a random blow. Then, worse, the torrent of abusive words, the unstoppable insults. Her tantrums did not begin with the dementia; if anything, they were weaker, more diffuse, in her later years. And I was not the only object: Dad, Corinna, her sisters, each took his or her turn. We never knew what would set her off. A dish placed on the wrong shelf could cause an outburst one time, a laugh the next.

I am still mystified by one incident. I must have been around eleven years old; Corinna wasn't with us yet. It was at the end of summer vacation, and I was home alone all day. Thinking to please my mother and father, I decided to make a cake for their common birthday. I'm sure I had never tried to bake anything before, but I got out the *Five Roses Cook Book* and carefully followed instructions. To my delight, the cake came out of the oven golden and light, but when I tried to get it out of the metal pan, part of it stuck. Maybe I didn't grease the pan properly or allow the cake to cool. Whatever the reason, the birthday cake looked good on one side and patched together and sloping on the other.

Mum must have been tired when she got home, disappointed to find a dirty pan soaking in the sink, upset, perhaps, that I had invaded her territory. She erupted. Screaming, she carried the cake and its dish into the yard and threw them onto the compost pile by the back fence. "You're useless," she said. "The only thing you know how to make is a mess. Stay out of my kitchen."

Useless, useless, useless. It was her favorite refrain, all through my childhood, along with "good-for-nothing" and "You'll never become a woman." She would also call me by a variety of names. From her tone, I could tell they were derogatory, but I didn't know what they meant until I was grown up and got an Italian dictionary. Then I was shocked. Did she know, for example, that *puttana* meant prostitute? That *mona* meant vulva? I couldn't believe that she did.

"Did you mean that?" I would say to her. (She couldn't. I still think that.) Or, "You should watch what you say."

"Watch? I'm your mother."

"Exactly, I'm your daughter. How could you call me that?"

"Call you what?"

I would pronounce the offending word.

"Me? I didn't say that."

"You did, you did, you did."

She assumed a long-suffering expression. "What—now I have to measure my words?"

That accusation became a favorite of hers. I was measuring her words. Or I was pressuring her to measure her words. The phrase came to represent all of our differences. I thought words mattered, that they should be used cautiously, accurately. That they reflected thought. She used them wildly, sloppily, creatively, mixing languages, fusing dialects. *Lui combackerà*—she'd say. (He'll come back.) *Osbondo* (husband), *frendyboy* (boyfriend), *tereeble* (terrible). To explain that she'd been working hard, she'd say, *working come un mus,* which confused me because I didn't associate moose with hard work. For Mum, words were an outlet, an expression of momentary impulses, of passing emotions. Words meant what she wanted them to mean. The lazy Susan in the cupboard, for example, was the *I-love-Lucy.* And my emphasis on restraint and accuracy proved again how cold and Canadian I was.

Now that she was beyond harassing me about my writing, I wished that she were still complaining. It might have roused me from my stupor. Trying to convince her that I was a writer, I might have convinced myself. For

I was no longer telling myself stories. I could still read; I was suffering from insomnia, and I spent many hours of many sleepless nights poring through book after book. But I couldn't write. My mind was dull and scattered. If I forced myself to concentrate, pushed myself to generate and arrange words, they lay inert on the page—imperme-able, clumsy, wrong.

In the mornings, I sat in the study, marked students' papers, surfed the Internet (particularly Istrianet), and stared at the computer screen. "No. No. No." I could hear Mum's voice through the floorboards, yelling at the home-care worker of the day. She screamed louder in the shower. She hated her face to get wet, hated to have a stranger help her shower and dress. Who could blame her? I'd learned the screams were not a sign that she was being mistreated. But I would twitch each time I heard them.

About an hour and a half after the helper left, I would go in to see her and offer her lunch. She'd be ensconced in her La-Z-Boy chair, her swollen feet up. Her walker was supposed to be in front of her so that she could, if she needed, push down the footrest and get herself up and moving. To her right, on top of a small foldout table, a cup of apple juice, a box of Kleenex, her upper dentures, and her hearing aid emitting a high-pitched squeal. On the wood floor in a semicircle around the chair, damp Kleenex she'd used to collect for the mucus she couldn't swallow. I'd put her hearing aid back in so that she could hear me, then use a dry Kleenex to pick up the wet ones.

How many times? Countless, countless. She knocked over her juice. I cleaned it up. I helped her into the bathroom. I guided her back to her chair. Repeated actions, repeated words, hers and mine. The view outside the large window on her left marked the passing of the year; leaves sprouted, grew, turned color, and fell. Mud and bare branches, snow, for months. Another season, another year. Time was wasting me. I was suspended, unable to move forward.

Once before, about eight years earlier, after a series of disappointments (bad reviews and too many rejections), I had suffered from depression and not been able to write, but this time felt different. This time I had the added sense of running out of time. I watched my mother's decline and felt my own mortality.

"I am worried about you," Tatiana said. "You look so stressed."

"So old," I thought, checking myself in the mirror.

"I'm moving out," Antonia said, "as soon as I can afford it."

"I read a new study on stress," Tatiana said. "They've discovered that chronically stressed caregivers of those with dementia have elevated risk of heart disease, arthritis, osteoporosis, and certain cancers for years afterward."

"I'm not surprised."

"Would you like me to e-mail you the URL site?"

"I believe you. Spare me the depressing details."

"How long can we do this?" Marco said. "Our house is no longer our own. All these home-care strangers wandering in and out."

"You always supported me on this."

"I know. I know. I'm just venting."

"She does have congestive heart failure," I said. "How much longer can she have?"

Over the last fifteen years, she had lost a raft of her skills: the ability to be a gracious hostess to a crowd of friends, to cook a delicious meal for ten in two hours, to keep a house spotless and ordered, to turn a length of cotton into a summer dress. And then, and then: to write a letter or a card to a relative or carry on a sustained conversation. To make a bed. To wash the supper dishes. To know the direction of the kitchen or her en suite. To walk unaided. To dress, to bathe herself.

She could no longer follow the arc of a story. Probably that loss meant less to her than the others. (I would have found it unbearable.) I noticed as I sat beside her in the evenings that she couldn't follow the plot of a television drama. Before Dad died and for a little while after, she had been obsessed with *Anne of Green Gables,* the miniseries about the orphan girl who makes everyone love her with her charm and goodness. She had watched the videotape over and over. But now it did not hold her attention. She couldn't remember ever having seen it. I found myself arguing that she had liked it/would like it. I explained the plot, identified the characters. Repeatedly. "Isn't there anything else?" she would ask.

She preferred a faster pace, streams of images, car chases, races, fights, motion, those speeded-up makeovers of rooms or people. The purpose of the activity did not matter. Sometimes she would laugh inappropriately.

She also could not read more than a sentence. I never had seen Mum with a book, although she claimed that in her youth *Little Women* and *Anna Karenina* had been favorites. But she used to peruse the Italian magazines that my aunt Enea sent, *Oggi, Gente, Amica, Famiglia*

Cristiana, from cover to cover. After Dad died, I noticed
that she was paging rather than reading. She would look
through both the weekly Italian newspaper from Vancouver and the daily Edmonton newspaper, reading a headline
out loud, pausing at a picture. Sometimes she would ask
me to read a story and explain the details. Rapes and mur-
ders caught her attention. She saw dangers everywhere.
"You shouldn't let them go out," she would say about Antonia and Tatiana. "You shouldn't leave them so free." There
was a world of bad men out there all intent on hurting her
granddaughters. "You'll cry. Mark my words. You'll cry."

Although she spoke often of crying, she seemed to
have lost that ability, too; she had shed no tears for my
father. But had she understood that he was gone?

ON A SUNDAY morning two and a half years after Dad's
death, Rosa woke up to his absence and her loss. I went
into her room to get her up and begin the morning rituals—I had no help on Sundays—and found Mum sitting
sideways on her bed, feet on the floor, a hand on the white
bar installed to help her get up and down.

"Where's Franco?"

I didn't know what to say. The cemetery? Too brutal.
"What do you mean, where?"

She stared at me, suspicious. "When is he coming back
from the hospital?" For the first few months after Dad's
death, she had cursed the hospital. "He was fine when he
went in," she'd said. "But the evil ones killed him." Then
she'd stopped, and now and then I had the feeling that
she'd forgotten Dad was dead. Or had blocked his death
out of her mind.

"Mum, Dad isn't coming back. He's . . . he's in heaven."
Her eyes were blank. "Don't you remember the funeral?"

"No."

"Corinna came. Marco gave the eulogy."

"No . . . I don't believe you."

"Before we built this room for you, and you came to live
with us."

"I don't remember."

"He's been dead for more than two years."

"Oh, oh, oh . . ." Her face crumpled. She fell back on
the bed.

I propped Mum back up, put an arm around her. "I
know, I know," I said, patting her shoulder. "Poor Mum."

"Oh, oh, oh . . ." Mum continued crying; that is, she
made little crying sounds without producing any tears.

Antonia appeared in the doorway. "Mommy, I'm feeling really sick."

"Still?" Antonia had been complaining for three days.
And I could see that she was getting worse. Her eyes were
glassy and her cheeks flushed.

She took a step toward me. "No," I said. "You might
be contagious, and Nonna's vulnerable." Mum's cries were
getting louder. I had to raise my voice so that Antonia
would hear me. "Get Dad to take your temperature. You
look feverish."

"He's got lots of marking. He has to finish."

I gave Mum a hug, then let go of her. As I got up, her
moans became shouts. "Oh, oh, I can't. I can't."

"Mum, please. I'll be right back."

"Alone. Alone . . . Alone . . . Francoooo."

I followed Antonia into the living room. I felt her forehead. Warm. "Go back to bed, and I'll bring you some aspirin."

"I can't swallow. It hurts too much. Even water."

"Oh, oh, oh . . ." From the other room.

Marco was coming down the stairs, holding a long fax message. "This came for you."

"Damn. I forgot this was the day we fixed—the other judge and I—to come to a decision on which book wins. He wanted to do it by fax."

"No e-mail?" Marco asked.

"My mouth has these sores," Antonia said.

"No e-mail for some reason. What a hassle. If I can just get that out of the way."

"Mommy. The sores—it's scary."

"If I take you to the medicenter, you know what it's like. Hours and hours of waiting. You're more comfortable here. You can see our doctor tomorrow."

"Caterina," Mum called. "Ooowoo." (Her standard sound for catching our attention.) If only Tatiana were here; but she was in Jasper with her girlfriends.

"Let me see," Marco said to Antonia. She opened her mouth wide. He looked and then took two steps back. "Not good."

"Caterina, ooowoo."

Antonia's eyes are filling. "Ohh—I'm so sick."

"Caterina," Marco said, "Look at this." I looked into Antonia's mouth. There were deep, raw holes along her gums and in her tongue.

"Oh my goodness. Hoof-and-mouth disease."

"Mom, gross."

"Foot-and-mouth, I mean." And indeed, after visits to three doctors, my diagnosis would be confirmed. But at that moment, I had an urge to howl and pull my hair.

My mother was at her doorway, taking a few wobbly steps toward us. She had pulled a blouse over her night-gown and was holding a pink cardigan in one hand. "I'm going to my house," she said. Her hands and legs were shaking. Marco and I managed to reach her, one on each side, as her legs gave way.

After I brought Mum her breakfast, I sat down with her. I read the fax, made notes for an answer, and cajoled her. "Come on, a sip, a sip." Mum took her pills but would not touch her toast or coffee. "I'm as alone as a dog," she said, not in her usual assertive tone, but tremulously.

I lifted my head: "No, you're not. You have me and Tati-ana and Antonia—"

"I've lost Franco..." She looked so stricken I wished she hadn't remembered. Better—or at least easier—to be disconnected, unaware.

26

I dissi che bisogna far valise
Che in primavera dovare pompar
Con quatro fazoleti e do camise
E con do braze che sa lavorar

We have to pack our bags
In spring we must leave
With four handkerchiefs and two shirts
And two arms that know how to work

Istrian song about the exile

readings

LONG AFTER I HAD given up hope of finding a collection of books about Istria, at least one that I could access, I came across a mention of just such a library. My propensity to read whatever comes to hand can cause me to fritter my time away. But it can also unexpectedly yield a novel idea, a different take, an odd fact, or an important connection.

I was sitting with my mother as I did most evenings. We were both half-watching television. I changed the channel frequently, trying to find something that would capture her interest. She would have been happy to watch videotapes of *The Three Tenors* or concerts by Andrea Bocelli every night. She would cry out in recognition of an aria or a song of her youth. Sometimes she would hum along or sing a phrase or two. Music remains when so much else has fled. But I couldn't stand such repetition. A few days in a row, and I felt desperate. I was afraid I would grow to hate the songs.

Click, click, nothing too sexy, violent, or talky. "Okay, Mum?"

"Stupid . . ."

"Very stupid. How about? . . . umm, not that . . . no . . ." I settled for one of those endless award shows, lots of pretty dresses and movement. I pulled a magazine off the pile on her side table: a *Messaggero di Sant'Antonio,* published by the Cathedral of St. Anthony of Padua and not at all my usual fare. Mum, who had subscribed to this messenger of St. Anthony as long as I could remember, nodded in approval. "The Saint saved my life."

"You told me." Many times, but only in the last year or so.

"I was at the hospital. I was going. Going. I prayed to him." That was believable. She'd always called out to him in times of stress or fear. *Sant'Antonio, prega per me.* "And I saw him, with these eyes. In his monk's clothes." She hadn't been in the hospital since she lived in Nanaimo. Why hadn't she talked of it then?

"He touched me. And I got better." Sure you did. In a dream. "I used to go to Il Santo." Referring, as they do in Padua, to the cathedral as the saint.

Most days she had no memories of her distant past, so I was startled when she remembered. Startled but interested. "When you were a girl?"

"I always loved Sant'Antonio."

"I know."

"There was a parade around the village on his feast day."
The village? "Only the men named Antonio carried his
statue."

Mum was confusing two different St. Anthonys: the
one who was born in 1195 and was a patron saint of Padua
and the one (Sant'Antonio Abate) born in the third century
and patron saint of Lussingrande. I almost pointed it out
but caught myself. Down, girl. What did it matter? Both
saints were monks. She could have conjured up either
one of them. "Do you remember the feast day in Lussino?"
I said.

She shook her head. Her eyes had gone vague.

"You would go to visit Maricci, right? Zia Cecilia, Zia
Giuditta? Armida—she was your friend."

She turned her head away. How did it feel to dis-
connect like that? From one moment to the other, the
fog rolled in. But the word "fog" by itself did not convey
the confusion and fear I now saw in her eyes. More like
the Sacramento fog I experienced the winter we lived there
with Marco's father: white, opaque, and dangerous. No,
more like the London fog in the fifties that Dad had told
me about: black, polluted, and smothering. A killer fog.

I got up to pat her hand, to kiss her on the top of her
head. "Your hair needs washing," I said.

The Messenger of St. Anthony is distributed in Italy, but
it seems primarily aimed at Italian immigrants around
the world, featuring a spiritual advice column, accounts
of the friars and their missionary work, articles about
Third World issues, and reports on the activities of various regional (Italian) clubs: the Calabria Club in Brisbane,
Australia, for example, or the Abruzzi Club in La Plata,

Argentina. Mum's favorite section—I took it out and passed it to her automatically—was the insert with its rows of snapshots, accompanied by announcements of baptisms, weddings, and anniversaries from all over the world. Each picture of an extravagantly dressed bride or baby, each smiling family group, represented a donation to Il Santo, an appeal for prayers and blessings. It was also a declaration of success: look how well our family, our daughter, our grandson is doing.

Paging through what was for me an unlikely source, I found what I needed. An article on the Giuliano-Dalmato Club of Toronto recounted that the members had assembled a collection of 250 books, a library on their homeland of Istria-Dalmatia.

In the spring, I was invited to Toronto to give a paper at a conference. This paper and this conference have disappeared from my memory—perhaps because, in my mind, the purpose of the trip was to contact the Giuliano-Dalmato Club and visit their library.

The members of the club welcomed me, thrilled that someone who was not an Istrian but the daughter of an Istrian (who didn't and did belong) was interested in their homeland and their story. In 2005, the library was moved to the Veneto Centre; but the two times I visited, it was still in a basement rec room, with a wet bar, glossy wood paneling, and two heraldic banners, both featuring the emblem of Istria, a yellow goat perched on a mountain peak. It consisted of a wall and a half of books, almost all in Italian and almost all published by tiny émigré presses. This room was in a member's house in the suburb of Weston, Ontario. Both times, Guido Braini, the president, drove into the center of Toronto from Weston—a trip that took at least an hour—to pick me up.

The library was a treasure trove. I spent hour after hour at a long table piled high with books I'd pulled off the shelves: skimming, reading, flipping pages, taking notes, cramming, cramming in as much as I could. Although my previous bibliographic searches had turned up nothing on the internment of Istrians in World War I except an unpublished thesis, just in case, on the first visit, I searched for anything on Istria and the Great War, including anything on the court-martial of Nazario Sauro and his men, anything—a paragraph, a sentence, a word, to verify, to situate, to contextualize my mother, my grandfather, and the family. I found no relevant connections, no clues, not even the names of Sauro's sailors on the submarine, but still facts aplenty—history, botany, music, poetry, and more.

On the second visit, about eight months later, I did not search for anything specific but tried to absorb everything I could about the culture that had shaped Rosa Pagan. Both times, Giorgia S. provided me with pots of coffee and plates of cookies. (Giorgia asked that I not print her name.) She hovered. "Are you warm enough? Do you have enough light?" And she talked and talked. She apologized for interrupting my reading. And still she talked, compelled to tell me her life story.

Late at night, as Guido drove me back to my hotel, he recounted *his* story—Koper to Trieste, to the tobacco fields near Peterborough, to Toronto, refugee to citizen, son to grandfather, fear to calm—while navigating the freeways of the greater Toronto area. Success, a happy ending of sorts, yes, but regret, too—regret still, nostalgia, loss.

Konrad Eisenbechler, who was born in Lussinpiccolo and is a professor of Italian at the University of Toronto, spoke with less urgency. He was a baby when he left Lussino. ("And let us not speak of Losinj; it was called Lussino for at least half a millennium.") Besides, Konrad told me, the people of Lussino were not political, a generalization that corresponded with my experience. Unlike many of the refugees not from the island, none of my relatives who left and became refugees cursed or criticized Tito or the Communists. (Which may explain why it took me so many years to become aware of the scope and significance of the exile.) It was as though they thought their lives were not worth talking about. Their tone had been impersonal, fatalistic. "We had to leave."

Eisenbechler may not speak of trauma or exile, but he is important to the Istrian community in Canada, taking time from his scholarly career to work on the club's magazine. Recently, he translated *L'Esodo: La Tragedia Negata degli Italiani d'Istria, Dalmazia e Venezia Giulia* by Arrigo Petacco, the first historical work about the Istrian exile, and published it under the title *A Tragedy Revealed* with the University of Toronto Press.

Like many Istrians, including many of those who left, Eisenbechler's ethnic background was not primarily Italian or Croatian. Although politicians and ideologues speak of Istria as being either Italian or Croatian, as properly belonging to either one country or the other, historically the region has also been home to people who identified themselves as Austrians, Romanians, or Serbs.

Besides, over the last hundred years, a certain percentage of Istrians of all ethnic backgrounds have claimed different identities, depending on who was taking the census. "Many. . . declared themselves Italian one day, Slavic the next, according to the benefits accorded them," Petacco writes in *A Tragedy Revealed*. Under the Austrians, it was better to be Croatian or Slovenian; under the Italians in 1941, a greater percentage declared themselves Italian. Sometimes the shifts in ethnicity are mysterious. The population of Veli Losinj did not change much between 1900 and 1910, increasing by 50 to 1,992. Yet in 1900, 60 percent of the inhabitants (or 1,174 inhabitants) claimed to be Croatian, and 24 percent (or 473) Italian, whereas in 1910, only 36 percent said Croatian and 43 percent Italian. I see this fluidity of identity not simply as opportunistic but as reflective of the multicultural and multiethnic nature of families in the old Istria. If you had an Austrian father and an Italian mother, did you have to choose one ethnicity over the other? Was identity necessarily singular?

Upon leaving Mali Losinj in the early fifties, the Eisenbechlers went to their so-called mother country, Austria, but Eisenbechler's mother found the German culture foreign. His parents had been educated in Italian schools and spoke Istro-Veneto at home and in their community. Rightly or wrongly, they felt Italian, at least culturally, so they joined their fellow Lussignani in Italy and then in Canada.

This second visit, I was in Toronto to publicize a slim volume of stories, all written years before. Since the title story, "The Island of the Nightingales," was set in Losinj, Guido arranged for the club to host a launch at the Columbus Centre. I met more Istrian-Canadians than I

could count, and like most of the participants of Istrianet, most were eager to tell their story, the true story (they
called it), the real story. They felt they had been ignored,
denied, silenced. Not even their children would listen to
them. And most mourned the indifference of the younger
generations. "What do they care about the past?" one man
said.

"They don't understand what our lives have been," a
woman said.

But a few were thankful. "The name Istria means
nothing to my grandchildren. And I am happy that they
are free of all that pain."

Each narrative unique, each the same. I heard certain phrases repeated again and again: *a silent migration,
an exodus of biblical proportions, the cities empty as ghost
towns*. The exiles everywhere used these words as badges,
talismans, incantations.

The most frequently used phrase—350,000. They say
half of a population of roughly 700,000 left.

Is this figure believable? I am not an expert. I guess it
might be somewhat exaggerated. It is generally accepted
that some towns and all the major coastal cities were
emptied. And that in some places no one left. Twenty
thousand—the only number I found in the University of
Alberta library—is ridiculous: at least that number came
to Canada alone through the International Refugee Organization. Petacco accepts 350,000. Darko Darovec, a historian from Koper who published *A Brief History of Istria* in
1998, with the support of the Slovenian Minister of Culture, says:

Any assumptions which may be made about the number of exiles in advance of an in-depth study of the problem is pure speculation. It will be possible to unravel this problem only with the aid of archives of the Yugoslav military government (which is in Belgrade) and of the state archives in England, USA and Italy, several of which are not yet available.

ALTHOUGH VISITING the library was valuable, most of what I have learned about Istria, what I've grown to rely on, has come through the stories people have told me in person or through Istria-talks. There was a certain turnover of participants on the Internet discussion group. Intermittently, someone would accuse Marisa, the Webmaster, or the group at large of being too pro-Italian or pro-Croatian and then unsubscribe. Others stumbled across the site and joined.

In my research, I had to adjust my belief that everything worth knowing could be found in a book. How pleased my mother would have been if I had come to such a realization ten years earlier, when she was still her old self. Not that I would have probably admitted she was even a little right.

Now, too late, I wish I had listened to my aunts, to my father, to Marco's father, and to my mother. I wish I had spent more time asking them what their lives had been. The death of an old man or woman is the destruction of a library.

27

And hundreds and hundreds were
killed or thrown into prison to
wither away, and they were not
fleeting flowers, but vigorous plants,
men and women in an Italian city
that disappeared like last year's snow.

Ianni Sabucco, in an unpublished
memoir, SI CHIAMAVA FIUME

what they told me

ON OCTOBER 15, 1943, three months after
Mussolini's government fell and one month after Italy
signed an armistice with the Allied forces, the German
military annexed as a province of the Third Reich an
extensive territory that stretched from Fruili to Ljubljana
and included Istria and Dalmatia. The area, named Adri-
atisches Küstenland—as Istria had been called under the
Austrian Empire—was occupied after a fierce week of
fighting that left at least fifteen thousand Yugoslav partisans dead. The Nazis ruled Istria "as brutally as they did
in every other territory occupied... There were countless
summary executions and public hangings (Petacco)." They
rounded up Jews and the leaders of the opposition for

the concentration camps. They instated a draft and, on a minor note, had the monument to Nazario Sauro in Koper dismantled.

The next two years were times of starvation in Losinj. Allied submarines, war boats, and planes patrolled the sea around the island, cutting off most supplies from the mainland and making fishing a dangerous occupation. The German ss seized most of the food grown locally. My cousin Leda remembers her mother (my aunt Maricci) walking from one end of the island to the other, bartering everything of value they owned in return for a sack of cornmeal or a bottle of olive oil. (Hence the story of begging for potato peels.) Like most of the other men, Maricci's son, Oscar, was taken away to the mainland to be forced to fight or to work as slave labor. At least three of these men died in German prisons. Oscar escaped, however, and joined the partisans, a choice that could not have been easy.

The month in 1943 between the surrender of the Italian Fascist forces and the takeover by the Nazis was one of great chaos. Partisan groups with varying ideological backgrounds (but led by Tito's Communists) battled the Croatian Ustashi, Slovenian Domobranci, and Catholic White Guard. At the same time, the anger created by two decades of Italian repression boiled over. Representatives and instruments of the Fascist regime—mayors, policemen, teachers, city clerks, and tax collectors—were tortured (the women raped), and they disappeared into the *foibe*. These reprisals (for the most part carried out by Tito's partisans) spread to other members of the Italian-Istrian middle class, to landowners and their families. It was a time of terror, and these wartime excesses were not justifiable but understandable. No doubt some people who simply got in the way were slaughtered. At least these *foibe* have been unofficially acknowledged, whereas the later ones, from 1945 onward, in which Italians were targeted for being Italians rather than Fascists, continue to be denied.

In Veli Losinj, during that chaotic month, no one was taken away and executed. Only one citizen, Antonio Cunei, who had been an officer of the Italian navy, was cast into a *foiba,* and that was at the end of the war, in May 1945. Still, the town learned the nature of Tito's partisans. A large group of Serbian Chetniks, who were loyal to their King Peter, were camped close by Mount St. John. Tito's partisans attacked them, even though they were technically on the same side, fighting the Germans. There was a fierce battle, and the Chetnik men were slaughtered. (A local four-year-old, Paolo Lettich, was also killed.) Several Lussignani told me that they never got over seeing those mutilated bodies on their hill. The captured Chetnik women and children were told they would be escorted back to their homes in Serbia. They sailed off in a ship, escorted by about ten of the partisans. In under an hour, the boat returned without its cargo. The partisans were still washing the blood off the decks and sides.

After the Italian armistice and the German occupation, a small minority of Giuliani (Italian-Istrians) continued to fight for Mussolini's government, now based in Salò. Many more joined the partisans, often surrendering their weapons to Tito's men. Sixteen thousand men formed themselves into an Italia brigade with a Garibaldi and Venezia division. By the end of the war, these battalions had all been dispersed; the soldiers were either absorbed by Tito's forces or killed.

Giorgia S., whom I met at the library of the Giuliano-Dalmato Club, said that her family did not think of leaving in 1945 when Tito's forces took over Koper, once Capodistria, the beautiful city a few kilometers along the gulf from Trieste. For several years, like most Italian-Istrians, the family remained. This was their home; their roots went back to the 1600s. They were not afraid of another change of regime. They had lived through four in the last thirty years—Austrian, Italian, German, Allied—and expected to survive the new masters as they had the others.

Giorgia was young then, a recent graduate of the *liceo*, the high school, and already had a good job working at the *Palazzo del municipio*, city hall. "I remember," she told me, "a municipal election. It must have been in '48. No one came. All day we waited with the ballots and the boxes, and no one came to vote. My supervisor was furious, ranting and raving. 'What about you,' he said to me. 'Go ahead. What are you waiting for? You vote.' But I wouldn't. I knew it was a farce, that all the candidates were members of the [Communist] party. And I'd heard that the winner had already been chosen. So I refused. And he picked up his umbrella, swearing at me in Slovenian. And he began beating me until he broke the umbrella on my back."

As a clerk, Giorgia was charged with issuing identifications and handwriting the births and deaths of the citizens of Koper into the big black volumes of the archives. Until one morning she walked into the record office, and 150 years of books (at least twenty volumes) were gone.

She stood and stared at the empty shelves, as if she could wish them back.

"Do you know where they are?" she asked a coworker. She thought maybe a supervisor had ordered them moved; perhaps they were being checked, reviewed. Or undergoing some process of conservation. Some of the books were hundreds of years old. She could hear the others talking around her, a buzz in her ears. Her stomach was flopping with anxiety, though she couldn't explain why.

One of the other clerks entered the office from a back door. "Come see," he said. "There's been a bonfire, out the back. . ." They found a small pile of ashes and several pieces of hardened and warped material that could have been the cloth covers of the books. Whoever had taken the books couldn't have burned more than one or two there on the street. There would have been more ashes, more dust. And it would have taken too long; the bonfire would have been big and noticeable streets away. So many books were gone.

Neither the historians nor the bureaucrats of Slovenia or Croatia admit that archives disappeared in the late forties. As I discovered in Mali Losinj, if you ask, for genealogical purposes, the absence is blamed on the Nazis or an accidental and unfortunate fire. Decades of church records also seem to be gone. Maria Lettich and Armida Baricèvic in Veli Losinj suggested that the local priest would deny me access because I was not Croatian. It was useless to ask, they said. And they were right, though not because I wasn't recognizably Croatian. Will Gladofich and Mario Majarich, who were Croatian, were both denied access to the records of the Cathedral of Veli

Losinj. Only in novels or in the stories that the refugees recount among themselves is the disappearance of the archives acknowledged and speculated upon.

"We suspected Tito's secret police," Guido told me. "Suspected that it was a deliberate policy—creating chaos in registries. Making it easy for them to claim that the Italians arrived with the Fascists, rather than being indigenous."

This was the time when in a few towns, the stone lions of St. Mark, the symbol of Venice, were toppled and smashed to pieces. And in diverse cemeteries of Istria, gravestones were defaced, the names, Italian names, chipped out of the stone. It was the time after the war, after the simple reprisals for the Fascist outrages. Tito was securing the Communist reign but also promoting Slavic nationalism. The Slovenian historian Darovec states that "the Commissions of Purification" were used to attack those who were "nationally inconsistent"—that is, the Giuliani.

The desecration did not stop with the death of Tito. After the civil war that accompanied the dissolution of Yugoslavia, *I Rimasti,* the small Italian population that was left, felt emboldened to claim concrete rights. (Under Communism, they had been used for propaganda purposes; their rights were token and somewhat illusory.) The citizens of Cres asked that the stone lion of St. Mark that had been destroyed in the forties be restored. Many communities in Istria instituted bilingualism, particularly bilingual town and street signs.

These minor changes enraged the Nationalist Croatian politicians. Croatia was for Croatians. Istra, as the Croatians called Istria, had always been only Croatian. The

Italians, according to a few of the Croatian historians, had arrived with the Fascists. And, the politicians claimed, Italy was again, in this twenty-first century, "reintroducing" Italians to Istria in order to turn Croatia into a colony.

A recent request by Furio Radin, the leader of the Italian community in Croatia, that all signs on government roads be bilingual has caused more hysteria. On Croatian newspaper Internet forums, one man told Radin to "get lost, you ugly monkey." Another spoke of "dumb, arrogant Italian extremists." Still another said, "Serbs are no longer a danger to us. Now the danger comes from sneaky Italians."

In May 2001, in a small, private graveyard, far from a church or a town but close to the quarry of Cise, between Motuvan and Traz, an altar and a crucifix were raised. The altar was inscribed with *Fiat Voluntas Tua;* the crucifix with the following poem: *Le candele per noi accese / si stanno spegnendo una ad una / La notte giunge ormai / Non ci sarà piu alba.* "The candles you have lit for us / are going out one by one / We are joining the night / There will be no dawn." This modest monument commemorated the twenty young men with Italian names who were executed and buried there on May 10, 1945. A few months later, Jonas Frykman, a Swedish professor and head of a research project on cultural identities, came across the graveyard. He found the white stones and the wooden crosses marking the graves scattered and overturned and the altar smashed.

Some regimes, the obvious example being Nazi Germany, keep careful records of those they have exterminated. Others have a less systematic plan, encouraging the unwanted to leave, to go somewhere else, to disappear.

Sometimes these unwanted are not a minority but a majority—a majority that has been rooted in a place for centuries. So how does the hostile force uproot these people;
how does it incite them to leave? By violence, by seizures
of property, by select executions, by terror, certainly. But
to ensure that they go away and stay away, to forestall later
claims, the regime destroys the records. Then it can claim
that they, the powerless, do not belong. It can claim that
they have no rights to the place, for they were never there.

"We decided we had to leave after the books disappeared," Giorgia said. "We didn't know what might happen next."

"There were other things," Guido later told me. "Our
world was changing so fast. Churches and schools closed.
The names of cities and towns changed."

"We heard so many terrible things in the war," Rita
Bertieri said in Edmonton. "What the Ustashi did to the
Serbs. We began to sense we would be next."

"We were battered by the war," Bruno C. said in Vancouver. "By the bombings and the starvation. By all the young
men gone forever. We were weakened and uncertain."

"In Capodistria all the windows of the shops owned
by Italians, the vast majority of shops then, were broken,
their goods looted," Guido said when he drove me back to
my hotel. "That was our *Kristallnacht*. Of course, people
started to disappear. Always at night. We would hear the
rumble of trucks taking them away."

"Later, in Italy, in the newspapers, it was said that only
the Fascists were taken. But that is not the way it was."
Giorgia's hand was trembling; her voice wavered. "Some of
those who had been partisans in the war were also taken."

"There was no pattern." I heard this over and over, on Istrianet, in the homes of Istriani in Canada, Italy, and Croatia.

"I suppose it was a way of getting rid of someone that you had a grievance against. Or if you coveted his property, you denounced him." Guido said.

"But it was more than that. No sense to it."

"Like the plague," Guido said in casual tone. "Like fate: implacable, inevitable." (*A chi toccava, toccava.*)

By this point of the communal narrative, Giorgia was breathing noisily, almost gasping for air. "A brother or a sister or even a father, suddenly gone. You couldn't find out where they were taken, what happened to them."

"There was no appeal," Bruno said. "So, we grew afraid."

"Afraid and lost," Rita said.

"All the leaders of the community, the intellectuals, disappeared or chose to leave," Guido said.

"Some officials seized the family bakery. My father had forty-eight gold coins, hidden, to help us start a new life," Rita said. "But somehow they found out. Someone told and a policeman confiscated all of them."

"We crossed the border in 1949," Giorgia said.

"We left Rovigno in 1951," Rita said.

"We got away in 1955," Guido said.

Milovan Djilas, who was Tito's right-hand man, writes in his memoir: "In 1945, Kardelj and I were sent by Tito to Istria. Our job was to induce all the Italians to leave by whatever means necessary. And it was done." (*E così fu fatto.*)

28

To be a witness, try to remember.
That cannot be done.
Nor am I doing it.
I only know it's gone, that city...

Czeslaw Milosz, "Wanda,"

NEW AND COLLECTED POEMS, 1931–2001

ruins

I IMAGINE A CITY as silent and still as a graveyard. Shops closed, corner cafés deserted, streets empty of
traffic. Churches, theaters, arenas locked, apartments and
houses shuttered. A statue toppled, a plaque defaced. The
piazzas and roads opening before me are both familiar
and strange. And I am overcome by the sense of eeriness,
of absence in the light and the dark.

A city of white stone and long shadows. I imagine only
one city, though there were many—one city, reduced to
the sounds of sea, wind, and rain, reduced to a landscape
of futility and ruin.

I don't belong here, I tell myself—don't look behind
the broken doors, don't peer into the cavernous entrances,
do not mount those stairs. They lead nowhere; that floor
is gone. Like the people who used to live here, gone—like

an old woman's past, gone. Turn back, get out. Down the hall, feel your way. Through the dark to the open air. Forcing my legs to move, to go forward, one step after the other. The echoes of my steps on the pavement stones, the sound of memory.

My city does not conform to an actual Istrian city. It is a sequence of images and apprehensions that remains fixed in my mind. Over 85 percent of the population of the coastal cities did leave during the exodus. Capodistria, Rovigno, Pola, Zara, Parenzo, and Fiume, as they had been, disappeared. They had emptied before, centuries earlier, once, twice, three times, devastated by the black plague, changed into sepulchers. Those times, the Republic of Venice had sent its sailing ships to the corners of its empire to bring new settlers, new citizens: Greeks, Albanians, Romanians, Croats, Serbs, and Italians.

Witnesses of the post–World War II exodus speak of how thriving and lively cities became ghost towns. That could not have been entirely true, but Pola (now Pula) was the closest to the desolated city of my imagination. The exodus of Italians, who made up almost 100 percent of the population, was "sudden and massive," according to Petacco. The Italians thought that they were safe and that the city, which was an important naval center, would not be handed over to Yugoslavia. When they realized in late January 1947 that Pola was to be transferred on February 10, the same day that the peace treaty was to be signed in Paris, they panicked. In a little over a month, they had fled. But they were quickly replaced. On the date of the transfer, the Yugoslav troops marched in to take over from the Allied forces and to confiscate what they could. As one community left, another was forming. People from the suburbs and countryside rushed in to take over the empty houses. Settlers were brought in from Macedonia and Bosnia.

Outside of the coastal cities, a smaller percentage of the population left. Besides those of Slavic ethnicity, who were not pressured to leave, some ethnic Italians, the *Rimasti,* also stayed, because they believed in the new order, in the Communist ideals. Or because they managed to evade persecution. Or because they could not envision life away from their particular place, their portion of land and sea and sky. And, except for Pola, the exodus was gradual, stretching from 1945 to 1956. (Afterward, people continued to leave, until the late sixties, but that emigration was of a different nature, more consistently economic than ideological, more rural than urban.) So many who eventually left wanted to stay. They hoped the situation would improve. They hung on and on, until they could not do so anymore.

ONE WINTER DAY a few years ago, I was comparing memories of Losinj with Miki Andrevicevic, a neighbor and friend. Both of us were reveling in our just-discovered link to that sunstruck island.

Miki had come to Edmonton as a participant in the most recent exodus, the one that followed the breakup of Yugoslavia, leaving behind a prestigious job as general manager of the Belgrade Symphony and a role in the artistic life of his city. Miki knew Losinj well; he had spent the summers of his university years there. "I've often told my wife how special, how magical, a place it is."

"It is. It is."

"I'm not sure she believes me."

"Marco neither."

Miki used to stay in Cres, not Losinj. "I was a student, and Losinj was expensive. A place for the rich and the important. Writers and artists. Many of the Belgrade elite. The conductor of the symphony, I know, had a summer home there. The houses used to be very cheap."

"I wonder why."

"There were so many empty houses. Abandoned. Apparently, you could get them for almost nothing."

I made a face. "Did no one ever question why there were so many abandoned houses? Ever mention all the Italians who were forced out?"

"No," Miki said. "We were told that they wanted to go. That they chose."

"Oh, sure," I said. "They chose. But why?"

"They did not all go. The family I rented a room from was Italian. So many of the inhabitants. That was where I learned my Italian—in Cres and Losinj, in the streets and the shops."

When Marco and I visited Losinj in 2001, I could not help but wonder about the Serbs that Miki said had owned vacation homes before the early nineties, before the dissolution of the old Yugoslavia through the bitter civil war. So when I managed to engage someone in conversation, I often asked, "So, what about the Serbs who owned houses here? Have they come back? Will they be able to come back? What will happen to their houses?"

Most did not answer me. One man shrugged; another shook his head. One woman turned away. They all looked uncomfortable. I suppose they thought that I was rude, that such things should not be talked of. Fifty years earlier, someone like me could not, would not, have asked such questions about the houses that belonged to the so-called Italians. Or, at least, not without consequences to anyone who didn't respond with the party line: "Those people opted out. They chose to leave." Or "Those houses belonged to foreigners, Italians, Fascists who came with the occupying regime. They didn't belong." Denying a thousand years of history.

I was lying on my stomach and naked when I questioned the young masseuse at La Punta Hotel. We were speaking English: she was from Zagreb and had lived for some months in the United States. "What about all the houses here owned by Serbs?" I said. On my back, her fingers stopped moving. A silence stretched between us. Finally, she said in a quiet voice, "If they had killed a member of your family, you wouldn't forgive. You can't forgive."

Conversely, cousin Armida reacted by leaning closer and nodding vigorously. "It's terrible, terrible, what happened. The war." (Meaning the recent civil war.) "Not here, thank God. A few boys went off to fight. But what I saw on the TV news from Italy."

I asked again about the houses owned by Serbs. Did Armida know of any?

"The one right behind me and two down, that one is owned—well, it was—by a fine gentleman. A Serb. Who knows? Who knows?" Armida then suggested, as did a couple of others, that the Serbian owners would get some sort of restitution from the Croatian government. From someone.

Those that left during the post–World War II exodus are still waiting for the restitution for their confiscated properties. A small settlement was mandated in the Treaty of Paris, signed in 1954, to be paid by Italy to the exiles as part of its war reparations, but it was rejected by the leaders of the exiles as too small. As Guido Braini explained, "We thought that if we accepted, we would be giving up our claim." The money remains in a bank in Rome.

One family abandons a house; another family claims it. A culture withers; another blooms. But not everything is refilled, replaced, renewed. Oblivion is not complete. Traces remain. Ruins speak.

And there are so many of them—ruined houses—in Losinj. I was surprised on the 2001 visit that I had not noticed before. These were not waiting for summer visitors, nor had they been recently vacated by ex-countrymen. These showed signs of decades of desolation. One, then another, and another, on the outskirts of Veli Losinj. One, then another, and another. All over Istria, I have been told, deserted homes. Windows, doors, rooms gone, people, pets, possessions gone. Now only an idea of shelter, a collection of absences, four walls of plastered rock, lines of stone where walls have once been choked by grasses, homes for maquis and laurels, thistles and reptiles.

The ruins, gray and rough, carried me back to my grandmother Caterina standing at the door of her house, turning the key in the lock. Thinking she will return. Hurrying because her children are afraid and the soldiers impatient. One bag each.

The ruins carried me back to my aunt Maricci throwing her key at the silver leaves of an olive tree. There.

Knowing she will not return. There. Directing the retreat, husband, daughter, cart, suitcases, you take that, and that, it's no use crying, no use. Bearing her granddaughter Corinna carefully, safely in her arms.

Decay does not begin; it is ever present, but with no one and nothing to oppose it, the corruption multiplies. Dust settles, shrouds. A window is broken, a door breached, chests and carpets taken. Mice nest in the matrimonial bed. The *bora* blows away a roof tile. Rain, dirt, and seeds enter; mold darkens, then weakens an inner wall.

Fifty years of ruination. The stones remain.

{ 29 }

Everything lies all jumbled
up in it, and when you look back,
you feel dizzy and afraid.
W.G. Sebald on the past,
ON THE NATURAL HISTORY OF DESTRUCTION

Va via ti che commando mi.
You go, because I am in charge
Angelo Cecchelin (comic) on the so-called democracy
and liberty after World War II, from a song on tape

lies

WHY SUCH A LONG SILENCE? As if those
intertwined events, the *foibe* and the exodus from Istria,
had never happened, as if any acknowledgment, any discussion, were taboo. A half-century of silence. I can
understand why the rest of the world did not take notice.
Considering the magnitude of events during those years,
the multitude of dead, the exodus was proportionately
minor. But why the silence in Yugoslavia and, more sig-
nificantly, in Italy, where everything is debated. Why?

Indifference. *Stop whining. Others had it worse.*

Elitism. *Some deaths are more important than others.*

Intellectual laziness. *We are busy talking of other things.*
The exodus is not fashionable.

The relative ease of thinking in slogans, of thinking en masse.

Ignorance. *That area was always Slav. The exiles were all Fascists.*

Ideology. *It wasn't ethnic cleansing but class warfare. The Italians were the bourgeois.*

Principle. *For peace. For the good of the party.*

Shame.

The journalist Anna Maria Mori writes that for many years, she would tell people she was born in Florence instead of Pola. To be an Istrian was something shameful, mistaken. You were branding yourself an outsider and not a proper Italian. Although she eventually confessed her true origins, she despaired of convincing any of her colleagues, and friends on the left, of the "tragedy of the Istrian people."

Only in the last few years, since the war over the breakup of Yugoslavia, has the story begun to be told. Because the old hegemonies were defeated: Tito and Communism on one side of the border, the Christian Democrats on the other. And because it was happening again in Kosovo—the ethnic cleansing. But this time there were television cameras and news reports. This time there were no handy karst pits, no *foibe*, in which bodies could be made to disappear.

SHAUL BASSI, a young professor of Canadian literature at the University of Venice with both a Jewish and an Istrian background, organizes for the city *Il Giorno della Memoria*, The Day of Memory, when the Holocaust is officially remembered. In 2004 he took on the organization for Venice of *Il Giorno del Ricordo,* the Day of Remembering, to mark the *foibe* and the exodus. He said, "They are not at all equivalent: one was genocide, the other an ethnic cleansing. Still, no one has ever been charged or tried for the slaughters in Istria."

Consequently, when not denied altogether, the executions (including those of women and children) are usually viewed as justified, acceptable. Shaul told me that to this day in a district of Marghera, which has the largest population of Istrians in Italy, threatening slogans are repeatedly sprayed on the piazza walls. "We should have exterminated all of you," they say in Slovenian. Or *"Vive le foibe."* So Shaul sees the need to commemorate the *foibe,* to have a Day of Remembering on February 10 of each year (the anniversary of the day that Pola was handed over to Yugoslavia). (Slovenia has declared a competing national holiday on February 10, a celebration of "The Reannexation of the Adriatic Littoral.") However, Shaul is distressed that in Italy the right-wing politicians have used ceremonies on that day as vehicles of propaganda.

Politics have poisoned the air for the post–World War II Istrian refugees since they began arriving in Italy. The postwar Fascists tried to use their plight to embarrass the left wing and to promote, to glorify, a mythical pure *Italianità*. They continued to claim that Istria had always been primarily Italian—rather than multicultural. They also did not admit to the excesses of Mussolini's regime, ignoring the earlier attempts to turn Slavs into Italians. Right-wing politicians trumpeted the superiority of Italian culture. Meanwhile, the more central Christian Democrats had betrayed the Italian-Istrians by giving in to Tito's and Stalin's territorial demands—that is, by handing Istria, including Pola, over to Yugoslavia. The Christian Democrats wanted to hide and forget that betrayal.

The Italian Communists were the most desperate. Tito was their hero and must not appear in a bad light. Even the party members who left Italy to live in the Socialist paradise and ended up either fleeing or spending years in a Yugoslav prison camp were pressured by the party to remain silent for the sake of their Communist ideals.

At the Bologna train station in 1947, the refugees were denied water; in Southern Italy, food relief. In Ancona and Venice, the exiles were greeted with the slogans *Fuori i criminali fascisti.* Away with the criminal Fascists. I believe these stories of harsh treatment by union members. To this day, Gianfranco Bellin, a leftist thinker, receives death threats for supporting the exiles' point of view, for telling their stories. And I have heard the continuing hatred in the voices of certain academics and journalists when they speak of these displaced people.

In 2005, at the University of Venice, I attended a lecture by a "scholar" on the *foibe.* When I got to the right classroom, it was filled to overflowing. Feeling conspicuous, I squeezed through the throng in the doorway and edged forward to a tight spot against a glass bookcase. Since the *foibe* had so rarely been discussed or acknowledged in Italy, I was expecting a debate about the statistics or the significance of the events.

Instead, I was listening to a *foibe*-denying rant. The journalist Claudia Cernigoi was arguing that almost no Italian ethnics were executed by Tito's men, and if they were, they deserved it, and if they were, they were certainly not thrown into the *foibe*. Anyway, the *foibe* were often mine shafts, the woman said with a smug expression, as if we should judge the executions differently if the victims were thrown into a man-made, rather than a natural, pit. Besides, she said, all the Italians had been Nazi-Fascists. Cernigoi did not assume the usual academic tone, calm and dispassionate. She sounded outraged and scornful, as if she or her family had been victimized. I was stunned by her venomous tone. When she finished speaking, I waited for someone—anyone—to challenge her or, at least, to question her assertions.

No one did. The three men who took turns speaking from the audience (from their tweed jackets and self-regarding manner, I marked them as professors) simply amplified the speaker's theme. It was ridiculous, one said, to claim that anyone was killed for being Italian when Tito's partisans saved a trainload of Italians bound for a Nazi concentration camp. Besides, said the next, the Italian workers of Monfalcone went to live in Yugoslavia. (*But they fled back. They found themselves persecuted. Imprisoned in Goli Otok.*) Besides, said the last, these so-called exiles, these Italian-Istrians, weren't real Italians, and they came and took jobs away from real Italians. Bread stealers.

And I thought, *damned for being too Italian, damned for being not Italian enough.*

At least two members of the audience, an elderly man and woman, were Istrian exiles. I could feel their distress. I waited and waited for them to speak. But an opening never came. This lecture was managed, perhaps even staged.

Half a century of silence. Yugoslavia and its brand of Communism are finished. Yet when the Istrians of the diaspora speak out, they are still being told that they are wrong, that they are lying about what they experienced or witnessed. *Shame on you,* posts a certain Ferdinando on Istrianet, addressing all those who left. *Shame on you,* writes this young Italian man, for leaving, for not embracing the revolution, for being (*admit it*) fat bourgeois pigs. *No one wants to hear your stories. No one believes you.* Every few months, his sneering messages reappear.

I type back: *the shame is all yours.*

30

Memory is the belly of the soul.

St. Augustine, CONFESSIONS

sisters

MUM WAS A CHILD when her mother sent her off into the world. I cannot imagine letting go of one of my daughters when she was ten years old. But it was what was done not just then but until recently. In times of difficulty, you sent your child off for the chance of a better life. That was how Corinna came to live with us—how she became my sister.

Corinna's grandmother (my zia Maricci), grandfather (my zio Erminio), and mother, Vilma, left their home in Losinj in 1950. Corinna spent her infancy and part of her childhood in the refugee camp in Tortona. After many years, the four of them moved into a cold-water apartment in Genoa built for the Istriani. The family remained poor. They'd had to leave everything of monetary worth— savings, belongings, even jewelry—behind. And in those postwar years, Italy was impoverished; unemployment and

consequently emigration were high. So Corinna's grandmother and mother earned the little they could, which
was not much, cleaning houses, while her grandfather,
Erminio, was ill with the tuberculosis he picked up in the
Yugoslav prison.

Corinna was a pretty child with thick chestnut hair,
bright eyes, and a bright mind. Italy had a sizable minority
of doctrinaire Communists in the fifties; Corinna's first-
year teacher was a true believer. The *maestra* alternately
ignored and picked on her. She was heard referring to
Corinna as a Fascist. "I didn't know what the word meant,"
Corinna told me. "I didn't know what I had done. Why
she didn't like me." Now, she realizes that the teacher
must have hated her for being one of those who fled the
people's paradise of Yugoslavia. Even though Corinna was
a baby when she left Losinj, she represented a challenge
to the teacher's belief in the manifest superiority of Tito's
way and therefore must be defeated and humiliated.

This experience was a common one for the Istrian
children of the exile, particularly those who ended up in
Genoa or (even worse) Bologna. For some Italians, the
children were tainted because they—well, their families—rejected the new Slavic order. They had chosen Italy.
For others (like Corinna's second-grade teacher) they
were tainted because they were Slavs in disguise, flooding
across the border, imposing upon Italy, taking jobs away
from real Italians.

To make her situation worse, Corinna's father (who
had remained in Losinj) was not married to her mother. "I
don't know how all the children knew," Corinna told me.
"But they did. And they jeered at me all the more."

What was to become of Corinna? Her grandmother was worried. Oscar, Corinna's uncle and the first of the Sambos to escape, was beginning a new life in New York City. He had been working as a mariner and had jumped ship to enter the country. Luckily, Caterina Lettich's niece Genni had been in New York since the twenties and helped Oscar get his green card. Back in Genoa, Maricci hoped that eventually Oscar could sponsor their immigration to the United States, but she knew the process could take years.

Corinna's mother, Vilma, met and married an Italian man, and for a short while, the promise of stability and belonging hovered. Guido Semensato adopted Corinna, gave her his name, as they say. But Maricci never trusted Guido, and indeed within a year he was in prison on a robbery charge. It was then that my parents agreed to bring Corinna to live with us, to adopt her in the hopes of providing a better future. It can't have been easy for her mother or her grandparents to let her go; they did it for her. It was difficult for Corinna to leave their love, especially her grandmother's, to travel to a strange country and join a family she hardly knew.

My mother helped her sisters in any way she could. On the infrequent occasions they managed to visit with each other, they fought, sudden summer storms of screams, slammed doors, and tears. Still, until the last few years, Mum never stopped sending money back. My parents took in two of Enea's sons, one after the other, when I was little in England.

They took in Corinna for the sake of my aunt Maricci, but they also did it for me. I was a lonely child—plump, bookish, and clumsy. In the early years in Canada, when

they were settling in, finding their way, we moved so often
that I went to twelve schools in seven years. I was never
anyplace long enough to develop friends or to feel at ease.
At least, that was my excuse. Like most immigrants, my
parents worked long hours—days, evenings, some weekends. When I was eight, nine, ten, Mum worked for other
families as a housekeeper and babysitter while I was home
alone. For years, she worked for the Kwong family. Mrs.
Kwong was very ill with a kidney disease, and Mum looked
after the two little girls. She particularly doted on Dale,
the younger. Now Dale, who is a playwright in Calgary,
tells me Mum gave her loving care. And all these years
later, I think, *Mum was more maternal to her than to me.*

Corinna was to be my companion (as Rosa was to have
been Lea's in Trieste). She arrived in Calgary on a bitterly
cold January night, a little girl with big, round, blue eyes.
She shrank from the new faces, the confusion of voices, the
arctic wind. By summer, she had slipped into a new culture, country, language, and family, as she had before and
would again, when she married into the Gonzales family.

Dad grew to love her in his nondemonstrative British
way. Mum was as conflicted, as domineering, as difficult,
as generous, and as angry a mother to Corinna as she was
to me. No wonder Corinna left as soon as she finished
high school. But Corinna has told me that she has had
a better life because she joined our family, that her life
would have been narrower, poorer, if she had stayed with
her mother. "I learned many things," she said.

However, I was the lucky one. When Corinna came to
Calgary, she diverted the laser of my mother's attention
from the back of my neck. And her companionship, her

example, her experience, and her sisterly love over the years broadened my life. There is a common Italian insult, *Va a malora,* the equivalent of "Go to hell" but literally calling down an evil time—darkness and ruin—upon the recipient. When Corinna's grandmother sent her to us, it was to save her from potential *malora.* And Corinna's two half-brothers did eventually go to ruin in New York City, becoming drug addicts. The older one committed suicide at twenty-five; the other one still lives under the shadow of addiction.

Still, I don't think Corinna needed us; she is one of those rare hardy flowers who will bloom wherever she is planted. At least I was no Pina or Lea. I recognized the importance of an ally; I welcomed the wayfaring girl. In that unhappy house (for my parents fought and fought) in that barren suburb, Corinna and I offered shelter one to the other; we created a point of reference, a grounding, an acceptance. Together, we were at home.

SOMETIME IN THE third year of my caring for my mother, she forgot who I was. She recognized me as someone familiar but no longer understood that I was her daughter, no longer called me by name.

"She asks about her sister all the time," Helen, a recent home-care worker, told me. "Asks where she is, when she's coming back." Helen was pretty and never condescending, and Mum talked to her more than to the others. "Today she said her sister took her to an expensive restaurant."

"Sister? No, that's me. We went to the top of the Chateau Lacombe last week for her birthday." I was surprised and pleased that Mum had noticed it was a good

restaurant and even boasted of it. I had found the outing
a strain. She wanted to go but as usual resisted my dressing her, insisted on an old silk dress that was now much
too big, the neckline falling off her shoulders, insisted on
pantyhose. I only got the pantyhose on with Tatiana's help;
we pulled, pushed, and yanked. At the restaurant, Mum
complained that the soup was too hot and the chicken too
salty. I was afraid she would take her top teeth out, the
only ones she still wore, put them on the plate of food,
shock the waiter, disgust Antonia, and embarrass the rest
of us. So I cajoled her, threatened her, *don't, don't, don't,*
and as soon as she took out her teeth, I snatched them up
in a Kleenex and hid them in my bag.

"Maybe it's time to give these jaunts up," Marco said.

And part of me longed to, oh yes, the petty part, *keep
her at home,* the childish part, *confined,* longed to scream
and storm and cry. *Look what you are doing to me.* My
hands itched to grab her shoulders and shake her. Those
frail, narrow shoulders. And now Helen was telling me
that the celebration dinners did make an impression on
Mum. How could I begrudge her an outing when she had
so little left in her life?

In the first year or two of care, I had arranged for visits by an old friend or a lady from the church. But Mum
was beyond making conversation, beyond wanting to see
anyone that she couldn't recognize as familiar, as *one of
ours.* She was declining day by day, becoming more inac-
cessible, hysterical, frightened. I was used to the repeated
questions and the delusions. But now the moments of connection were shrinking, the symptoms of dementia more
prominent and persistent.

When I came home from an evening out, if I asked whether Helen or Jody had come, she would insist three women had appeared to help her wash and prepare for bed. "I'm tired of all these people," she'd say. If she saw Antonia, Tatiana, and me, she worried about *the other one*. Where was she? she would ask three, five, ten times. And, resurrecting the old obsession, who was the girls' mother?

"Me," I would say. "I'm their mother," hauling out the photo albums.

"No, their real mother."

"That's me. Look, here's a picture of me and Tatiana when we just got back from the hospital."

"Impossible. You never had children."

And it hit me—Mum wasn't assigning me to the generic role of sister. She thought I was Giaconda, unmarried, childless, annoying. The family pain in the ass. They had always fought, the two sisters; when Aunt Giaconda came to Calgary for six months, when we went to Italy in the summer, they couldn't stop themselves. They squabbled, lobbed nasty comments back and forth. *No, no,* yelled one. *No, no, no,* yelled the other.

What a melodrama, said Gina, wife of my cousin Lino. We were all in Veli Losinj that time in 1970, on a month-long vacation—sea, sun, barbecued fish, dancing on the beach (for me), romance (for me), eating and laughing under the stars, the whole gang of us, aunts and cousins and friends. And on each almost perfect day, the sisters argued. No, no, no. It's like the opening of the Mina song, Gina said. (Mina was an Italian pop star.) Each "no" is one note higher and louder.

On my parents' last trip to Venice, a little over a year before my father's heart attack, the conflict between the sisters deepened into estrangement. They fell out over their different versions of the past, different presentiments of their respective futures.

In her later years, Giaconda became obsessed with money or, more precisely, with her lack of it. She had worked at low-paying jobs most of her life and faced old age with a modest state pension and a $40,000 nest egg. As long as it was in the bank, she felt that (as she put it) she would not end up on the street. She'd lived for over thirty years with Lino, her nephew, and Gina. More than other nieces and nephews, they (and their two children) were her family, her "comfort in old age," her home. Then the owner of their apartment died, and his heirs decided to sell. Giaconda shared Lino and Gina's desire to remain in their home and neighborhood. Like them, she dreaded the thought of moving out of Venice to the cheaper and nastier Mestre. She understood that their own means were modest, that they needed her contribution to manage the purchase. But as soon as she handed over her life savings, she resented Gina for having asked and Lino for pressuring her. She felt the harsh winds of scarcity buffeting her about.

She wrote to those of her nieces and nephews who lived in the United States and Canada, for she knew— oh, she was sure—that everyone in America was rich and problem free. She wrote letter after letter begging: a hundred dollars, twenty, anything would help. She was old and ill and could not manage on her pension. Venice was ruinously expensive. She should have left long ago, but where could she go now, at her age? Most, including Corinna and me, sent her the odd fifty.

The day after Dad and Mum arrived on their last visit, Giaconda took her brother-in-law aside. As usual, she flattered him: he was so good, so intelligent, not hard like Rosina. "You must promise me a monthly stipend. It is the least you can do."

"We'll see," Dad said, later claiming he'd been jet-lagged and not thinking straight. He would have answered the same way, probably, even well rested. Everyone in the family knew he had trouble saying no.

When he told Mum, she screamed so loud, Gina said, she could be heard across the *calle*. And she challenged Giaconda. "How dare you? I worked hard for my money. Do you think I found it on the ground? That all I had to do was bend over and pick it up?"

"Your money? Your husband's money, you mean. And he wouldn't be your husband if it wasn't for me. I made your marriage for you. You owe me."

Mum, who was starting to forget large chunks of her past, was positive that Giaconda had not introduced them. "You are making it up." (And my aunt had never made this claim to me.) Dad, who showed no signs of dementia, admitted he could not remember.

Giaconda wouldn't let it go. Each morning when Dad came down to breakfast, she would be waiting in the lobby. She'd watch him eat, then follow him back up to the hotel room and wake up Rosina. "I never sleep in," Giaconda would say. "She spilled the milk; I never do that. She can hardly stand. I can walk all over the city. She doesn't deserve Teddi; I know how to treat a man like him." Giaconda spoke softly, as if to herself; Mum often didn't hear the comments. But she got the gist.

She yelled at her sister, who yelled back. Bad, bad, bad, Giaconda said.

Insupportable, Mum said. *Va a remengo,* she said. (Go to ruin, go wander, which was cruel under the circumstances.) Please—both of you—please, Dad said. Sometimes Mum punched her sister in the arm or the chest. And Giaconda would pinch or scratch. The two old women flailed at each other in a way they never had as children. And after, Giaconda would be smug, satisfied. You see, you see how she is.

Day after day, the sisters fought about what had and hadn't happened at the end of the war. They were never reconciled. After Mum and Dad returned to Edmonton, Giaconda sent them a series of raging and incoherent letters. I can see now that her desperation was a sign of her encroaching dementia. As Mum's stinginess was a sign of hers. She had never been hard in the way that her sister accused her; she was known for her generosity. But both felt the other was lying out of perversity and spite; both were ruled by a foolish, yet frightening, anger.

31

Memory is imagination
pinned down.

Mason Cooley, CITY APHORISMS

on the lagoon

IN 1945, MY MOTHER and Giaconda were roommates, sharing a tiny attic apartment in a palace on the Grand Canal. But in Mum's story of how she met Dad that spring, Giaconda was never mentioned. I had the impression Mum was living alone, as she had for many years, when the fateful meeting occurred. It was Lino who, in pointing out to me where his aunts had lived, confirmed—at the very least—Giaconda's presence. "Those years," Lino said, "we all took refuge here in Venice."

Venice was not immune to the effects of the war. After the Italian government capitulated to the Allies and the Nazis occupied the area, much of the sizable Jewish population of the city was deported to the concentration camps.

And one of Mum's standard stories was the time she witnessed ss officers retaliating for the killing of one of their own. It was early morning; she was on the vaporetto on her way to work. The German soldiers rounded up the first ten males they could find, pulling some of them out of their beds. They were mostly boys, a couple of old men. Several of them were still in their pajamas. The driver of the vaporetto had been ordered to remain at the station. The passengers were supposed to watch, to learn not to support the Resistance. The ten were lined up at the edge of the canal. The wives and the mothers were held back but begging, begging. Children, Mum would repeat, little boys. "Then they were shot—so fast," she would tell me. "So fast it hardly seemed real. And the screams, you don't forget them. Oh, I can still see them, those boys, floating in the canal. You don't forget."

But Venice felt safer than the mainland—less likely to be bombed or to suffer fighting in the streets—and consequently the city was overflowing with refugees, jammed with ten times the population it has today. Enea and her family moved from Chioggia to the Lido, and Giaconda left Padua and took shelter with Rosa. (In her version, Rosina was not helping her out; she was helping Rosina by moving in with her, contributing to the rent money.)

Did they get along then? I can't imagine it. Mum was only a couple of years older, but she had more experience of the world; she hadn't remained a shopgirl in Padua. She'd gone abroad, lived in Tunisia. And she would not have refrained from telling Giaconda how naive she was. She would try (and fail) to boss her little sister around. Still, they stayed together in those close quarters. What choice did they have?

Until my father arrived and kicked them out. The story was told so often that it passed into family myth. Dad met

Mum when he took over the house in which she was living for officers' quarters.

Dad had been in North Africa; then he was part of the Allied invasion of Italy, landing in Ancona and moving north. By the time he reached the Veneto, he had been at war for three years and had obtained the rank of captain. He'd also learned how to speak Italian, the only man in his company to do so, and so became the unofficial translator and liaison with the natives.

When the Allied forces entered Venice, the different armies were not concerned about any possible opposition from remaining pockets of German soldiers. Their common objective was to secure the best place for headquarters. The New Zealanders, for example, whose general had visited Venice before the war, planned their entry carefully. They captured the Royal Danieli, which was (and still is) one of the world's great hotels. The Royal Engineers were obviously more used to building bridges and defusing land mines than strategizing invasions; they had to settle for the Palazzo Grimani to house their headquarters and the undistinguished Palazzo Giustiani-Persico, near San Toma, for officers' quarters. All the inhabitants from the countess on down were displaced.

Mum never said where she (or Giaconda) went. I imagine they moved in with Enea, her husband, and their five children in their small apartment on the Lido. Certainly, there would have been little room for her things. Luckily, the pleasant Capitano Eduardo (as she then called him) told her she could leave a few boxes in her room. And since most of her clothes were still there, she had to return to the palazzo frequently.

The capitano—Teddi she was soon calling him—was courteous, attentive. When he invited her to an officers' party, she accepted.

That was it—their story, a "How We Met" column in the daily newspaper, a founding myth. But Giaconda remembered it differently, or at least she did by their last visit. She was insistent. She had met Capitano Teddi first, for she was the one who kept returning to the Persico to pick up her and Rosina's clothes. Her sister, always the lazy one, had sent her. The capitano was courteous; he smiled and joked with her. And one day he invited her to the officers' dance. But she was working that evening, and besides, she was seeing that jeweler's son, the one who turned out to be a thief. She only wished she had known at the time. So out of the goodness of her heart, she suggested that he take her sister, whom he had met once or twice. And she persuaded Rosina to keep the appointment and even lent her a dress, her violet silk. "I introduced them," Giaconda said. "If it wasn't for me, that marriage would have never happened."

When they began to date, it was Giaconda who encouraged Rosina, Giaconda who told her to ignore nasty gossips, Giaconda who said you're old enough to know your own mind, Giaconda who advised her to ignore her brothers. Ermanno and Santo had no right to wave the specter of family honor, no right to forbid Rosina to keep company with an English soldier. "Now they were concerned?" Giaconda said. "And what could they do from Trieste?"

I suspect Mum didn't need much encouraging. I can see how much she was enjoying herself in the snapshots from the time. And Dad too. He was only twenty-four,

twenty-five, during his time in Venice, younger looking than his fellow soldiers in the surviving photos and
already assigned to a special commission and in charge
of all watercraft for the port. He had mahogany water
taxis and sailing yachts at his disposal. His leather-
covered album with the neatly printed caption provides
a clear photographic record. Under the label "At Work,"
small photos of tugboats, cranes, military trucks, and
launches. Under "At Play," yachting, pictures of a sailboat,
The Santa Barbara, in dock and out on the lagoon. In the
latter, Frank is at the helm, or smiling under the sail, the
only one of the group of soldiers wearing a shirt; he could
get sunburned in five minutes. Under "Officer's Mess,"
snaps of various angles of a palatial room with a carved
marble-front fireplace and a half-dozen pillowy divans.

The war was over, and for thirteen months—what
could be sweeter—Venice was his, theirs, Frank and
Rosa's—Capitano Teddi and Rosina's. They felt the city
and their future were open and available. The salons of
the elite, the bar at the Gritti, the parties under the chan-
deliers of the Danieli. Places where Rosa had never dreamt
she would go—not as a guest, at least. The deck of *The
Santa Barbara* on outings to the far islands of the lagoon.
The back of a private launch, the boatsman navigating the
maze of canals, *Look at me, you nasty cows.* The capitano
had his own driver and his own valet—a batman he was
called—to take care of his things. *Talk all you want. An
Englishman, so there.*

I never saw this album until after Dad was gone, when
I was clearing out the condo. Why? Could they not bear
to look at the way they used to be? The pictures do feel

private—the two of them, together on the motor launch, in a garden on the Lido, at a ritzy restaurant with fresh flowers, a bottle of wine, and plates of gnocchi on the table and two white-coated waiters hovering. In a larger professional picture of a crowded dance floor, I find them in midstep. A fox-trot, slow, slow, quick, quick, the music rises up from the glossy surface of the photo, from the uniforms and the evening dresses, the gilt chairs and the marble columns: "You've Got to Accentuate the Positive"—promenade, close, spin, close. Rosa's expression is carefree, happy, unlike before, precourtship, unlike after, postmarriage, unlike her wedding pictures when she looks apprehensive and determined. These photos tell me that then—May 1945 to July 1946—then she was happy.

She wrote to Teddi, "You brought me happiness." I found the phrase and other more intimate expressions in a small book with a blue-flowered cover. The book is dedicated to Capitano Eduduar (no one seemed to manage Frank William Edwards), to remind him of his time in Venice, and is signed by a Marina Buonamici. And on most of the pages of thick cream paper, someone has glued in standard views of Venice, but toward the end, Rosa has written her messages of love. "Don't forget me." I was surprised. Mum gave me the impression that they were engaged before he left Venice for a new deployment in Trieste. Instead, Rosina was uncertain of his commitment. I was even more surprised by her diction. "I was a thirsty flower awaiting the sweet kiss of rain." Where did such words come from? They seem so foreign to the mother I knew. A book, I suspect, a romance. *Grilli per la testa.* Crickets in the brain.

I'm not sure what the Royal Engineers were doing in Trieste in the summer of 1946, but the city, unlike the rest of Italy, was still not at peace. It was under British and American armed forces command, claimed by Italy and Yugoslavia, an official area of strain. I wish I'd asked my father about his experiences in Trieste. I wish I'd asked him about all of his experiences in the army—North Africa, the Adriatic coast of Italy—and about Venice. I was interested in listening to his stories only after I could no longer do so. During his last years, he spoke often of writing his memoirs. If he had, they would have been worth reading. He had an easy, clear prose style. But how could he, ground down as he was by the daily care of my mother?

It was the Royal Engineers, during nine days of October 1954, who measured out along the so-called Morgan Line the border between Yugoslavia and Italy, dividing villages, farms, and even homes in half. Of course, Dad did not take part; he was back in England by then.

At some point during his time in Trieste, Frank went back to Venice on a break and gave Rosa an engagement ring. They were married in Great Doddington, Northamptonshire, England, in June 1947, a month after Dad left the army.

THE SUMMER BEFORE Dad died, Giaconda's dementia progressed from subtle to obvious. On the first night of a holiday up in the mountains, Giaconda went down for dinner clad only in underpants and a bra. Before Lino managed to arrive and collect her (he'd been phoned at once), she was spotted naked walking down a corridor.

Husbandless and childless, Giaconda had been the backdrop to the lives of others. If (as I cannot help thinking) the actions of a person suffering from dementia are not random but carry some sediment of meaning, Giaconda's public nakedness was a step onto center stage. *Look at me.* Or was it a provocation?

You nasty cows. Once, in the rest home where she died, she smeared the walls of another resident's bathroom with her feces. *I showed them,* she told Gina.

When I told Mum of Giaconda's death, she would not believe me. "It was quick," I said.

"No," Rosa said.

"A good way to go. Drinking her *caffelatte* in the evening. That is what Gina told me."

"No, she was here."

"What should we send? Flowers or a telegram, or both?"

"No. They're trying to trick us."

"Who? Gina? Lino? And why would they?"

"They want my money. So they are saying the woman's dead."

"Your sister, my aunt Giaconda, is gone. They just wanted us to know."

"I don't believe it," Mum said, shaking her head slowly. "You can't fool me. I saw her."

Even a few months earlier, I would have tried to find the meaning in her denial of her sister's death, but now I was exhausted, numb. Whatever, I thought—like some sullen teenager—whatever.

32

Thus we sailed up the straits,
groaning in terror, for on the one side
we had Scylla, while on the other the
mysterious Charybdis sucked down
the salt sea water in her dreadful way.

Homer, THE ODYSSEY, XII

a difficult passage

BY THE THIRD YEAR of caring for my mother, I was losing patience. I couldn't go on, yet what was the alternative? By the Third Year, by the Fourth Winter: I began capitalizing the units of time to mark and make significant their passage. Because my days felt both trivial and endless. Because I was losing hope and conviction. I was losing myself and my mind.

For some time after Mum had moved into our house, our relationship had been easier. I adjusted; she calmed down. But by the third year, she feared not the dark man who entered in the night but me (*her sister*). By then, she accused me of poisoning her. All her pills, she was sure, were poison, and when she needed antibiotics and the doctor prescribed liquid because she could not swallow such large pills, she was even more recalcitrant. I would beg her, *please, you need your medicine, please.* But sicker and weaker than usual, she was also crazier. She'd purse her lips and shake her head. *You take it.* I stirred the liquid into juice and crushed pills into butterscotch pudding. I held a spoon in one hand and a piece of chocolate in the other. Eventually, I would win, but the battle exhausted me.

And sometimes, and not just because of the medicines, she cursed me: *Va a remengo, va in mona.* Go astray, go to ruin, be lost. *Crepa.* Drop dead. I couldn't allow myself to analyze her words. A symptom of the Alzheimer's, I told myself. Nothing personal. It's not worth thinking about. It's not worth reacting.

Crepa. Che ti vien un colpo. Drop dead. May you be struck down. She had used such words before, not just when I was a girl. But those times were infrequent, and I usually could walk away. Leave the house, retire to my room. Now I had to stop myself from reacting. Swallow my emotions.

Now and then, she tried to hit Mila, who was the soul of patience, and more often, Sandra, who was the home-care worker Mum disliked the most. The woman was a dog trainer and eerily efficient in getting Rosa to do what she didn't want to do.

One hundred demons per (red) hair, my mother used to say to me, when I lost my temper as a child. *Cento diavoli per capel.* Then she had infuriated me as no one else could or ever would. Now, bound again to her needs and moods, I was subject to embarrassing fits of anger. At least I nearly always managed to control them. My face would flush red, my heart would pound, but I would act and speak as I should. Still, part of me longed to let go, to shriek and stamp and frighten her. To make her understand how terrible the situation was, how hard and frustrating for me, how dire for her. To break out of my indenture.

In Italian, *volere bene* is the phrase used for non-passionate love—to wish well or good. *Mi vuoi male,* my mother accused me. You wish me evil. And I would deny it, indignant after all I was doing for her. One of the times, she was incontinent, and I was trying to clean her off, but there was shit everywhere. I hadn't said a word, but she must have read my face. She said, "You wish I was dead." I didn't answer, didn't reassure her, because in that moment I did wish her gone. She began to scream that I was killing her, killing her.

"No, you're killing me." The unmeasured words slipped out of my mouth.

Every day for two weeks, she claimed I was trying to kill her. This in addition to her usual comments that the pills were poison. I would try to soothe and jolly her. The truth was I did long for her death. I imagined it. When I went to bed at night, I would envision walking into her room the next morning and finding that she'd died in her sleep. But once I conjured the image of finding her small, shriveled body lying there, rigid and cold, I would be seized with dread. Then I was afraid that it would happen.

And I was afraid that I was dying, too. "We're all dying," my doctor reminded me. But my fear was more primitive; it was her death, the decay of her mind, then her body, that was burrowing into me. I had to fight the urge to run away, to save myself. I had to steel myself to touch her gently, to give her a goodnight kiss or hug. And if she flinched, if she looked at me with frightened eyes, I wondered how we had become death for each other.

I was lost on the sea of duty, navigating between a stone cliff and a whirlpool. *Crepa.* Shipwreck.

The doctor prescribed an antipsychotic for my mother and a new antidepressant for me. The little pills, yellow for her, purple for me, calmed both of us. She didn't take her medicines any more willingly; she grumbled about the extra pill. But she did take them and her habitual exclamation—*veleno*—sounded like a comment on the medicines rather than on what I was trying to do to her. At the same time, I was less irritable. I could express unforced affection and concern, could care for her with care.

"*Brava,*" she said once or twice.

"Your mother always was a manic-depressive," said my friend Karen, who had known me for more than thirty years. Her comment had the force of revelation. Why hadn't I seen it before? All that nerve-fed energy. All that whirlwind activity. Manic, unpredictable, yes, yes, no, no—work, work, work.

Mum had cleaned and washed and ironed for family and boarders. She had made her own fresh pasta and bread, pies, and jams. Let me give credit where it is due. She sewed clothes for herself and for Corinna and me. (A bit too big, so that we could grow into them; a bit frumpy, so that our body shapes were obscured.) She crocheted doilies, knitted scarves and sweaters. Let me celebrate as well as complain: the feasts of food, the three-course meals, the cases of peaches and apricots she canned (with my and Corinna's help), the abundance of tomatoes and peppers she bottled into sauce. And this besides working at a full-time job, first as a housekeeper and nanny, later, when she was the age I am now, as part of a janitorial crew, cleaning offices downtown. No wonder she judged my reading to be mere idleness. No wonder she told Giaconda that she worked hard for her money.

"We think she has been on antipsychotics before," said the neurologist at the Glenrose. "Because of the tardive dyskinesia."

"But she had the chewing symptom when she was on the antidepressant Zoloft, not the antipsychotic Rispedral. Thank goodness."

The doctor shrugged. "Some sort of mood-altering drug."

I didn't believe it. My father slipping my mother a pill without her knowing? She would never have admitted she needed to be medicated. She used to call her sisters, husband, and daughter crazy. She was sure she was the sane one.

VA A REMENGO. Without knowing a word of English and against the advice of her brothers, employers, and friends, Rosa Pagan followed Capitano Teddi back to his hometown. Frank did not, as many feared, play the role of the soldier and abandon her. Although he was an Anglican, he immediately married her in the closest Roman Catholic church. Still, Rosa was never welcome in Earls Barton, a Midlands village of two pubs, a Saxon tower, a village green, and five shoe factories.

She was an Eyetie, wasn't she?

One of them, the enemy.

Over the hill and no better than she should be.

And our Frank, the only Barton boy to go to Northampton Grammar on scholarship.

Our Frank.

What was he thinking?

Our Frank.

My grandmother Ada was particularly hostile to this man-trapping war bride, this, this *foreigner*. ("Your grandma wasn't one to hang back," said Brian, one of my English cousins, when we visited him in 2007. "She spoke her mind.") In the first months, until the newlyweds bought the row house next door, Frank and Rosa lived with his parents. Rosa was not allowed in the kitchen. After all, they were an English family; this was a meat, spuds, and veg house. They would have none of your nasty spaghetti, none of your oil or your garlic or other foreign muck. Not in this house. And not in Rosa and Frank's either. Thank you very much.

Grandfather Fred was kinder to Mum. He didn't just speak over or around her. He tried to communicate through gestures and repetition. When she was pregnant, he hoarded rations to bring her the odd banana or chocolate bar. "He was excited about you," Mum told me. "He couldn't wait for your birth. He was sure you would be a girl, so he would try to pronounce your name. We planned it ahead—Renato for my father if it was a boy, Caterina for my mother if it was a girl. But he couldn't say it right, so he'd call you Katey." (And that was all right. It was what my grandmother was called too, Katé.)

Mum's first pregnancy had ended in a miscarriage. He was a boy, she would tell me for the next fifty years. "I lost my boy." She was soon expecting again. I was due in mid-November, but days and weeks passed and nothing. On December 3, my grandfather, who was in his mid-fifties, had a heart attack and died. After the funeral, Mum finally went into labor. "It was difficult and long; three days. I suffered with you," she said. But she never screamed or groaned. She knew that the cold-eyed nurses expected her to: *those Eyeties make such a fuss.* She would confound them. (Despite her hysterical character, Mum was always stoic about physical pain. When I was a teenager, she twice passed a kidney stone at home without making a sound.)

A specialist was brought in from Northampton. Dad was told that he had to choose between mother and child and that he might lose both of us. We were saved through a high-forceps delivery. I was so bruised and battered that the decision was made to keep me from my mother. No use upsetting her. She'd lost so much blood. She was weak and not herself.

She begged to see me. The nursing Sisters pretended not to understand her, though she repeated "baby" and "please" over and over. Mum's breasts leaked, and the head Sister brought her someone else's baby, a boy, to nurse. My father tried to reassure her that I was fine, a healthy, red-haired girl, the biggest baby in the nursery, but he seemed distracted, halfhearted. Mum began to fear that I was dead and that they were keeping the news from her until she was stronger. The Sister said, "Tomorrow we'll bring her to you." But tomorrow came and passed and the next day and the next, and the witch was still saying tomorrow.

Now Mum knew that the nurses, the doctor, and Ada were all conspiring against her, plotting to take her baby away, to give her to someone else, someone English to raise. Or they had stolen her already. Teddi, too; he was in on it. He wasn't stopping them. He wasn't defending his wife.

Mum waited until the other new mothers on the ward were asleep. When she stood and took a step—it was her first time without help—she saw black spots. She moved slowly with one hand out to help steady herself. The floor shifted, the corridor tilted, but she pressed on. Clinging to the shadows, past the bright nursing station, past an empty desk, drawn by the distant sound of the newborns. She heard their cries. Heard my wails. Her breasts responded, wetting the front of her nightgown. Past the nursery Sister. Finding me worse than she thought, finding me swollen black and blue and red, finding me under an open window, the cold dark air beating down.

They were trying to kill me.

Even years later, Mum could not see that it was all a cultural misunderstanding. In Italy, a current of cold air, of December air, is considered dangerous for a strong, healthy adult, let alone anyone ill or newborn. In Britain, because of Florence Nightingale's influence, fresh air is thought to be good for you. Mum remained convinced that either the nursing Sisters set out deliberately to murder me or they would have killed me through their carelessness and neglect. Their ill treatment of me sprang from their hatred of her, because she was a foreigner. She thanked Mother Mary and St. Anthony, who gave her the strength to save me.

In the photographs taken of Mum during her years in England, her unhappiness is obvious. She does not look like the same woman who smiled from the snaps of the courtship in Venice or posed in the wedding portraits. Two years later, admittedly after two pregnancies, she looks forty pounds heavier and a decade older. Her clothes are no longer crisp and elegant but drab and shapeless. I am in each photograph, usually in my father's arms. He smiles at me or the camera. My mother does neither. In one of them, taken by a street photographer in the rain, Grandmother Ada and Dad are in front. They have half-smiles and seem in mid-chat. I am against Dad's shoulder, pointing off to the side. Mum is trailing behind, glowering.

Dad would take Mum up to London to go to the opera or visit some Italian friends they had there. ("Well, I never," Grandmother Ada used to say, thinking the trips were extravagant.) But in the village, Mum felt alone and friendless. She thought when she went out people were whispering about her. They were.

"It was your dad's fault," one of his cousins told me fifty years later. "He should have made your mother speak English."

"Well, your grandma would tell your dad he shouldn't speak Italian to Rosina," explained Brian, who was less judgmental. "But it wasn't so easy for your mum. We all spoke a very strong dialect then. Must have been confusing. Even in Wellingborough [a nearby town], people spoke different from here in Barton."

Dad worked all week, and most weekends he played bass fiddle in a jazz band. Mum wanted him to quit; she hated being left behind with me. He was reluctant. He was deeply musical and loved playing. Still, eventually, as Mum put it, he had to give in.

Until I began writing this chapter, I never considered that Mum might have suffered from postpartum depression, that during my infancy she might have been not just unhappy but clinically depressed. When I had my girls and began hoarding each detail of their development, I did wonder why Mum had no observations, no memories, no stories of my early years. I asked, if only to compare, as I had compared our respective experiences in pregnancy, labor, and nursing, but she could not remember my first words, steps, or tastes.

After Mum came to live with us, she expressed unease each time I told her I was going out. "Where are you going?" she asked. "When are you coming back?" I could feel her fear that I would abandon her.

One of Dad's stories was how, when I was a baby, Mum would abandon me in various places. He'd chuckle. "I'd come home from work and ask, 'Where's Caterina?' And your mum would say, 'In the backgarden'—she did leave you out there a lot. But I'd go and look and look and not find you. I'd panic." Another chuckle. "And she'd realize she must have left you at the shops again. And I'd run and find your pram outside the door of the grocery and you screaming your head off."

"I guess I'm lucky I wasn't kidnapped. Or hurt."

"No, no. This was Barton. Everyone knew who you were. Your Mum would just forget you places. Go in one door and out the other, I guess."

"I guess," I echoed, wondering why no one ever picked me up out of the pram and comforted me. Wondering why, knowing where I belonged, no one ever carried me home.

33

After so long an absence,
he failed to recognize it [Ithaca].

Homer, THE ODYSSEY, XIII

O terra natia, o Istria aspra e rocciosa, addio
To my native land, to bitter
and stony Istria, farewell

Franco Alitalia, unpublished poem

going home

I WANT TO GO HOME. During the Fourth Year of Care, my mother became more insistent. She had been asking since she moved into our house, *take me home,* but now once a week had become once, twice a day. And she said the words to herself besides. *Home.* I would overhear her as I passed her doorway. *Home.*

What was going on in Rosa's head when she used that word? Because the Italian word for home, *casa,* is the same as the one for house, I often flashed through the houses she had lived in. Was she remembering one of those? The condo, just blocks away, crowded with a lifetime of furniture? The modest bungalow, dark under the Nanaimo rain and looming trees? The split-level in monotonous suburban Calgary that was my childhood home? The vertical slice of the old ironstone house in Earls Barton? Not all the rooms, small and often shared, in the homes of others, where she passed her childhood and youth—not them, but the house on the island of Losinj, the house with the orange tree, spacious, well-proportioned, solid, whitewashed, and shining under the Adriatic sun? It was clear in my mind's eye, if not hers; I was recently returned from my visit to Croatia. None of the later ones matched that first one.

I want to go home. I couldn't bundle my mother up, coax her into the car, drive her over to the condo for a visit. The apartment had been partly emptied and rented out. (Many of her things were in the storage unit.) If I'd told her that I had decided to let strangers live in her home, she would have been furious. Even if she could no longer remember where that home was or what it was like, she would have protested. On two separate occasions, I'd asked her permission to sell my father's piano to a close friend, who would treat it well. (It was in the condo unplayed, neglected.) She'd been agitated for hours. A year later, when Mum saw my friend at Christmas, she remembered: "That woman tried to take Franco's piano."

So I knew I was going against Mum's wishes. I felt guilty. But the rent money was needed to cover the condo fees, utilities, and part of Mila's salary, and I was in charge.

I want to go home. Rather than question Mum as to what she meant, I would explain to her again why she needed to live in my house. You need my help, I'd say, prompted by the foolish wish she could, on some level, understand the state she was in and the consequences for me. Mum would insist she could look after herself, she didn't need me, and we'd have one of our useless, circular discussions. I'd have done better to distract her, for on some level, she did understand. That was why she was overcome daily with the unease she expressed in asking to go home.

The repeated request to be taken home is considered a symptom of the second stage of Alzheimer's. It's connected to the loss of an essential body sense—that of direction, of orientation. As I write these words, I am sitting at a desk on the second floor of my house, facing a window. I can see what is before me, but I can feel what is behind me, below me, to my left, past my bedroom. I know where I am. I am aware of my presence, my positioning, in this specific space and place. And this is at the root of my sense of being comfortable, at home.

Mum had lost such body awareness years earlier. And she was ever more disoriented. *This way.* Not at home, even when in her home. She needed to be guided to the kitchen and to the living room. *This way.* When she was in her chair and thus facing away from her bed and bathroom, she did not remember where they were. *Right here, Mum.*

Those suffering from Alzheimer's often wander. They do not "get lost." They are lost, permanently. And since everything around them is unrecognizable, they search for a place of certainty and familiarity that they (and we) call home. Fortunately for me, my mother was not strong or mobile enough to get out of the house and wander. Once I did find her halfway down the basement stairs. *I want to go home.* Another time, she was fumbling with the front doorknob. *Home.*

Managing Mum's physical care, ensuring that she was clean, safe, fed, properly medicated, and reasonably calm brought me both closer to her and farther away. I knew her body, the narrow shoulders, the hollow above her sagging breasts, the rounded, slack stomach, thin legs, swollen ankles and feet. I knew the wrinkles and the moles, the purple clusters of broken veins, the brown spots on her chest and cheek, the iron smell of her hair when it needed washing, the wispy hairs in her armpits and between her legs. I knew her flesh, her matter, as if it were mine. And it did not disgust me (as even less intimate glimpses did when I was younger) or make me want to turn away. Taking care of her body, I grew to accept, to acknowledge it as my first home and a preview of my last one.

And sometimes, unfortunately not always, my touch became gentler, less hasty. But the physical intimacy was mocked by the growing mental estrangement. And it was her mind that I wished I could nurse, restore, know. At four, at forty, at nine and ninety, how did it feel to be Rosa?

I CAME ACROSS a clue while on a different search. I was reading anything I could on the concept of nostalgia, the malady named by Johannes Hofer in his medical dissertation of 1688, in which he combines two Greek words—one that means return to one's country and the other that means pain (so the pain generated by the desire to return to your land). I started with that dissertation and continued all the way to the twentieth-century treatises on nostalgia.

Nostalgia, *le mal du pays,* exile, homesickness. *Unheimlich:* the opposite of belonging to the house or being at home. Freud defines *unheimlich* as "the uncanny. . . all that is terrible" in his 1919 essay of that name. Based on individual cases, he posits that the uncanny "is that class of terrifying which leads back to something long known."

It springs from the repressions of the infantile mind (particularly of recurring anxiety) wherein the familiar becomes unfamiliar.

This theory of repression didn't interest me. But my attention was caught by Freud's observation that people who are oriented in their environment, who know where they are, are unlikely to suffer from the impression that there is something uncanny in the objects or people around them. So a person who was not oriented, because of displacement or, worse, dementia, was more susceptible to the sensation of the *unheimlich,* to "all that arouses dread and creeping horror." More likely to turn a shadow into a dark man or a person into a demon.

And I felt Mum's terror, a cold flame. As I sat in the university library holding the leather-bound book, for a few loud heartbeats, I felt the fear.

The porous border between familiar and unfamiliar, neighbor and stranger, *heimlich* and *unheimlich.*

Between at home and lost.

WHEN MUM AIMED one of her favorite insults at whomever irritated her, *va a remengo,* she was wishing on others what she feared the most for herself: wandering, ruination, homelessness, disorientation.

Mum's disorientation in old age was not the result of a lifetime of displacement. But it was an apt correlative. After she was exiled from Lussingrande, through the years in Caltagirone, Chioggia, Padua, Earls Barton, Kathyrn (Alberta), Stettler, Edmonton, Calgary, Nanaimo, and Edmonton, she never found an unequivocal home. She did feel settled in Venice, which is why that city is not on the list. I cannot blame all these moves for her failure to adjust or to assimilate. I can't ignore the example of Corinna, who took on protective coloring, fitting in wherever she went, adapting to major shifts in culture with goodwill and determination. At some point, perhaps very early, Mum had come to believe that she would not or could not belong, no matter how she tried. So she didn't try, and she didn't fit in. In Italy, England, Canada, too often, those around her literally did not understand where she was coming from. She was misunderstood and misjudged. By her daughter, among all the others.

Because I've lived in Edmonton for many years, as well as having taught a myriad of students, I'm often recognized at the grocery store, a movie, or a yoga class. Someone will say to me, "You're Caterina, aren't you?" Mum spoke of this happening only once, when I was about eleven. She'd been on a bus in Calgary, coming home from one of her many jobs. An older woman was walking down the aisle. She stopped before Mum's seat and looked and looked again. "Rosina Ponaronzo," this stranger said, identifying her by the Pagan family's nickname. "Rosina from Under the Orange Tree."

The lady was Giovannina Francovitch of Lussingrande; she and her husband, Miro, had arrived in Calgary from a refugee camp in Italy in 1958 (two years before she saw my mother on the bus). Mrs. Francovitch recognized Mum not from their childhood, which after all had taken place forty-five years earlier, but from the holidays Mum took in her home village, especially before World War II.

In the spring of this Fourth Year of Care, before I told Mum that Marco and I were planning to visit Losinj, I wondered if she would even recognize the name. And the first time that I said, "We are going to Lussino," she did not respond by word or gesture. Her eyes remained blank. But I brought the trip up again; I did have to prepare her for four weeks in the extended-care hospital. "We want to see how Lussino is now," I said. And then, rather than trying to explain my search, I added, "I'm thinking of writing a book."

"You and your books," Mum said, her face crumpled into an expression of distaste. The next time I mentioned Lussino, she made the connection. "I want to go. I want to see my people."

My people? I had never heard her use that phrase before. My people—when she didn't know those who were with her every day, Marco and me, for example. My people: did she mean her relatives—nearly all dead or gone? Or a broader kinship? A vaguer longing that she attached to the name Lussino?

She had always been proud to say she was from Lussino. She would declare that she was Italian but add Venetian/Istrian/Lussignan. She never hid that fact, never denied her origin, as so many Istrians did, claiming they were born in Florence rather than Pola, Venice rather than Fiume. Because they were ashamed; because they'd been shamed. ("You are from there," I would say enthusiastically. And he or she would deny it, flaring up, "Not me, no, not me.")

I was packing her suitcase for the extended-care center when she surprised me again. "Take some good coffee," she said.

"What? When?"

"To Lussino. And aspirins."

I didn't bother arguing. I smiled at the suggestion, pleased that my mother was aware enough to make it. But it wasn't 1954 or 1970, when packages from those who had left helped support those who remained.

Her people: I looked for them on the island of Losinj. I found churches and piazzas, captains' villas, Hapsburg homes, an emperor's jetty, a walled graveyard on a cliff over the sea, a medieval tower with a concrete balustrade, all bearing witness to what had been, to the old multiethnic place. The broken walls, the ruined houses, the fences of white stone all told a story but in a language few were left to understand. *Cosa ti vol?* What do you expect? St. Anthony's bells tolling the hours, the waves beating on the shore, the oak leaves rustling in the wind. Like the cries of the seagulls, Istro-Veneto, rising, falling, dying away.

Suso e soso: up and down, round and round.

The cities and the towns of white stone were empty, abandoned. Once? Twice? Ten times?

Her people were scattered to the four corners of the earth. And the culture—the last embers glowed in a club in Sydney, flickered in a restaurant on Long Island, flared bright in a kitchen in Seattle. And on the Istrianet Web site, under the direction, the blood, sweat, and tears, of Marisa Ciceran—a virtual rebirth.

A new people came to the island, once, twice, in the last sixty years.

It's always up—then down, round and round. Everything made by man and woman, everything of man and woman ends in ruins.

34

*Returning home, Ulysses does not
put an end to leaving. He thinks
of future odysseys... Ulysses both
returns and does not return.*

Vladimir Jankélévitch, L'IRRÉVERSIBLE ET LA NOSTALGIA

*Because its cities are empty,
its population dispersed*

Czeslaw Milosz, "The Fall"

what remains

MY MOTHER DIED at the end of that fourth year. My duty to care for her was done, but not my responsibility. I still struggled to understand the story of her life, to recover a few of her lost memories, to braid that rope bridge of stories over a sinkhole of oblivion.

In a speech that Triestine writer Claudio Magris gave on May 1, 2004, to mark the signing of the accord that opened the border between Italy and Slovenia, he stated that memory is a fundamental value. The border, which had been surveyed by the Royal Engineers in October 1954 after years of bloodshed, acrimony, and diplomatic maneuverings, separated more than two countries: it divided one part of Istria from another. (Of course, the border between Slovenia and Croatia that went up in 1991 still separates two other sections of the region.) Magris, a major European writer, has had a long connection to the region, and his wife, Marisa Marieri, was an exile from Fiume whose family, in his words, "had to leave, losing everything." He reminded the assembled dignitaries celebrating the new Europe that the violence and, above all, the victims of "these *our* lands" must be remembered.

"Memory is a fundamental value: it is not nostalgia for the past but a defense and rescue of life, a sense of the presence of every life and every value." He quoted the poet Marin: *All is present (the past does not exist)*. Magris noted the difference between this memory that frees us and a bitter, obsessive memory, which obstructs growth by keeping a grim account of wrongs suffered. (And certainly I came across too much of this type of memory during my research, on both sides.) A glorying in one's status as victim, an attitude that Magris described as: "I killed your brother, but you, thank God, killed two of my brothers."

A FEW MONTHS after Mum's death, I saw on Istrianet that some archives from the islands of Cres and Losinj had become available through the Church of Latter-Day Saints. All I had to do was drive to the closest Mormon temple, pay five dollars, and order the microfiches for Lussingrande from Salt Lake City. It was anticlimactically easy. Threading the film through a loop, turning a squeaking handle, and peering at a lighted screen had none of the romance of perusing the archival books of Venice.

I went twice to look at Veli Losinj indexes and spent all afternoon both times. As I had been told, the island's archives from the latter part of the nineteenth century and the early part of twentieth were missing. But I went through all the records that had survived and been copied, including the baptisms and weddings from 1824 to 1957. There were numerous Lettiches, who I presumed were not direct ancestors, since my grandmother's family had originally (I was told) come from San Pietro dei Nembi, a neighboring island. And to my surprise, a number of Pagans, the dates stretching back to the 1840s, and several with the first name Rosa. (In the Ellis Island records, I also found a Rosa Pagan from Lussingrande, who entered the United States in 1920. And inevitably I wished I knew the details of her life. She must have been some sort of a relative.)

I found the right Onorato Pagan and family (residing at house number 96) in the Austrian government census of 1912 that recorded the inhabitants of Lussingrande by domicile and listed names, birth dates, and ethnicity. I laughed when I saw the dates, startling an elderly gentleman, who was conducting his own genealogical inquiry in the next booth. According to the census, Mum had been telling the truth when she claimed that her passport was wrong in declaring she was born on August 30, 1910. And if so, her birth certificate, which bore the same date, was also wrong, even though it had been issued by the Archdiocese of Zadar.

In the census, her birth date was down as August 30, 1908. Had she fooled us all? Including the parish priest of the village? After all, the church records had been destroyed, and the census was probably not available to Monsignor Haracich when he signed the birth certificate in 1947. Or was the census wrong? It listed my aunt Enea, mother of four, as male. It also classified (at house number 90) my grandmother's family—her mother, Giovanna; her brother, Filippo; and her sister Antonia—as ethnically *Slav*. Yet my grandmother Caterina was classified as Italian. So what accounted for the switch? Did marriage do it? Did Caterina herself decide her identity? Or was it simply an error? And was the error in the classification of Giovanna and children or in that of Caterina? Hadn't Maria Lettich in Losinj said that "our family of Lettich" always spoke Italian, meaning Istro-Veneto? But did that make them Italian? And how reliable was her memory? She was ninety-three when I interviewed her. And what about the nickname, Ponaronzo—that was Croatian—meaning not of the orange tree, as I had been told, but under the orange tree.

Round and round, this shell game, find-the-identity, was both dizzying and foolish. Round and round, faster than the eye could see or the heart could know. And yet, the wager had been a home, a country, a life.

My presumptions about my grandfather were even more circular, even more confused. He drowned, he didn't; he fought, he didn't. I had clung to the theory that he had been one of Nazario Sauro's men, because it gave him a ready-made identity. I could imagine him in that submarine. It fit symbolically. The records of Sauro's court-martial had been destroyed in 1929 by a fire in the Judenplatz in Vienna.

Gradually I had to give up the idea that he had died in that way. Surely the children of such heroes would not have been shunted off to Sicily. And surely the widow Caterina and her children would have been given some sort of pension and not been so destitute. In my mind, I moved him from this side to that. He was born in Italy. He was living under Austria. He could have drowned while on another boat. All kinds sank because of mines in the Adriatic Sea, from torpedo boats to a luxury liner, the *Baron Gautsch*, which did the Lussinpiccolo-Trieste run.

I discovered that many Italian-Istrians were drafted to fight for Austria. The military command did not deploy them on the Italian front, so close by, stretching from outside Trieste along the Isonzo River (now in Slovenia), across the tops of the mountains of the Eastern Dolomites to the Altopiano. The Giuliani could not be trusted to fight the Italian troops, to make (vertical) war on soldiers who could literally be their neighbors or brothers. So they were expedited to the other end of the Austro-Hungarian Empire, forced onto Russian battlefields.

My grandfather could have been one of these reluctant soldiers. I wrote to the Austrian military headquarters for information, and they answered me, six months later, saying I should hire a specialist to search the archives in Vienna. And I was still considering this expensive proposition when I was nudged back in the opposite direction.

In May 2004, Marco and I were visiting Armida's son, Antonio, in Koper, Slovenia. He was showing off various treasures of Lussino, ancient maps and drawings, when he pointed to a framed portrait. "That's my mother's father," he said. "Your great uncle. Vincenzo."

"He's in uniform," I said. "Must be from the Great War."

"Yes, he was in the Battle of Kobarid." Antonio was speaking English with a marked Slavic accent.

"Caporetto? He was with the Austrians, right?"

"But not at all. His uniform, you can see—it is Italian."

So if one brother made his way to Italy to fight, had the other? Onorato was much older than Vincenzo. My grandfather was forty-one and had eight children when the war began. I realized that it didn't make sense for him to enlist on either side. But he may have had no choice.

The answer arrived while I was rechecking information on the camp in Caltagirone. My cousin Leda, Aunt Maricci's oldest daughter, relayed what she had been told: "The last time Mamma saw her father, our grandfather, she was so afraid, she said she could never forget."

THIS IS WHAT I now believe happened:

APRIL 1915

Rosina's legs are trembling, trembling. She can't make them stop. Mamma and Papa are already down the aisle heading for the doors of the church. Rosina feels a pointy finger in her back. "Go. Go." Her brothers push by, and she almost falls back onto the seat. And Santo stomps on her foot.

"Aiii," Rosina says.

Her big sister Maricci gives her a little shove: "You're blocking the way." Mamma and Papa are walking out with the rest of the people into the angry buzz of the piazza. They don't look back. And Rosina knows its bad, what's outside the cathedral doors, bad. And her legs tremble and her feet can't feel the floor, but she is moving. Maricci is scooping her along. At the font, Maricci dips her fingers in, then crosses herself. And Rosina stretches her hand up. She can just reach the holy water, so cool and slippery. *In the name of the Father.* Outside someone is shouting, a voice like grating metal, shouting over the buzz.

Then Rosina too is stepping out into the brightness. And she stumbles. She sees white—for a long second, then a confusion of dark against the white. And finally, the piazza, packed with people. By the quay, a carriage and four horses. In front of the *caffè,* instead of tables, a black motorcar. And everywhere, *gnoci,* Austrian soldiers, though they aren't like lumps today—no, they are straight and sharp in gray uniforms. Standing in lines like fences, dividing the crowd. The men on one side, women and children on the other. And they hold guns, balanced on their right side, rifles topped with knives that glint in the sun.

Rosina pulls away from her sister. "Papa." She flies down the steps. "Papa." She sees him among all the other men. His mouth is moving; he is talking to a soldier. And Rosina knows, knows, knows that the soldiers will take him away. She starts to scream, though she only finds this out afterward when she is told: "You screamed and screamed." She feels nothing, sees nothing, but one soldier thrusting her papa away from her, back into the group. And she is on him, punching. Half a gasp, and she finds herself on the hard ground. Hurting.

The *gnoco* points his rifle at her face, the shiny end so close, his voice so loud.

THE SOLDIER SAID, "Shut that brat up, or I'll do it." At least, that was what Leda told me her mother had told her. At least, that was the report I received ninety years after the event. Maricci spoke German; she'd learned it in the

Austrian school. So she understood, and in desperation, she put her hand over her little sister's mouth to muffle her screaming. With Ermanno's help, she dragged Rosina away.

All her life, Maricci remained convinced that if she'd not gagged Rosina, her sister would have been seriously injured or killed. (Her screams were so loud, and she wouldn't stop.) I cannot believe that to be true. I suspect the soldier was unnerved by the child's screams. So he made a threat he would never have carried out.

The Austrian army was rounding up the men who remained: those not yet away at war, those not fighting for either the Hapsburg Emperor or his enemy, the Italian King. This population of older boys and middle-aged men were forced into conscription. If they were judged to be Italian irredentists, they were imprisoned or used as forced labor. Those men whose loyalty was less in question were pressed into the Austrian infantry, bound for Russia.

I still do not know how Onorato Pagan died or where he was buried. He could have fallen ill at a prison camp in Czechoslovakia. Or, like millions of others, he could have died on a distant battlefield.

His family last saw him that morning, rounded up, behind a line of soldiers. Then he vanished.

(In the next World War, the scene would be repeated. That time, it was German soldiers who arrived during Sunday mass, so as to be sure they could trap all the remaining males. And it would be Onorato's grandson, Maricci's Oscar, who was taken for slave labor. Providentially, he escaped and joined the partisans. And Oscar escaped again—this time from the Tito's men—and found his way to America and an American wife, to Long Island, three children, and seven grandchildren.)

Still, what remained with Maricci, what she never forgot, was the fear. Leda said Maricci never talked to Mum about the incident, for she didn't want to remind her sister of what was best forgotten. And although Mum did not remember the day their father, Onorato Pagan, was taken away, she carried the helplessness and the fear she felt on that day for the rest of her life.

IN THE END, it was not me, but Tatiana and Antonia, who sat the death watch with my mother. I'd taken Mum into the General on the Friday evening for a five-day stay. Early on Saturday morning, Marco and I left for a conference in Chicago. We'd barely checked in to the hotel when Tatiana phoned to say Nonna had suffered a stroke. I couldn't get a flight back until first thing Monday morning. (I tried, but I didn't move heaven and earth.) My father's death had been so drawn out and painful that I expected this passing too would be long. And this time, I was weaker, exhausted from the years of care. So I dreaded what lay ahead.

Tatiana and Antonia stayed with Mum for those two days, leaving only to sleep. They talked to doctors, talked to her, even though she was unconscious, held her hand and stroked her hair.

I arrived in the late morning, straight from the airport. (Marco stayed behind at the conference.) I greeted the girls with hugs and a series of questions. Had the doctor seen her that morning? Should I speak to the head nurse? Had they called a priest to perform the last rites? Then I sent them off for a break.

Although I had been warned Mum was in a coma, I somehow hadn't expected her to look so white and so still. I leaned over to kiss her cheek. "I'm here, Mum," I said.

I pulled an armchair right beside the bed so that I could sit and still keep a hand on her arm, skin to skin. I continued to talk, though I don't remember what I said. Nothing of consequence, I expect. After a few minutes, I trailed off, stood, and picked up a women's magazine from a side ledge. Mum's breathing changed, became a rattle. Then silence. Was that it? It couldn't be. I had just got here. All over? Finally? Couldn't be. She hadn't seen the priest, hadn't been absolved, anointed, blessed.

She looked the same, unlike my father, who had changed so utterly from the moment before to the one after. And I sat for a minute or five. The girls came back. Antonia hovered at the door; Tatiana paused at the bed, then came around to me. "Mommy," she said, touching my shoulder, "what are you doing? Nonna's dead."

She had been waiting for me, in the end, only me. She hung on until she heard my voice. "I'm here, Mum."

The words freed her to go, to escape the fear and confusion. To begin her final passage home.

Looking back on her last difficult months, when her decline became ever more obvious and disturbing, I see that like Jacob wrestling with the angel, not letting go until he was blessed, I hung on to her until she blessed me. And she had—a couple of months before her death, one evening when I was tucking her into bed. Uncharacteristically, she had matched my kiss on the cheek. "Thank you," Mum said.

"What?" I was taken aback.

"Thank you. Thank you for everything you have done for me."

I have returned to that moment many times, reassuring myself that it did happen, that I had not imagined it.

But my allusion to Jacob is not completely apt. She blessed me, she passed away, but I still hung on. For years. Until I arrived at Rosina Ponaronzo. Until I knew her. Until I wrote this book.

acknowledgments

WRITING IS a collaborative art—all the more so in the production of this book, which tells the fate of a people. It took more than one village to raise it.

I was lucky enough to attend the Literary Journalism program at the Banff Centre for the Arts. Working on the trip-to-Croatia section, I was encouraged and challenged to test my limits by then director Alberto Ruy-Sánchez. I also received guidance and concrete advice from Ian Pearson, my editor, and Moira Farr. For the first time in my writing career, I felt at home.

Also at the Banff Centre, at a writing retreat, Genni Gunn read a first draft of the book and, friend to friend, informed me I had "no through line," convincing me to toss the draft out and begin again. Not only was she right, she handed me the needed narrative line. Next, I am grateful to Kay Stewart, who responded to each chapter as I produced it as well as (a few years earlier) provided a sympathetic ear while I cared for my mother. The members of my neighborhood writing group, Katherine Koller, Bev Ross, and Debby Waldman, accompanied me on my journey. I also appreciate the input of the two who joined me later on: June Drew-Jeffries and Mar'ce Merrel.

Thank you also to Nancy Flight, my insightful and sensitive editor. And I am deeply grateful to John Pearce, a prince among agents.

A grant from the Canada Council and one from the Alberta Foundation for the Arts provided some financial assistance in the writing of this book.

In Croatia, in Italy, and in Canada, as well as over the Internet and through the Giuliano-Dalmato Club of Toronto, many Istriani (both those who left and those who remained) shared their experiences with me. I feel the privilege and the responsibility of telling their stories. Many of these people are named in the text. Some have passed away or lost their memories since they spoke to me. I must single out Marisa Ciceran, the Webmaster of Istrianet, which became an essential tool for contact and research, as well as Etty Simicich, who promptly answered all my questions about Lussino, even when she had just been released from the hospital, and Guido Braini, who twice drove me from downtown Toronto to the Giuliano-Dalmato Club library in Weston and back.

I learned much about the current issues in Istria through ten years of reading both the newspapers and newsletters of the exiles, such as *L'Eco di Fiume* and *El Boletin,* and the online Croatian papers, *Glas Istre* and *Vecernji List,* translated from the Croatian mostly by Pino Golja and posted on Istrianet. An essential book for an outline of the exile was *A Tragedy Revealed: The Story of Italians from Istria, Dalmatia, and Venezia Giulia, 1943–1956* by Arrigo Petacco. For the geographic facts about the island of Lussino, including the flora and fauna, I used *Cherso e Lussino* by Nadir Mavrovic; for a deeper understanding of nostalgia, *Nostalgia: Storia di un Sentimento,* edited by Antonio Prete. *Nazario Sauro, Il Garibaldi dell'Istria* by Ranieri Ponis was given to me by Professor Marina Petronio of Trieste. I relied on many old and rare books, with stained and even missing pages, published by tiny presses, including *Lussingrande* by Steno Szalay, *Arie di Lussino* by Elsa Bragato, and, for an early history, *Storia Documentatat dei Lussini* by Matteo Nicolich, first published in 1874.

I was inspired and emboldened by the books of the masterful writers of the borderland: Carlo Sgorlon, Claudio Magris, and Fulvio Tomizza. The quotations from *The Odyssey* are from a translation by E.V. Rieu. The translations from the Italian are mine.

I could not have told my mother's story without my raft of cousins, who fed and humored me and answered my questions when I mined their memories: in Venice, Liliana Locatelli, Lino and Gina Bullo, and Mario Bullo, who figured out where my parents met and sent me a picture of the palazzo; in Koper, Slovenia, Antonio Baricèvic; in Earls Barton, England, Brian and Hillary Bailey; and on

Long Island, Mary Sambo and Leda Vlacci, who provided the missing piece to the puzzle.

I am grateful to Corinna Gonzales, who gave me the impetus for the book and steady support. And last, but also first, I thank my immediate family: Marco, Tatiana, and Antonia, who kept me going when I despaired. They make all the rest possible.